Thirty Years of Public Sector Reforms in Africa
Selected Country Experiences

D1807547

Editors

Paulos Chanie (PhD)

Paschal B. Mihyo (Prof.)

Organisation for Social Science Research
in Eastern and Southern Africa (OSSREA)

FOUNTAIN PUBLISHERS
www.fountainpublishers.co.ug

Fountain Publishers
P.O. Box 488
Kampala
E-mail: sales@fountainpublishers.co.ug
          publishing@fountainpublishers.co.ug
Website: www.fountainpublishers.co.ug

Organisation for Social Science Research in
Eastern and Southern Africa (OSSREA)
P.O. Box 31971
Addis Ababa, Ethiopia
E-mail: ossrea@ethionet.et
Website: http//www.ossrea.net

Distributed in Europe and Commonwealth countries outside Africa by:
African Books Collective Ltd,
P.O. Box 721,
Oxford OX1 9EN, UK.
Tel/Fax: +44(0) 1869 349110
E-mail: orders@africanbookscollective.com
Website: www.africanbookscollective.com

ISBN: 978-9970-25-232-9

Contents

About the Authors

Paulos Chanie, has a PhD in Development Studies (2007) from the International Institute of Social Studies, Erasmus University, The Hague, Netherlands. During his career, he has been teaching at the Addis Ababa University, doing research and consulting local and international organisations in the areas of public policy and administration, development management, decentralisation and civil service reform. He has published in the areas of public service reform and management, ethnic politics, neo-patrimonialism and fiscal federalism. He is currently an Assistant Professor at Addis Ababa University and Director of Research at the Organisation for Social Science Research in Eastern and Southern Africa (OSSREA).

Paschal Mihyo, a Tanzanian, is a lawyer by profession. He is a Professor of Politics and Administrative Studies with an LL.B., LL.M and a Ph.D. in Public Law from the University of Dar es Salaam. Between 1975 and 1988, he taught in the Faculty of Law at the University of Dar es Salaam. Between 1988 and 2004, he taught and served as Dean at the International Institute of Social Studies at Erasmus University, in The Hague. From April 2004 to September 2005, he was Director of Research and Programmes at the Association of African Universities in Accra, Ghana; after which he joined the University of Namibia as a Professor from 2006 – 2008. From 2008 to February 2012, he was Executive Director of the Organisation for Social Science Research in Eastern and Southern Africa (OSSREA) and then moved to Nairobi to join PASGR in February 2012, shortly before he resumed the same position back at OSSREA as of December 2012. He has published eleven books and thirty-one journal articles on law, human rights, higher education and politics in Africa.

Joshua Kivuva, is a Fulbright Scholar and Alumnus of the University of Pittsburgh's GSPIA programme. In addition to his teaching position at the University of Nairobi, Dr Kivuva is a researcher and consultant with the Society for International Development (SID), and the Center for Law and Research International (CLARION). He heads a development studies team on a UNDP/UNECA project on

Elections and the Management of Diversity, and is a member Afro-barometer studies team. He is widely published.

Claudious Chikozho, is the Exxaro Business and Biodiversity Leadership Programme Director at the Albert Luthuli Centre for Responsible Leadership, University of Pretoria, South Africa. He holds a PhD in Applied Social Sciences, a Master's Degree in Public Administration, and a BSc in Political Science from the University of Zimbabwe. He has 15 years experience in applied social science research and postgraduate teaching in development studies. His current areas of special interest include public sector leadership and service delivery; environmental sustainability; adaptation to climate change; and technology transfer processes.

Matteo Rizzo, is a Lecturer in the Economics of Africa at the School of Oriental and African studies (SOAS), University of London, UK, and has taught at the LSE, Oxford and Cambridge. His main research interests are urban transport; informal labour under globalisation; the political economy of agrarian change (past and present); and development aid. He is currently completing a monograph entitled "Being taken for a ride: Neo-liberalism, informal labour and transport in an African metropolis", 1983–2010.

Kassa Teshager Alemu, is a PhD candidate in Development Studies at the University of South Africa and Lecturer at the Ethiopian Civil Service University, Department of Development Management. He has a Master's Degree in Local and Regional Development from the Institute of Social Studies (ISS), The Hague. Kassa has published widely, and his research interests include local government and governance; rural livelihoods; food security; social protection; MSEs; rural development; local economic development; urban and rural poverty alleviation; private sector development; and NGOs.

Shawel Asfaw Yosef, is a Lecturer at the Ethiopian Civil Service University, Department of Development Management. He has a Master's Degree in Business Administration (MBA); and Bachelors Degree in Business Education from Addis Ababa University. He has worked as a Lecturer and Assistant Lecturer at Unity University and Mekele University and as an Accountant and Loan officer for Awash International Bank. His research interests are corporate governance and management of human resource, business, projects, and development.

Abebe Walle Menberu, has an MBA from Addis Ababa University. He is currently working as a lecturer at Bahir Dar University, Ethiopia, where he has served as Dean of the Faculty of Business and Economics; Head of Plan, Budget and Finance; Business Process Reengineering Team Czar; and Advisor to the President on BPR. His main research area is change management in the public sector.

Leonada Mwagike, has been a Lecturer at the School of Business, Mzumbe University, Tanzania, from 2000 to date. She is a PhD candidate at Sokoine University of Agriculture (2008 to date). Her publications include 'Exploring seven Cs as supplementing factors in supplier evaluation and selection' and 'Adding value through contract management'. Her research interests are education, gender, poverty, social capital, procurement and contracts management.

Mamkwe Claudia Edward, has been a lecturer at the School of Business, Mzumbe University, from 2000 to date. She is a PhD candidate at Sokoine University of Agriculture (2008 to date). Her research interests are poverty, climate change, food security and gender.

Muhajir Kachwamba, is a Lecturer of Institutional and Development Economics at Mzumbe University, Tanzania. He is currently a PhD student in International Management at the University of Agder, Norway. His areas of research interest include international trade; cross-border activities of firms; information economics; and institutional economics. He has published on various topics including 'Evaluating the cost-benefits of E-government projects', 'Internet marketing in the public sector', 'Impact of E-government on transaction cost and FDI inflows', 'E-government in marketing a country', and 'Internet-based information and FDI location decision-making'.

Roberts Kabeba Muriisa, is Associate Professor at Mbarara University of Science and Technology, Uganda. He has a PhD and Mphil in Public Administration from the University of Bergen. He has been a visiting scholar at the universities of Bergen (2008), Oldenburg (2011) and Stavanger (2012). In 2008, he partnered with other scientists on a publication *Reshaping research universities in the Nile Basin*. He has published widely on higher education. Other research interests include HIV/AIDS; migration and security; and public policy and governance.

Verena Tandrayen-Ragoobur, is a Senior Lecturer in Economics in the Department of Economics and Statistics at the University of Mauritius. Verena has a Master's Degree in Economics and International Economics from the University of Nottingham, UK, and a PhD in Economics from the University of Mauritius. She has published widely and worked as a consultant and conference organiser. Verena's research areas are international trade; foreign direct investment; labour markets; public sector reforms; poverty; economic development; climate change and gender issues. Verena is the chair of the WTO Chairs Programme.

Kesseven Padachi, is a Senior Lecturer in the field of Accounting and Finance at the University of Technology, Mauritius. He has a PhD in small business finance and is a Fellow of the Chartered Association of Certified Accountants. His research interests include PBB and Corporate Finance, particularly on issues relating to capital structure. He has published in international academic journals including: *International Review of Business Research Papers, Journal of Applied Finance, Journal of Internet Business, International Journal of Business Research,* UNU-WIDER publications, and the *International Journal of Finance and Economics.*

Keene Boikhutso, is a Lecturer in the Faculty of Education at the University of Botswana. He teaches Social Studies education courses in the Department of Languages and Social Sciences Education. He also supervises research projects at undergraduate and graduate levels. Keene Boikhutso obtained his PhD in political studies at the University of Cape Town, in 2010. His research interests are in the areas of education and development; curriculum studies; political studies; ethnicity and ethnic identity.

Maxwell Chanakira, is a Telecommunications and Management Consultant who has worked in the academic and telecommunications sectors of SADC countries for more than twenty years. Maxwell lectures in Strategy and Organisational Leadership at the Harare Institute of Technology, Zimbabwe. The thesis for his Doctorate in Organisational Leadership from Tshwane University of Technology, South Africa, created a conceptual framework to analyse the strategies of telecommunications enterprises investing in Africa. His interests focus on strategy and leadership in private, as well as public and multilateral organisations.

William Muhumuza, is a professor in the Department of Political Science and Public Administration, Makerere University, Uganda. He has a PhD in Political Science from the University of the Witwatersrand, Republic of South Africa (2004). His areas of specialisation are Political Economy of Development and Governance. He has undertaken various researches in Uganda, especially on topics of rebuilding community in post-conflict areas and Uganda's political institutions, democratisation and citizen engagement.

Nicholas Awortwi, is currently Director of Research at Partnership for African Social and Governance Research (PASGR), based in Nairobi, Kenya. Before joining PASGR in January 2012 Dr Awortwi was a Senior Lecturer in Development Management at the International Institute of Social Studies of Erasmus University, The Hague, and a Visiting Lecturer in Suriname and Uganda. His research and advisory services are in public sector reforms and management; governance and the private sector; governance of public services provision; decentralisation and local governance and municipal governance and management.

Acknowledgements

We are indebted to SIDA, NORAD, DANIDA and the Royal Netherlands Government's Ministry of Foreign Affairs for their financial assistance and encouragement in the production of this book, and indeed their unfailing support during the past three decades of OSSREA's research and capacity-building programmes.

We greatly appreciate the work of the dedicated researchers in sub-Saharan Africa who devoted their precious time and resources to writing the chapters and presenting them to a policy workshop, and who responded with diligence and understanding during the editing process. It has been a privilege to work with them.

We are also deeply grateful to Gavin Bennett for his thorough and substantial editing of the chapters, and to Abiye Daniel and Matebu Tadesse for copy-editing and reviewing the edit.

Foreword

Prof. Gelase Mutahaba

Over the past three decades, African countries have been reforming their public sector with a view to improving efficiency, effectiveness, accountability and transparency as part of efforts to improve the delivery of public services. The reform actions have included privatisation, public/private partnerships, commercialisation and adoption of private sector approaches in managing public organisations. This book, published by OSSREA, reviews measures taken by African countries in that regard, the extent to which the measures have achieved their intended results, as well as the factors behind the failure to achieve the results, where this was the case.

The contributions by the authors indentify four major reasons for the failure to achieve the intended results.

The first is the lack of government and private sector capacity in terms of capital, inputs, equipment and other crucial resources, as well as capabilities in terms of knowledge, skills, information, experience and other soft skills. In this book, it will be seen from various cases that various public sector reforms failed to improve delivery of services due to severe capacity and capability gaps. In some cases, because the markets were weak, the reforms seemed to be replacing a sick and ailing public sector with a weaker and more inefficient private sector. The case of contracting out in Tanzania and Ghana explained in this book provides examples on the same.

The second is the lack of political will on the part of government reflected by the weak readiness of top government officials to 'let go' or to transfer some powers and functions to the markets and to the lower levels of government. In most of the cases covered by this book and other works, the decision to 'let go' has remained very difficult to make, for many politicians and bureaucrats in the region. The case of business process re-engineering and health sector governance in Ethiopia, the organisational reforms in the universities of Botswana and Makerere and the public service reforms in Zimbabwe show that without political will to 'let go', key functions and decisions reforms will be less effective.

The third is the weakness of the institutional arrangements for effective public sector reforms. In this book, we see cases where privatisation was introduced without any law being put in place that could guide the procedures and processes of privatisation. That vacuum created space for chaotic privatisation and gave room to those in charge of deciding which enterprises to privatise and how — a case in point discussed in this book is the South Africa telecom reform. This led to unintended consequences. In all cases in this book, however, it is clear that the legal, regulatory and other institutional frameworks are critical in giving adequate direction, pace and rhythm for reforms.

The fourth is the weakness in involvement of the concerned public in the design and implementation of the reforms. This has been the Achilles' heel of many of the reform processes in Africa and perhaps elsewhere. Citizens are not organised well enough to exercise influence on service delivery. Where they are organised, the organisers are part of the elite and not ordinary citizens. Consumer organisations are still very weak in Africa and in some countries they do not exist at all. Civil society organisations exist but they are pre-occupied with issues within their mandates. They are restricted to perform by draconian laws, and do not have enough resources of their own to enable them to pursue agendas that go beyond the issues they are funded for. As a result, they have been missing from action. While power has been shared with difficulty between governments and the markets, very little of it has been shared with the citizens. The major lesson we take from here is that the reforms, as part of the process of power-sharing among the three major actors, will remain lopsided until citizens have a bigger role to play in evaluating the quality of service delivery.

In spite of the above four and other limitations, however, I would like to end by saying that thirty years of public sector reforms in Africa have not been in vain. As this book shows, against all odds, reforms have transformed the way the public services systems work and have potential to transform the provision of public goods in Africa. In every country, ministries have developed strategic plans, service charters and mechanisms for grievance handling. In most countries, ministerial structures of decision making, planning, budgeting, monitoring and evaluation have been rationalised. Human resources management systems have been rationalised and wage and incentives reforms introduced that have been accompanied by reduction of the working force and the retention of fewer but better paid staff; and the introduction of integrated payrolls and personnel information systems. Ethical practices and standards have been established — aiming at increasing transparency in recruitment, promotion, procurement procedures, and materials management. In several countries, performance management policies have been established and results-oriented assessment and advancement procedures put in place. Almost all the countries in Africa have embraced new financial performance improvement systems which harmonise and link resources availability with development objectives – bearing in mind issues of equity between regions and social groups. The adoption of Medium Term Expenditure Frameworks has increased financial management discipline, political commitments to budget processes and procedures, predictability of funding sources and services, manageability of budgets and their limitation to affordable levels, monitoring of expenditure and periodic accountability to stakeholders. These and many other changes create room for hope that continuous reforms will ultimately raise levels of efficiency, accountability and transparency. As a person who has spent over thirty years either doing research or providing technical assistance on public sector reforms in many African countries, I have reason to believe that Africa's public sector has changed for good and the future of Africa's public service delivery is very bright.

Prof. Gelase Mutahaba

Introduction

Paulos Chanie

OSSREA has a mission of enriching an African research tradition that responds to national and regional socio-economic, political, and technological challenges and opportunities. Accordingly, it is conducting various research projects through actively engaging budding African scholars. One of the research projects is examining the three decades of public sector reform in sub-Saharan Africa.

As it is well known, the performance of public administration is central to any country's wellbeing. The lessons of history in this respect are stark. Where governments deliver cohesive policies and develop efficient public service systems, countries thrive – socially and economically – but the converse is equally true. Almost all countries in the world have been making efforts to enhance their system of public administration through designing and implementing various reforms. The recent wave of reform in public administration is the one which has been with us for the last three decades and is wide-ranging and complex and various studies indicate that some have been successful; some are a complete failure; while others are in-between. Focusing on sub-Saharan African countries, the chapters included in this book present what different countries and public institutions are trying to do; what seems to work and what does not; and why; through a series of case studies that cover a wide range of different circumstances and details.

These chapters journey across 30 years and through nine countries, namely; Botswana, Ethiopia, Ghana, Kenya, Mauritius, South Africa, Tanzania, Uganda and Zimbabwe. They explore public sector reforms ranging from telecommunications and public transport, to higher education, agriculture, city management, and health services. They travel through issues of decentralisation, restructuring, outsourcing, corruption, electoral processes and security. The chapters also examine various managerial techniques, including project-based budgeting, business process re-engineering, performance management, e-governance, new public management, contract management, and private-public partnerships. This research assesses inputs, outputs and, above all, the outcomes of the reforms; and also analyses the relative impact of both design and implementation.

Each chapter tells its own complete story with its own perspective, data, findings and conclusions. Together, this array of different projects and authors offers a considerable body of knowledge, information and ideas in an intensive package from which readers can readily draw. For members of the research community, policy makers, administrators and the general public, the book presents a scientifically robust set of studies which, either individually or in compendium, offer a wealth of experience on what works, what does not, and why.

Chapter 1

The Trajectory of Public Administration in Africa: Background

Paulos Chanie

Africa is in a phase of momentous change to solve social and economic problems, develop capacity, and align itself with global performance standards. One of the central components of Africa's determination to catch up and line up is "good governance" — policies and administration that optimise sustainable long-term development outcomes for the people. The waves of Public Sector Reforms in Africa over the past 30 years are part of this agenda. The ultimate objectives are clear. The question is what should change, and how, to achieve them. The answers must be sought through both a vision of the future and the wisdom of hindsight: why, after some fifty years of independence and with the putative efforts of the Western world trying to help, is so much still unimposing? Having a handle on those reasons is pivotal to any solution. So, to put current public sector reform in context, a rear-view mirror is necessary.

The objective of this background chapter is to reflect upon the trajectory of African public administration. The attempt is not at all to provide the chronological outline of the history of African public administration as it unfolded across the diverse countries of the continent. The great depth and diversity of the past and modern systems of public administration in Africa makes writing on a unified African public administration system a challenging task. This chapter is, however, a very short background to this very big topic. It is written based on the assumption that the African countries possess shared stories that allow identifying common general trends in their systems of public administration. Accordingly, the history of public administration in Africa can be positioned in four main phases, namely: i) Pre-colonial, ii) Colonial, iii) Development Administration, and iv) New Public Management. The following section provides brief summaries of these phases to help capture the overall context on which the present book is largely anchored.

Pre-Colonial Public Administration

As the historical path to state formation and the resulting state forms in pre-colonial Africa were diverse and complex, identifying common or country-specific features and experiences of public administration is challenging. The experience of pre-colonial Africa is not only diverse but also contradictory or, as Mamdani (1996) states, the pre-colonial tradition is constraining rather than illuminating. Nonetheless, there are two opposing views on African pre-colonial public administration. The first view assumes the non-existence of any form of public administration in Africa and considers African societies as stateless, primitive, and basically characterised by incessant wars, plunder and anarchy (Mukandala 1996)[1] or "tyranny-ridden Dark Continent" (Mamdani 1996,36). The second view argues against this stereotypical assumption. However, there is an acknowledged view that holds that pre-colonial Africa had varied and complex patterns of public administration[2]. According to the latter, thus, pre-colonial African societies generally comprised either large empire states[3] that put together different ethnic groups under a centralised authority, or smaller states[4] identified with a single ethnic group. The larger empire states, either formed through conquest or internal differentiation, had centralised and hierarchical state structures with an administrative, judicial and coercive apparatus (Sandbrook 1985, 43). Many of the smaller states were less hierarchical but were organised as sub-groups and living and working together under the umbrella of common rules and customs (Mukandala 1996).

Many of the large and small states in pre-colonial Africa performed different functions, like providing internal order, defence, and the protection and regulation of the land and other property. Dia (1996) points out that traditional heads of states or kings were obliged to assist their followers in need and to guarantee the welfare of the group. The states were also financed either through resources generated from agriculture, proceeds from plunder, revenue derived from long-distance trade, or a combination of these (Sandbrook 1985). The state apparatus in the large empires was hierarchically organised with kings at the top of the hierarchy and chiefs at the level of the field administration. The relationship between the kings and the chiefs, however, had not been a master-servant type. Mamdani (1996, 43) notes, "... even if the nineteenth century administrative chiefs were the king's appointees who could not stay in office without the king's pleasure, their power was not just circumscribed by the will and capacity of the king". Rather, he states that the chiefs were constrained by tradition, peers and the people; were despised; and risked removal if they did not execute their functions properly (*Ibid.*).

Although difficult to generalise, in many of the larger empire states, the manner in which the kings and chiefs were assuming state power was not tyrannical. Dia (1996) testifies that in many of the states, "...the rulers were not self-appointed but selected by specific bodies whose choices then had to be approved by a council of elders or a similar body". Whitaker (1988) asserts that the process of ritual and political legitimacy, as well as the systems of checks and balances, characterised the historical monarchies in Africa. The kings at the top of strongly centralised systems were not left to perform their activities as they wished as there were different mechanisms in place for ensuring their accountability[5]. Dia (*Ibid.*) indicates that special agencies played an important role in upholding the authority of rulers, and at the same time constraining their abuse of power; popular uprisings were also an institutionalised and expedient way of getting rid of unpopular rulers. Moreover, checks on potential power abuses were maintained by rotating the kingship among the lineage, imposing fixed terms of rule, and ensuring that failure on the part of rulers to discharge their functions satisfactorily was followed by retribution or removal (*Ibid.*). An important feature in the system of pre-colonial African states is that public administration was collective and participatory[6]. In many of the larger empires that are known for their hierarchical system of traditional government, most of these entities were generally governed by consensus and broad participation, involving group representation at the central level and village councils at the local level. This translates into the fact that the rulers had authority but shared power (Dia 1996, 39). Chazan (in Soremekun 2000, 271) also highlights that the notions of representation were deeply embedded.

Taking the practice of larger states like the Ashanti (West Africa) and Buganda (East Africa), Chazan (*Ibid.*) points out that youths, traders, artisans, religious leaders and heads of kin groups had their own delegates in ruling councils. In a similar fashion, a practice of consensual decision-making and broad participation was also found in small states. Dia (1996) notes that when important decisions had to be made, chiefs tended to consult village councils and to seek unanimity, even if doing so required very lengthy discussions. Chazan cited in Sremekun (2000) points out that in small states such as the Kikuyu in Kenya and the Tiv and the Igbo in Nigeria, "...adults participated in almost Athenian fashion in the planning and implementation of communal affairs and in the adjudication of disputes". Whitaker (1988, 35-36), too, posits that there were effective local governments that fused the politics, religion and economic life of the community.

As can be discerned from the foregoing discussion, then, it is evident that pre-colonial Africa had a complex and varied public administration system that provided different services for members of the society and generated resources from various sources. The system, especially in the larger states, had a centralised hierarchical structure but with different arrangements of checks and balances to monitor the use and misuse of power by the kings and chiefs. Participation in decision-making and representation were also the basic features of many of the states, albeit with differences in degree. This system of public administration in pre-colonial Africa was dismantled by the advent of colonialism which introduced the Western model of public administration as shall be discussed in the following section.

From Pre-Colonial to Colonial Public Administration

Modern public administration, as practised in the Western world, was introduced into Africa at the end of the nineteenth and the beginning of the twentieth centuries. The colonial Master's instituted a system that somehow resembled the Weberian rational bureaucracy[7]. But, the manner in which it was practised and the purpose it served were different. The rules and procedures that were developed generically in and for colonising countries were applied indiscriminately in colonised countries, often with little regard to local conditions and aspirations (Hyden 1975, 147; Gardiner 1975, 14).

The colonial public administration, which was highly centralised and based on spoils and sheer force, was structured to serve primarily as a tool to subjugate the territories. The system was devised to maintain law and order and ensure compliance of the local populace, as well as an uninterrupted extraction of resources to meet the needs of the colonising countries rather than to provide development-orientated services (Perera 1978, 27). Gardiner (1975,15) observes that "...in many ways the colonial civil service was considered as an extension of the Armed forces" and "...the colonial governor was both commander-in-chief and the senior civil administrator". Olowo (1988, 220) states that the colonial bureaucracy could be characterised by "...high concentration of political power in administrative officials, elitist and racist orientation, and narrow preoccupation with law and order". Moreover, there was very little distinction between politics and administration or, as Baker (1990) states, the relationship between policy and administration was blurred. It should be noted, however, that while there were some differences in terms of the system of administration followed by disparate colonising powers (Belgium, Britain, France, Portugal, and so on), they all had certain features in common. Most noticeable among these were, the emphasis on domination through law and order; exploitation through extraction and taxation; and protection of the colonising country's interests and institutions (see Rothchild and Curry 1978, 50; Turner and Hulme 1997; Whitaker 1988, 37).

The colonial system of public administration lacked political and moral legitimacy as well as accountability. In the whole system of administration, no provision was made for legislative and judicial checks and balances to limit the discretionary power of the colonial governor (Dia 1996). The indigenous checks and balances system that had been prominent in the local government administration system was dismantled. Appointed from above, the administrative chiefs were given the power to administer the local governments in a manner required by the colonial Master's without restraint. Their powers were diffuse, with little functional specificity. Meredith (2005, 6) notes that, "...scattered across vast stretches of Africa, lone district administrators became virtually absolute rulers of their domain, functioning simultaneously as police chief, judge, tax collector, head of labour recruitment, special agent, and meteorological observer". Mamdani (1996) also argues that, "...by undermining both popular checks on state authority and traditional constraints as embodied in traditional chiefs, the colonial state really liberated administrative chiefs, from all institutionalised constraints, of peers or people, and laid the basis of a decentralised despostism". Turner and Hulme (1997, 163) also note that under the colonial local government system, power was in the hands of the non-indigenous, centrally-appointed officers and "...there was minimal interest in devolving power to local representatives because the colonial ideology defined Africans as lacking the intellectual apparatus for modern governance".

There are differing arguments regarding Africa's colonial public administration system. Some consider it as having been an efficient system, which was later spoiled by the leaders of Africa who assumed power after independence. Hence, Hyden (1983, 60), maintains that, "the colonial powers left generally well-functioning administrative machinery behind when they abandoned control over their African territories." Others, by contrast, contend that the colonial public administration disrupted traditional social orders and left a system of public administration that was unaccountable to the society that lacked transparency and was unregulated by legislative checks and balances. Adu (1975, 21), Baker (1990) and Dia (1996) say that the colonial period left behind such a wave of destruction that Africans are still suffering from its multifarious impacts - not only on their politics and economics but also on their culture and their very identity. Perera (1978, 27) also states that, "... the political heads who replaced colonial masters were themselves reluctant to introduce immediate changes; many of them belonged to a common elite class insulated from the masses; the administrative structure seemed to satisfy their immediate interest of maintaining a degree of peace and order as would help them to remain in power" (See also Baker 1990.).

When colonised countries became independent states, numerous administrative reforms had been considered and attempted. One of the prominent reforms was Development Administration, which is the focus of the next section.

From Colonial Administration to Development Administration

In the 1950s and 1960s, newly independent African countries adopted a system of administration, labelled 'Development Administration' (DA). This was part hand-over and part reform, but, ironically, it enlisted Western experts to help with their models of bureaucratic organisation, training and technical assistance (Turner and Hulme 1997, 154). The DA movement was based on the assumption that "... the primary obstacles to development are administrative rather than economic"[8]; and thus, using ideas and mechanisms of the developed world, public administration could be instrumental in social and economic development in Africa. Gant (1979, 18) observes that the preceding system was not designed to respond to demands for social and economic development, whether in colonies such as Indonesia and Nigeria or in kingdoms such as Thailand and Ethiopia. Another justification for DA was the inadequacy and irrelevance of the colonial public administration, which was considered too centralised and hierarchical, obsessed with law and order, irresponsive and unaccountable in its application , based on directive principles and ponderous procedures, and fraught with inadequate systems of personnel, materials and budget administration.

DA was grounded on the prevailing concepts of development and classical administrative theories[9]. Among the intellectual bases, the most important was the modernisation theory, and specifically 'Rostow's stages of economic growth' (Baker 1990), which, inter alia, emphasises the need for capital-intensive and technologically-orientated agriculture, urbanisation, and industrialisation in the developing world. Alternative models from the Eastern, Marxist nations that espouse managerial rationality and centralising assumptions in both political and economic areas were bases for the DA movement (Turner and Hulme 1997). The push for DA by the Western World, especially the USA, was introduced not only to bring growth or modernisation, but also to accelerate capital formation within a liberal democratic framework and to counter the communist threat (Dwivedi and Nef 1982; Baker 1990).

The main elements of DA were impartial management, bureaucratic rationality and neutrality, planning hierarchy, management by objective, planning, programming and budgeting (PPB), civil service professionalisation, centralised authority and job specialisation. The central government was also expected to play an entrepreneurial role in development and have a good measure of commitment to the national objectives, a willingness to take risks, and accessibility to the public. Some of the specific reforms under DA included the following:

- Strengthen the centralised and interventionist state to plan and implement socio-economic development. The state-at-the-centre was accepted as the prime actor in bringing change and accelerating economic growth, to act as leader, investor, regulator, innovator (Chapel 1977 and Baker 1990, 356) and, not least, as implementer.

- Overhaul management of public finances, which included re-orientating the system of budgeting for development programmes and introducing performance budgeting with new accounting and analytical techniques (Chapel 1977; Gant 1979, 195–220);

- Provide for effective personnel administration, including introduction of different categories of personnel (scientific and technical, entrepreneurial and managerial) in addition to traditional generalist administrators; and improving the personnel system and work environment to attract, retain and efficiently utilise qualified civil servants (*Ibid.*);

- Reorganise government agencies and their subdivisions in terms of specialisation — planning boards, nation-building departments (agriculture, industry, education, health), public enterprises, cooperative organisations, community development programmes, farmers' organisations) — and instituting a clear system of delegation and lines of communication in the government structure to permit effective and expeditious decisions and performance (Gant 1979, 24–28) and

- Introduce a model of devolved local government where sub-national governments were expected to be constitutionally separated from the central government and were given powers, including: providing a range of significant local services; raising own revenue; deciding on own policy and internal procedures; having own treasury, budget and accounts; employing own competent staff and having the power to hire, fire and promote. The central government was expected to serve purely as external advisors and inspectors (Turner and Hulme 1997, 160).

While these reforms were intended and even instituted in many Third World countries, their implementation, impact, and outcome was disappointing. Dwivedi and Nef (1982, 60) capture this phenomenon neatly saying that DA was a dismal failure responsible for anti-development, bureaucratic authoritarianism and seemingly everything that was wrong with development. Likewise, Loveman (1976, 616) indicates that "...development administration, inspired by United States doctrines, had reinforced or increased income disparities and inequalities, made the poorest even poorer in absolute terms, led to anti-development and to progressively more authoritarian regimes". Many others similarly state their disillusionment with the system pointing out its various fallacies and false premises, arguing that DA, largely exercised through various technical assistance programmes, was adopted without a careful examination of its applicability to the unique Third World setting. For instance, Riggs cited in Hyden (1983, 760) notes that DA did not consider the limitation inherent in the social and political environments of public administration.

Many of the reform measures were attacked from different corners. The belief in the superiority of the bureaucracy and the heavy emphasis on central planning were dismissed as being irrelevant (Hyden 1983, 64-67)[10]. The rules, regulations and procedures that defined and structured public sector activities and conditions of employment, too, were criticised for being inflexible and unduly complicated. The theoretical base of development administration or the assumptions of the modernisation theory, that is, the dream of a linear process of development towards democracy and economic development, was considered as unpragmatic and unattainable. As pointed out by Turner and Hulme (1997), the neo-Marxist assault on modernisation theory identified DA as a device to legitimise and promote the interests of the bureaucratic bourgeoisie and other dominant classes and/or elites.

In the same way, counter arguments to the above view credit DA for its contribution in improving the system of administration (the application of knowledge, techniques and skills in decision-making and problem-solving) and economic development in some countries (Gable 1975, 5). According to this stand, the failures of DA are basically attributable to the crises in the political leadership and institutional factors in Third World countries. As Khan (1984, 177) states, many governments in the Third World countries only paid lip-service to reforms and had no real desire to see major reforms; they only like to talk about it because of the political gain involved. Instances of institutional obstacles cited as setbacks included, lack of conscious strategy, lack of political stability, shortage of trained personnel, absence of proper institutionalisation of the reform effort in government machinery, and lack of a symbiotic relationship between planning and administration — all of which the DA was designed for, but not implemented, to remedy.

Nevertheless, in many of the African countries, the systems of government organisation, budgeting and personnel administration were structured according to the DA ethos and are still widely practised. Despite criticisms, it may be hard to dispute the DA premise that effective administrative mechanisms are important to national development. As will be seen in the following discussion, this understanding is still prominent in the New Public Management (NPM) movement.

From Development Administration to the New Public Management

After four decades of experimentation with Development Administration, the New Public Management (NPM) movement emerged in both developing and developed countries in the late 1980s. As was the case in the DA movement, the fundamental premise of NPM, especially for developing countries, was that there is a need for major changes in the political and administrative structures as a prerequisite for economic and political development. As Turner and Hulme (1997, 230) indicate, NPM was introduced by major donors (the World Bank, USAID and ODA) who came up with their own prescriptions for developing countries to address the crises in public management. Thus, developing countries were required to sweep away existing public administration, that is, elements of administration imported to Africa during the colonial era and the DA movement and replace it with NPM to improve public sector management.

The NPM, which has been in place for the last three decades, is used as a shorthand for many of the new trends or reforms in public administration that have taken place in many of the developing and developed countries. It is basically considered as a rival to, a substitute for, or a synonym of public administration (Bozeman 1993, xiii) and is given different labels, such as 'deregulating government', 'reinventing government', 'entrepreneurial government', and 'public sector managerialism' (Behn 2001). NPM is a new global paradigm and is claimed to transform traditional public "administration" into a new set of public management "techniques and practices". The changes are meant to transform the management of the public services in all parts of the world irrespective of differences in governance, economic and institutional environments.

The emergence and development of NPM reforms have been driven by a combination of economic, social, political, and technological factors in both developed and developing countries. In the developed economies it has been inspired by different factors, especially the crises of the welfare state, a factor which was reflected by the rising government expenditure, coupled with poorer economic performance, the collapse of near full employment, shrinking government budgets as well as the sharp increases in social inequality and social exclusion. The other main influence was the neo-liberal ideas (the 'New Right' ideology), which questioned the excessive and direct interventions of governments in the economy and believed that the market could offer superior mechanisms for achieving efficient supply of goods and services, with less direct involvement of governments. The development of information technology and the imperatives of globalisation were the added justifications for applying NPM (Minogue 1998 & 2000; Mackintosh 1998; Labri 1999; Heady 2001; Behn 2001).

Although the underlying philosophy is similar to that of developed market economies, in developing countries the following were some of the peculiar forces for the adoption of NPM. As discussed by many, for example, Mackintosh (1998, 79), Labri (1999), Polidano (1999), Minogue (2000) and others, these factors are:

- the economic and fiscal crises - reflected in unsustainable external and domestic debts, deteriorating real terms of trade, high inflation, low levels of savings and investment, shortage of consumer goods, deterioration in terms of trade and the like;

- the existence of policy deficiencies, bad and excessive management of the economy, large-scale institutionalised corruption, weak and demoralised public services, low productivity, political instability, worsening deprivation, and so on;

- policy-based lending by multilateral institutions and the implementation of structural adjustment programmes used as an instrument to encourage developing states to embark on reforms that were pro-market and pro-private sector; and

- the need to restore capacity and promote effectiveness and efficiency as well as to search for ways in which public administration systems could be made adequate to the task of recovery and adjustment.

Generally, NPM in both the developed and developing economies is intended to overcome the shortcomings of public sector administration through the adoption of market-based operations, private sector values and techniques of management, as well as through changing the role of government from acting as the principal vehicle for socio-economic development to guiding and facilitating that development. The literature indicates that NPM has a strong intellectual paradigm based on different theoretical foundations. Labri (1999), for instance, points out two broad orientations of NPM. The first orientation stresses adoption of business-type managerialism in the public sector. The second orientation is based on the 'new-institutional economics' movement, which has its theoretical foundation in public choice, transaction cost and principal-agent theories. In a nutshell, the arguments of the theories can be summarised as follows (see also *Ibid.;* Common 1998, 59):

- Public choice theory assumes that all human behaviour is dominated by self-interest and individuals are rational utility maximisers. It endorses political agendas, which are the bases for NPM, such as minimising the role of the state, selling the state's commercial assets, and curbing the functions of government agencies (Keraudren and Mierlo 1998). As a basic foundation for NPM, this theory also stipulates that the reward system in the public sector does not prompt effective performance. This often leads to waste of resources, growth of expenditure, and rent-seeking behaviour by bureaucrats, their clients and politicians (Gray and Jenkins 1995; Labri 1999).

- Agency theory rests on the notion that social and political life can be understood as a series of contracts. The agent undertakes to perform various tasks on behalf of the principal and in exchange the principal agrees to reward the agent in a mutually acceptable way (Shand 1996). This theory is at the heart of NPM's decentralised management system, which is concerned with such issues as selection of agents, the design of remuneration systems and the choice of institutional arrangements. It also states that traditional public administration has directly or indirectly resulted in the failure of 'principals' to effectively monitor the behaviour of their 'agents' (Kelly and Wanna 2000).

- New institutional economics postulates that transaction cost emerges as a function of the institutions through which economic exchanges are mediated, with markets and hierarchies forming the two ends of an institutional continuum (Brinkerhoff 1997, 4). The theory emphasises that efforts should be made to reduce transaction costs by moving towards the market end. This is another important base for the attack on the traditional model of public administration and promoting the reform measures of NPM.

- Managerialism also provides an important theoretical base for NPM. It advocates the adoption of private sector management techniques and practices such as risk taking, customer focus, and restructuring of organisations to deal with the problems of the old public administration.

NPM also constitutes a comprehensive set of elements that involve the whole area of governmental structure and activities, to address the inefficiencies of the traditional model of public administration and to enhance effective management of social and economic development. The reform measures involve issues related to decentralising management, restructuring government, provision of public services through market, privatisation, government budgeting and finance, human resource management, information technology and the like. These reform measures, as discussed by Gray and Jenkins (1995), Common (1998), Minogue (1998 & 2000), Labri (1999), Heady (2001) and Behn (2001), can be summarised as follows:

- Redefining the relationship between political policy-making and administrative policy-implementation by distinguishing the roles and responsibilities of senior administrators from politicians;

- Making government withdraw from direct provision and instead focus on a steering or enabling role, and enhancing the measurement and monitoring capacity of government over public service delivery;

- Increasing use of markets and competition in the provision of public services (contracting out and other market-type mechanisms);

- Introducing various forms of decentralising management within the public services (see especially Labri 1998, 189);

- Breaking up monolithic bureaucracies by disaggregating separable functions into semi-autonomous agencies, involving a split between a small strategic policy core and large operational units;

- Organisational unbundling or delayering of vertically integrated organisations, replacing traditional 'tall hierarchies' with flatter, flexible and more responsive structure and a new form of corporate governance on "a board of directors model";

- A shift of power to senior management in public organisations by designing a clear responsibility and accountability relationship - assuring managers of the availability of the needed human and technological resources and making them appreciate the value of competition;

- Devolving budgets and financial control to decentralised units by creating separate budget centres or spending units in order to give managers greater control over resources;

- Changing the restrictive and control-orientated budget process, which was skewed towards measuring inputs, into a system that considers results, efficiency or the effectiveness of government programme outcomes (see especially Kelly and Wanna 2000);
- Harnessing information technology in areas such as revenue collection, financial management and accounting, inter-departmental communication, human resource management, and delivering improved services to the public; and
- Revising public service personnel management and instituting systems where, among others, open recruitment procedures are emphasised; vacancies are filled on the basis of skills and competency; a shift from high security careers, shaped by lengthy service and seniority, towards short-term employment contracts; and achievement-orientated promotion with incentive packages which ensure skills and personal achievements are recognised and rewarded.

In summary, NPM is concerned with injecting the ideas of democratic participation, accountability, empowerment and decentralised management. As pointed by Behn (2001), the features of NPM can be summarised as:

- market government — which focuses on decentralisation, pay for performance, and other private sector techniques;
- participative government — which emphasises flatter organisations, total quality management, and teams;
- flexible government — which features virtual organisations and temporary personnel; and
- deregulated government — which stresses greater managerial freedom.

During the past 30 years, countries in sub-Saharan Africa have undergone different stages of public sector reform with the support and assistance of Bretton Woods Institutions and other international, bilateral and multilateral donor agencies. Ayee (2008) specifies three stages of the public sector reform in Africa: the first phase —1980s to early 1990s — focusing on macro-economic stability; the second phase — mid-1990s to 2000 — focusing on performance and civil service management; and the third phase — 2000 to the present

— focusing on efficient and effective service delivery. Technically, the reforms are expected to enhance efficiency, representation, and participation; introduce more competition and private market discipline into public administration; transform bureaucratic culture; promote more open, accountable and results- and citizen-orientated governments; and create a market-friendly, liberalised, lean, decentralised, customer-orientated managerial and democratic state. The specific public sector reforms include a myriad regulatory interventions and institutional arrangements. Some of these are decentralisation, privatisation, public finance management, strategic planning, performance budgeting, business process re-engineering, procurement management, human resource management, public service delivery, information technology, revenue administration, overhauling the executive and judicial sector, and anti-corruption.

Studies on public sector reform in sub-Saharan Africa show mixed results. Some indicate improved efficiency in the allocation of a country's resources due to decentralisation and privatisation, enhanced accountability of the public service through performance-based contracts, Citizens' Charters and Public Reporting, creating lean and mean autonomous institutions to cater for various government activities, and improvement in public service delivery in some sectors. Yet, there are strong voices of concern that claim public sector reforms have resulted in downsizing the public service, cutting state budgets, surrendering public assets, scaling down public services, taking from many and giving to a few, promoting an autocratic state, commercialising public goods, undermining trade unions, privatising public functions including the military, police and other human security functions; and eroding the state's capacity to carry out its regulatory and distributive roles, including maintaining social order. There are also claims that privatisation measures have reinforced networks of corruption, undermined the social contract, and contributed to de-industrialisation; that the pricing of basic social services beyond the reach of an ever-growing number of people has also created social grievances; and that most of the reforms are not contextualised to their country's realities. Some allude to a perception that the performance of reforms in Africa remains hindered by a multitude of factors, including lack of political will, absence of accountability, ineffective management practices, and corruption — all giving an impression that the imperfections of the non-market system have been transferred to the new system (Therkildsen 2001; Economic Commission for Africa 2003; Omoyefa 2008; Olufemi and David 2010).

The Organisation for Social Science Research in Eastern and Southern Africa (OSSREA) launched a book project in 2011 with the understanding that the foregoing arguments could be much generalised and there is a need for more focused studies on various public sector reforms. Accordingly, OSSREA made a call to researchers in sub-Saharan Africa to conduct comparative studies on specific public sector reforms in their respective countries with the aim to understand the processes, outputs and outcomes of the reforms, their weaknesses and strengths, and to draw lessons. In response, 62 researchers submitted abstracts and all these were given the go-ahead to write and submit draft articles, and 42 did. Of the 42 draft articles submitted, 16 were selected after internal and external review. These papers were presented in a policy-research workshop in Harare, Zimbabwe in July 2011. All the authors revised their papers based on the inputs from the workshop. The draft papers were thoroughly edited and 13 papers were accepted for publication. Each constitutes a chapter of this book, and starts with a short abstract for readers' ease of reference.

Notes

1. As pointed out by Mukandala (1996), Africans were perceived as animals, jungle-men and primitive, with minds in which the irrational element predominated, and where natives were constantly at war of all against all. He also underscores that Africans were considered as stateless societies plagued by perennial chaos and anarchy, and even where there was an attempt at rule-making and enforcement, the rules were fuzzy, covered only a few activities, and were constantly broken.

2. Some argued that public administration with bureaucratic features had existed in Third World countries before Max Weber observed their emergence in Europe. A case in point is the Old Kingdom of Egypt where complex patterns of delegation, specialisation and institutional longevity were evident before 2180 BC (Turner and Hulme 1997, 85).

3. Some of the larger states were mediaeval kingdoms of Western Africa, such as Ghana, Mali and Songhai; the ancient kingdoms of the Nubians in Kush in the Nile, and the Ethiopian in Axum; the kingdom of Buganda in the seventeenth century, the Ashante and others can also be mentioned (Sandbrook 1985, 44).

4. Examples of the small autonomous communities included the Ewe of eastern Ghana, the Ibo (or Igbo) of eastern Nigeria, and the Nuer and Dinka of southern Sudan (*Ibid*).

5. Mamdani (1996) points out that even when centralisation had gone too far, as in Buganda, the organised power of clans continued to function as a popular mechanism to check on both the king and the appointed administration.

6. Davidson (in Mamdani 1996, 40) asserts the common feature that underpinned the African states is the quest for a unifying force, depending on a system of participation that must not only work but must also publicly be seen to work, combined with 'a systematic distrust of power'.

7. The features of Weberian Bureaucracy include: a) clear separation between politics and administration (distinct role between political leaders and state officials); b) continuous and predictable administration based on written and unambiguous rules; c) administrators recruited on the basis of qualification; d) organisations with division of labour and hierarchical arrangements of tasks and people; e) all resources belonging to the organisation and not to the individual working in the organisation; and f) a guiding principle for all employees being a sense of duty and public interest (Minogue 2000; Heady 2001).

8. See Doland Stone (1965) - cited in Turner and Hulme (1997, 12).

9. These include Tailor's scientific management theory, Fayol's administrative theory and the ideal type of bureaucratic form of organisation.

10. Hyden (1983) argues that political leaders used it as a defence against the many pressures; facilitated governance by timing future prospects in order to secure needed compliance in the present; and created an opportunity for political leaders to have rapport with outside donors.

References

Adu, A.L. 1975. The administrator and change. In *A decade of public administration in Africa,* edited by Anthony H. Rweyemamu and Goran Hyden. Nairobi: East African Literature Bureau, pp.21– 30.

Ayee, J. R. A. 2008. *Reforming the African public sector: Retrospect and prospects.* CODESRIA Green Book. Dakar: Council for the Development of Social Science Research in Africa (CODESREA).

Baker, R. 1990. The role of the state and the bureaucracy in developing countries since the World War II. In *Handbook of comparative and development public administration,* Ali Farazmand (ed.). New York: Marcel Dekker, Inc., pp. 353–366.

Behn, D. R. 2001. Rethinking democratic accountability: Performance and the new public management (book excerpt).Web: http://governing.com/ rdachap2.htm.

Bozeman, B. 1993. Introduction: Two concepts of public management. In *Public management: The state of the art,* edited by Barry Bozeman. California, Jossy-Bass Inc.

Brinkerhoff, W.D. 1997. Integrating institutional issues into policy decisions. In Stuart S. Nagel and Derick W. Brinkerhoff (eds), *Policy studies and developing nations — Policy analysis concepts and methods: An institutional and implementation focus* (Vol. 5).

Chapel, Y. (ed.). 1977. *Administrative management for development: A reader.* Paris: UNESCO.

Common, R. 1998. The new public management and policy transfer: The role of international organizations. In *Beyond the New Public Management: Changing ideas and practices in governance,* edited by M. Minovue, C. Polidano, D. Derick, and W. Brinkerhoff. London: Jai Press Inc., p.1–18.

Dia, M. 1996. *Africa's management in the 1990s and beyond: Reconciling indigenous and transplanted institutions.* Washington, D.C.: World Bank.

Dwivedi, O.P and Nef, J. 1982. Crises and continuities in development theory and administration: First and Third World perspectives. *Public Administration and Development,* Vol. 2, pp.59–77.

Economic Commission for Africa. 2003. Public sector management reform in Africa. http://unpan1.un.org/intradoc/groups/public/documents/uneca/ unpan014953.pdf.(accessed on December, 2005)

Gable, R.W. 1975. Development administration: Background, terms, concepts, theories, and a new approach: Design of training module for the Development Studies Program. Washington, D.C.: AID.

Gant, G. F. 1979. *Development administration: Concepts, goals, methods.* Madison, USA: The University of Wisconsin Press.

Gardiner, R.K.A. 1975. From colonial rule to local administration. In *A decade of public administration in Africa*, Anthony H. Rweyemamu and Goran Hyden (eds.). Nairobi, East African Literature Bureau, pp. 3–20.

Gray, A. and Jenkins, B. 1995. From public administration to public management: Reassessing a revolution. *Public Administration Review*, pp. 76–99.

Heady, F. 2001. Public administration: A comparative perspective. New York: Marcel Dekker, Inc. pp. 275–313.

Hyden, G. 1975. Reforming the structure in the public service: Introduction. In *A decade of public administration in Africa*, Anthony H. Rweyemamu and Goran Hyden (eds.). Nairobi, East African Literature Bureau, pp.147–157.

——.1983. *No shortcuts to progress: African development management in progress*. Los Angeles: University of California Press.

Kelly, J. and Wanna J. 2000. New public management and the politics of government budgeting. Available from: http://willamette.org/impn/test/issue1/lellyo1.htm. (accessed on December, 2005)

Keraudren, P. and Mierlo, H.V. 1998. Theories of public management reform and their practical implication. In *Innovation in public management: Perspectives from East and West Europe*, T. Verheihen and D. Coombes (eds.). Cheltenham, Edward Elgar, pp. 143–158.

Khan, M.M. 1984. Administrative reform. In *Development administration*, S.P. Verma and S.K. Sharma (eds.). Delhi: The Indian Institute of Public Administration. Swatantra Baharat Press, pp. 1–16.

Labri, G.A. 1999. The new public management approach and crises states. Discussion paper No, 12. United Nations Research Institute for Social Development. Geneva.

Loveman, B. 1976. The comparative administration group, development administration and antidevelopment. *Public Administration Review* 36,(6), pp. 616–621.

Mackintosh, M. 1998. Public management for social inclusion. In *Beyond the new public management: Changing ideas and practices in governance*, Martin Minogue, Charles Polidano, David Hulme (eds.), Cheltenham, Edward Elgar.

Mamdani, M. 1996. *Citizens and subject: Contemporary Africa and the legacy of late colonialism*. New Jersey: Princeton University Press.

Meredith, M. 2005. *The state of Africa: A history of fifty years of independence*. London, Simon & Schuster UK Ltd.

Minogue, M. 1998. Changing the state: Concepts and practices. In *The reform of the public sector*, Martin Minovue, Charles Polidano, David Hulme (eds.). Cheltenham, Edward Elgar.

——.2000. *Should flawed models of public management be exported? Issues and practices*. IDPM, University of Manchester. Available from: http://www.man.ac.uk/idpm. (accessed on December, 2005)

Mukandala, R. 1996. African public administration. Web: http://aaps.co.zw/
publications/africa.html.htm. (accessed on September, 2002)

Olowo, D. 1988. Bureaucratic morality in Africa. *International Political
Science Review* , 9(3), pp. 215–229.

Olufemi F. J and David, A. K. 2010. Public sector reform in Africa: Issues,
lessons and future directions. *Journal of Sustainable Development in
Africa*, vol. 12, no.8.

Omoyefa, P. S. 2008. Public sector reforms in Africa: A philosophical re-
thinking. *Africa Development*, Vol. XXXIII, No. 4, 2008, pp. 15–30.
Council for the Development of Social Science Research in Africa.

Perera, M. L. M. 1978. Problems arising from the existence of dual
administrative systems in African countries. *African Administrative
Studies*, no 19, pp.28–35.

Polidano, C. 1999. The new public management in developing countries.
Public policy and management working paper, no. 13. University
of Manchester, Institute of Development Policy and Management.
Web::http://idpm.man.ac.uk/idpm/ppm-wp13.htm. (accessed on
September, 2002)

Rothchild, D. and Robert L. Curry Jr. 1978. *Scarcity, Choice and Public Policy
in Middle Africa*. Berkeley: University of California Press. http://ark.
cdlib.org/ark:/13030/ft9p3009f9/.(accessed on January, 2011)

Sandbrook, R. 1985. The politics of Africa's economic stagnation. Cambridge:
Cambridge University Press.

Shand, D. 1996. New Public Management: Challenges and issues in an
international perspective. Paper presented at the conference on Civil
Service Reform in Francophone Africa, 23–26 January, Abidjan.

Soremekun, K. 2000. The international dimension of governance. In *African
perspective on governance*, Goran Hyden, Dele Olowu, Hastings W.O.
Okothogendo (eds.). Trenton, NJ: Africa World Press, Inc., pp. 267–293.

Therkildsen, O. 2001. Efficiency, accountability and implementation: Public
sector reform in East and Southern Africa. *Democracy, Governance and
Human Rights Programme* Paper Number 3. United Nations Research
Institute for Social Development. Available from: (http://unpan1.un.org/
intradoc/groups/public/documents/un-dpadm/unpan044443.pdf)
(accessed on December, 2005)

Turner, M. and Hulme, D. 1997. *Governance administration and development:
Making the state work.* London: Macmillan Press Ltd.

Whitaker, J. S. 1988. *How can Africa survive?* New York: Harper & Row
Publishers.

Chapter 2

Reforms without Change: Kenya's Unending "War on Corruption"

Joshua M. Kivuva

Abstract

Corruption persists in Kenya despite numerous initiatives to eliminate the vice. This intransigence can be attributed to poorly developed laws; institutional weaknesses and ineffectiveness; the lack of political will to fight impunity; a political culture that not only condones corruption but also glorifies it; and inappropriate incentive structures and other bureaucratic pathologies within the public sector. Anti-corruption institutions have been ill-prepared and ill-structured; delivering measures either half-heartedly or not at all. The legal mechanisms and rules involved are flawed. In sum, institutional mechanisms created to combat corruption are doomed to failure, some purposefully so. However, attempts to rein in corruption are not without hope. Ongoing institutional reforms (which are part of Agenda 4 Reforms), the legal provisions and the spirit of Kenya's new constitution provide important institutional structures and sanction mechanisms that might greatly enhance the fight. The new constitution, in particular, has made it possible to implement salient aspects of existing anti-corruption laws. This, with the changing political environment and checks imposed on executive excesses, make the "war" against corruption winnable.

Introduction

The ruling party KANU first officially recognised the existence of corruption in government in 1978 and subsequently declared "war" to root it out (Chweya 2005, 12). However, this verbal declaration

23

was not followed by practical action. Indeed, the struggle for Kenya's second liberation in the 1980s was partly prompted by the high incidence of corruption (Throup and Hornsby 1992; Chweya 2005, 13). In the 1990s, under pressure from the International Monetary Fund (IMF), the World Bank and other bilateral donors, Structural Adjustment Programmes (SAPs) created a number of anti-corruption legislations and institutions — some action, but still no effect. The estimate that some 30 per cent of all government revenues in president Daniel Arap Moi's regime were lost in shady deals, embezzlement, unauthorised spending and (selectively) lax revenue collection (Ross 2004, 22) may be conservative.

That level of corruption, both grand and petty, has continued unabated for decades, despite the introduction of the multi-party political system and public sector reforms, both of which were introduced in the early 1990s, and despite the introduction of opposition politics and some transparency in government. Indeed, even after the "Moi Must Go" campaign (based above all on public fatigue with government vice) brought Mwai Kibaki to power in 2003 with a new raft of anti-corruption legislations and other measures, corruption in government persisted. The Goldenberg Scandal of 1990–1993, the Anglo-Leasing Scandal of 1997–2006 (Kivuva and Odhiambo 2010, vii) and the more recent Triton and the Free Primary Education Funds scandals have all taken place in the midst of the "government's war against corruption". There have been numerous other less notorious or unreported "harvests", some on vast scales. Not one of the culprits has been apprehended and successfully prosecuted.

This chapter seeks to answer some of the questions: Why has corruption persisted in Kenya despite efforts made to eradicate it? Why have the institutional and administrative reforms of the past 20 years been unable to stem national larceny? To what extent has the new constitution provided the necessary institutional framework for a more successful fight against corruption? How can the optimism brought about by the new constitution provide impetus?

Using documentary and other secondary sources, mainly government documents and other published and unpublished materials, this chapter argues that despite the failure of past efforts to end corruption, ongoing constitutional and institutional reforms instituted since the 2007 general elections hold an important key to controlling corruption in Kenya.

The rest of the chapter is organised into four sections. The first section conceptualises corruption and public sector reforms in Africa, and reviews the literature. The second section deals with the anti-corruption and public sector reforms during the Moi era, while third section conducts the same exercise during the Kibaki regime. The last section provides conclusions and recommendations.

A Quick Look at Corruption and Public Sector Reform in Africa

If the Nobel laureate Chinua Achebe had been writing about Kenya in the past 20 years, he would say what he said of Nigeria; that corruption in Kenya "has passed the alarming" and has entered the "fatal stage"; that the country "will die if we keep pretending that she is only slightly indisposed". Achebe blames this state of affairs not just on poor leadership but also on those who are close to power – "the sharks and crooks that surround these leaders" (Achebe, 1984). Political support is bought with fiscal favours on an all-pervasive and colossal scale.

As in Nigeria, corruption in Kenya permeates the entire socio-economic and political fabric of the nation. Indeed, the entire Kenyan public is "encapsulated in corruption" (Kibwana *et al* 1996, 34). Corruption is part of everyday life (Anyang-Nyong'o 2006, 26). In the past 20 years (and especially the most recent seven years of President Kibaki), the government has undertaken a number of reforms without significant effect. Transparency International's Corruption Perception Index (CPI) since the Kibaki era has consistently put the country among the world's most corrupt nations. Kenya was ranked 144th (out of 159 in the world) in 2005; 150th (out of 179) in 2007; and, 147th (out of 180) in 2008[1].

Studies on the drivers and impacts of such rampant corruption in Africa, in general, and Kenya, in particular, view corruption from two perspectives.

Firstly, corruption is viewed as a relic of colonialism (Kiai 2003), citing policies that turned a blind eye to the malfeasance of the colonial administration[2]. The failure to establish strong, independent institutions that could check against corruption is considered a deliberate move by the colonial administration to ensure its continued domination. Both the motive and the method are echoed in independent Kenya. Advocates of the "colonial legacy" perspective point out that the foundations of the Kenyan state made it more susceptible to corruption by establishing a powerful presidency, a weak and parasitic legislature, and a puppet judiciary. The manner in which the latter two institutions were established made them not just unable but, more importantly, unwilling to check the excesses of the executive, and that has been the bedrock of corruption ever since. The legislature and the judiciary have been ineffective; indeed they have acted as partners with the executive in perpetrating the vices. The judiciary in particular has provided sanctuary to those accused by ensuring that corruption-related cases are never finalised (Anyang-Nyong'o 2006).

Secondly, corruption is viewed as a logical outcome of the kind of politics practised in Africa in the post-colonial period: politics of patronage; politics of extraction; politics of 'rent-seeking' and personality rule, born of the absence of participatory governance (Kibwana *et al* 2001). The preponderance of governments throughout Africa that do not encourage transparency, accountability, or integrity in the conduct of public affairs is to blame. Patronage politics, personality rule and the politics of extraction are all characterised by the absence of an institutional framework to check over-centralisation and over-concentration of power – factors at the centre of corruption in Africa. This paper adopts this second view. It argues that political patronage, over-centralisation and excessive power within the executive are at the root of corruption – and its persistence – in Kenya. This is not a new discovery. It was 150 years ago that Lord Acton coined the immortal phrase: "Power tends to corrupt, and absolute power corrupts absolutely."

The many studies on the subject of corruption have not provided a unified definition, but descriptors of the modern form do share primary common features (Odhiambo 2010). For the purposes of this study, corruption means "dishonest or irregular transactions of official business for direct or indirect personal gain, which is perpetrated by individuals in formal positions of authority" (Chweya 2005, 3). Corruption involves the "theft of public assets by officials charged with their stewardship" (Mullei 2000, 44). Of the many forms, key practices include pocketing tax revenues, bribery and kickbacks – both in disposing of public assets for reduced prices, or using public funds to purchase assets at inflated prices. There are instances where both kickback mechanisms are used, in a constant cycle, even sometimes involving the same asset! Corruption is, therefore, extremely costly to an economy and has remained one of the main causes of poverty and a "major impediment to economic development" (Kibwana *et al* 1996, xv).

In Africa, anti-corruption strategies have been undertaken as part of broad public sector reforms aimed at creating a leaner, more efficient, motivated and productive civil service to facilitate better service delivery. Since public service reforms began in Africa in the 1980s[3], different countries have adopted a variety of measures to curb corruption. Ghana, Namibia, Nigeria, Tanzania, Sudan, Zambia and Zimbabwe have experimented with the institution of Ombudsmen, anti-corruption bills and a variety of institutional mechanisms to enforce ethical behaviour (ECA 2003). Ethiopia and Nigeria provide good examples of the institutional route[4]. Public sector reforms (including anti-corruption measures) have generally been limited in scope, speed and quality. A 2003 ECA study singled out corruption as "by far one of the biggest challenges in the public sector". Other challenges that have hindered public service reforms and the fight against corruption include multiple accountability, inadequate resource utilisation, inadequate institutional capacity, lack of political will, and poor coordination mechanisms (ECA 2003, 35).

An Economic Commission for Africa (ECA, 2003:35) cites institutional weaknesses (Mbaku 1998, 27), lack of political will to fight the problem, bureaucratic pathologies within the public sector (Chweya 2010), the erosion and compression of salary scales of public servants (Hope 2002) and a political culture that condones corruption. To McCormack (1997), corruption usually takes place "behind the screen" and is not easily detected. Kiragu and Mutahaba (2006, 12) identify low pay as the major single factor responsible for the rise of petty corruption in Africa. The UNECA report gives three reasons why public sector reforms are not effective instruments in fighting corruption: firstly, many of the public sector reforms in Africa were introduced in an overall political environment that was not sufficiently conducive to the success of the measure; secondly, some of the anti-corruption measures introduced have been partial in nature, focusing mainly on sanctions and not the source; and thirdly, many of the institutions established to promote ethics and accountability often lack the resources, public visibility, impartiality and public support that are crucial to their success (ECA 2003, 35).

The Public Service Reform Programme (PSRP) in Kenya dating back to the early 1990s was initially designed to be a civil service reform programme (CSRP) and its implementation covered 1993 – 2001. This programme was expanded later to include the judiciary, local authorities and parastatals (Oyugi 1996, 37). However, the reform initiatives under the core civil service were the central focus and consumed most resources. These were a continuation of reforms government had been undertaking since independence to improve the public sector and make it more efficient. Not uncommonly, the performance of government remained poor, inefficient and ineffective in service provision (Oyugi 1996, 37).

Although Kenya's public service was bedevilled with all these problems, "there is no evidence that they (problems) directly influenced government's reforms in 1992 (Oyugi 1996, 42; Republic of Kenya 1992). Rather, it was "somewhat by coincidence" (Oyugi 1996, 44) that the government, concerned about mismanagement of public resources, established a committee in 1981 with the sole purpose of reviewing public expenditure. To Walter Oyugi, it was the cost-saving measures recommended by this committee that provided the platform upon which the reforms in the civil service would be based (Republic of Kenya 1982). Kenya's reform agenda was also influenced by decisions made by the Commonwealth Heads of State meeting in Harare in 1991, which strongly supported the Commonwealth Principles of democratic development (Kaul 1995).

Corruption during the Moi Era [1980–2002]

Moi became president in 1978 and promised to follow Kenyatta's footsteps (*nyayo*). He certainly did in matters of corruption. Just as Kenyatta had condoned corrupt practices by his clients, and even used them as a resource for his patronage politics, the Moi regime was not keen on legislating against corruption and did not undertake adequate measures to eradicate it. While Kenyatta tacitly sanctioned corruption within limits, Moi's "*nyayo* philosophy" advanced that licence to a level of apparent impunity. Unlike Kenyatta's *magendo*, Moi's clients began what would later develop into looting of public institutions by public servants who "sold their authority", not only for irregular practices, but even before they would perform their proper duties. Even in the judiciary, the dispensation of justice became a commodity that could be purchased. Moi's "war on corruption" was words, not action.

Official corruption at the start of Moi's presidency was covert and in the form of nepotistic promotions, ethnic-based recruitments and selective award of lucrative government contracts to politically preferred individuals. Like the Kikuyu during Kenyatta's time, people from Moi's Kalenjin community seemed to get a disproportionate share of the available appointments – ethnic, regional and other characteristics took precedence over merit, qualifications and experience. Many with the ability and experience to merit recruitment and promotion were denied.

This ethnicisation went hand-in-hand with the selective issuance and denial of licences (trade, import, and export licences) and tenders which were awarded to the politically well-connected. These benefits became the regime's rewards for 'good behaviour' - support for Moi. The recipients gained access to public resources that they could extract (through corrupt means) to further benefit themselves and their clients. As corruption became common in the civil service, tenure could no longer be guaranteed by ability, diligence and hard work. So the holders of these offices were encouraged to enrich themselves quickly as insurance against unpredictable removal. It is this uncertainty caused by nepotistic recruitment and promotion that helped "push corruption to a whole new level" in Kenya during the Moi era (Kagwanja 2009, 18).

The politics of multi-partyism in the late 1980s and early 1990s made a bad situation worse, because it brought even more uncertainties - the threats of unregulated political competition which "opposition" posed to the Moi regime polarised the division between the pro- and anti- Moi groups; not just within the political elite but also in the public and other sectors of the economy. Moi obsessively staffed key institutions of government (judiciary, executive and even the legislature)[5] with loyalists, and they traded that for opportunities to enrich themselves. The pressure for political funding from official corruption increased, as Moi had not only to satisfy the appetites of his supporters, but also finance measures to undermine his opponents. Unlike Kenyatta's clients who were already well-positioned politically and well-entrenched economically, many of Moi's clients were novices in politics and were not (yet) wealthy (enough).

To rid the public sector of opponents, Moi granted what amounted to a blank cheque to his allies to do whatever it took to ensure his government survived the multi-party onslaught. Between 1990 and 2000, Kenya witnessed the institutionalisation and elevation of corruption to levels comparable to those of Nigeria, commonly regarded as the champion of corruption in Africa. Corruption became the most profitable aspect of working for Moi's government. A peak of this was the Goldenberg Scandal, which involved "an intricate collusion between the executive, legislature, judiciary and relevant government regulatory agencies" (Kagwanja 2009, 20; Kivuva and Odhiambo 2010).

Prior to the 1990s, public debates and discourses on corruption, like any other political debate in Kenya, were quite restricted (mostly through the self-censorship of pragmatism). Information on corruption, particularly the extent to which it had spread, was scanty in the public domain. Official statistics were simply not available. Those involved in high-level corruption were not just senior in government but socially powerful individuals who could easily threaten – even the lives - of any anti-corruption crusaders. Before multi-party democracy and public sector reforms offered a good measure of freedom of expression, public debate and dialogue on corruption remained muted. The only reports on corruption were from the Comptroller and Auditor General, the donor community and a few local NGOs.

Any corruption cases reported were handled through the traditional criminal legal system – investigations by the regular police and by normal courts under the directorship of the Attorney General who had absolute power to decide who could or could not be prosecuted.[6] In all the years the anti-corruption war had been waged, not a single high-profile corruption case had been fully prosecuted nor a conviction secured. Many of the cases that reached the court system were dismissed, delayed or withdrawn by the Attorney General (Anyang-Nyong'o 2006).

Quite apart from this "insider" veto power, government and others responsible for checking corruption did not pursue key suspects in any serious manner. Clearly, the law was a very limited tool for fighting corruption in Kenya (Kibwana *et al* 2001, 26). The office of the Attorney General was pivotal. Even where public or external pressure eventually forced the arrest of powerful individuals, the Attorney General could always intervene with "insufficient evidence" or "incomplete investigations" – unilaterally.

Public Sector Reforms and Moi's Anti-Corruption Measures

Things changed in the 1990s during what Huntington (1991) calls the Third Wave of democratisation, as important developments made issues of corruption mainstream. The demands for multi-party politics, pressures from the donor community, efforts from civil society organisations, public sector reforms and the presence of opposition MPs in parliament offered an opportunity for the people to discuss corruption, particularly official corruption in government. The 1990s saw increased domestic and international pressure for the government to institute anti-corruption legislations and to enforce existing ones. The introduction of Structural Adjustment Programmes imposed by the donor community demanded a more transparent and accountable government. Resistance by the Moi government led to the withholding of important development funds by major donors. It was the desire/need to ensure resumption of donor funds that forced the Moi government to institute public sector reforms and other changes presented as a meaningful response to corruption. The following are some of the public sector reform measures considered during the period of president Moi:

- The strategic vision of the CSRP (1993 – 2000) was the rationalisation of ministerial structures and function; effective decentralisation; retention of fewer but better-paid staff and improving ethical standards in the civil service (Republic of Kenya 1992,10). This was revised in the Civil Service Reform Medium-Term Strategy (1998 – 2001), whose vision was the achievement of good performance and high quality service delivery (Oyugi 1996, 46). This programme neither improved public service delivery nor reduced the government's wage bill. Nzioka (2002) found public service delivery deteriorated as a result of the programme's narrow focus. A new strategic Plan for Public Sector Reform was introduced in 2001, emphasising the restoration of efficiency and effectiveness (Nzioka 2002,16), and CSRP was expanded to a more inclusive Public Sector Reform Programme (PSRP), establishing a Project Coordinating Unit to help government improve public service institutions and support improved performance of the judiciary. With the oversight of the World Bank, the Government of Kenya committed itself to annual review in four key areas: a) Public service reforms; b) Public finance management; c) Legal sector reforms; and d) Project management. The CSRP from 1993 to 2000 was not integrated with budgetary reforms and generally did not have the required downward impact to reduce the government wage bill (Oyugi 1996, 50). The pace of implementation was slow and not far-reaching. The structure of PSRPs did little more than change the acronym (Kiragu 2002).

- Multi-partyism made parliament more assertive in demanding accountability from the executive. The revival of the committee system made parliament's oversight role more functional to demand openness in executive actions. The Parliamentary Public Accounts and Parliamentary Investment committees were especially active in demanding government acton on individuals and institutions cited in the Comptroller and Auditor General's reports. After the exposure of the Goldenberg Scandal where the public lost more than US $400 million[7], demands for action against corrupt individuals became public. The Goldenberg Scandal was the first mega-corruption scandal that was well publicised and the people got to know the extent of government involvement, despite attempts to shield those at the heart of the scandal.

- Three government departments/sections - procurement, accounting and auditing - were targeted for anti-corruption measures. An Efficiency Monitoring Unit (EMU) was established in 1990, followed by the inclusion of an anti-corruption section in Moi's 1992 election manifesto, in which his ruling party

(KANU) promised to take firm measures to "eliminate corruption and other unethical practices in the civil service".[8] Yet, in July 1997, the IMF and the donor community (the Paris Club) re-imposed suspension of aid to Kenya due to the government's failure to rein-in corruption. This was prompted by the government's unwillingness to prosecute the masterminds of the Goldenberg Scandal[9]. The government then amended the Prevention of Corruption Act (Cap 65) to establish the Kenya Anti-Corruption Authority, with Harun Mwau as its first director. He was suspended one year later and resigned in November 1998. He was replaced by Aaron Ringera, but following the arrests of senior government officials on suspicion of corruption, KACA was declared unconstitutional in December 2000 and subsequently dissolved. As well as conflicts between government and the IMF/World Bank, there were a number of collaborations in reforming the civil service. Following the second multi-party elections in 1997, and buoyed by the government's willingness to negotiate with the opposition, as exemplified by the Inter-Party Parliamentary Group (IPPG) Agreements, the World Bank helped government to reform public procurement. The most important assistance was the formulation and implementation of the Public Procurement Reform and Enhanced Capacity Project[10] intended to streamline and enforce public procurement and public tendering procedures. In 2001, further reforms were instituted through the Exchequer and Audit (Public Procurement) Regulations, which provided for the establishment of tendering committees, the establishment of the Public Procurement Complaints Review Board and the Procurement Appeals Board. Reforms in government accounting departments between 1997 and 2000 focused on major avenues for corruption, and key areas through which the government lost substantial revenues. Collaboration between the IMF/World Bank and the government identified the key areas as disregard for accounting procedures, poor data management, inadequate budgeting systems and inadequate and at times irregular monitoring of government expenditures. With IMF and World Bank technical assistance, teams were seconded to improve the financial accounting and financial management systems,[11] leading to the reorganisation of accounts departments at various levels of government, stricter controls of petty cash, and stronger internal audits of government finances in all areas. These audits became "the focal points for reform in the public service" (Chweya, Tuta and Akivaga 2005, 28–9), which improved the government's ability to safeguard public finances.

- The Public Service (Code of Conduct and Ethics) Bill in 2001 sought to outlaw bribery and other contraventions of rules and procedures, establish standard operating procedures for public services, prohibit public servants from taking part in areas where they had personal financial interest, require public servants to conduct their personal affairs with integrity, and encourage meritocracy in both recruitment and promotion. If these measures to seal loopholes were enacted, many legislators would lose major sources of campaign funds and lose their control over clients in the public service. The bill was not passed in parliament. The Attorney General submitted a revised bill, but parliament was dissolved in readiness for the 2002 elections before it could be debated. The bill was later passed by the Kibaki government that succeeded Moi.

- Responding to domestic and international pressure, the government created a special police unit — the Anti-Corruption Squad — with a mandate to investigate corruption cases and advise the government. The squad was under the command of the Police Commissioner, and under the direction of the Attorney General. At this time, the police force had the reputation of being the most corrupt institution in government. Appreciating this irony, international pressure to institute an independent agency to deal with corruption cases did not relent, even with the subsequent establishment of the Anti-Corruption Police.

- In 1992, the Attorney General appointed a 15-member reform task force to review and update laws and, in 1998, the Chief Justice appointed a Legal Sector Reform Coordinating Committee (the Kwach Committee) to make recommendations on how the judiciary could be made more effective and efficient. Its report, submitted in 2000, focused on "more institutionalisation." When the IMF made the setting up of an independent authority to tackle corruption a condition of aid resumption, the government created the Kenya Anti-Corruption Authority (KACA)[12], seen as "the most far-reaching" measure "to address the problem of corruption by the Moi government" (Kibwana *et al.* 2001,31). The IMF demanded that the people selected to head the KACA had to be appointed in consultation with the Law Society of Kenya (LSK), the International Commission of Jurists (ICJ) and other key civil society organisations. By an August 1998 Kenya Gazette Notice, the government conceded to IMF demands and agreed to an Advisory Board to recommend who could be appointed to head the KACA. The government also accepted that those to run the KACA would be "people of outstanding honesty and integrity, knowledgeable or experienced in law; having experience and knowledge in monetary and financial matters, accountancy and fraud investigations" (Ng'weno May 15, 1998, 33). But the government's commitment to facilitating the KACA was questionable right from the start. The KACA was under the control of the executive, with its key positions being held by people appointed by the president. The executive resisted any attempts to anchor the KACA and other anti-corruption agencies within the constitution, and resisted attempts to have the KACA leadership vetted by parliament. The KACA was also denied powers to prosecute and remained subject to the Attorney General's veto. The KACA also relied on the Kenya police for its investigations and on the judicial system for trial - institutions firmly under executive control. In practice, the Attorney General, the police and the judicial system acted more to protect suspects than prosecute them. Whenever the KACA did get suspects to court, almost all cases were undermined by the Attorney General's veto. The KACA therefore remained a "toothless dog" (Ng'weno, May 15, 1998)[13]. (The judiciary would finally make it a dead dog.) While still breathing, the KACA lacked a sound financial base and adequate staff and was never fully operationalised. It acted more as a smokescreen than a spotlight on looters and corrupt leaders. Among leading public figures with enormous wealth from dubious sources was the first director of the KACA itself.[14]

So while KACA plainly lacked political support, it did not have popular support either. When the new director did charge some high-level government officials,[15] the Attorney General and the Finance Minister acted to have the director removed, and although this did not instantly happen, an alternative strategy that left him with nothing to be director of was successful. In December 2000 the authority was declared unconstitutional.[16] In response to subsequent and heightened public and international pressure, the Attorney General published a number of anti-corruption bills.[17]

• Parliament plays three key roles: legislative, representative and oversight. With the reintroduction of the multi-party system, parliamentary committees were reintroduced and reinvigorated. Two committees, in particular, the Public Accounts and the Public Investment, took a lead role in the fight against corruption. The two made annual reports to parliament detailing many corruption cases that needed to be investigated. In addition, parliament appointed ad hoc investigatory committees[18] as well as a Parliamentary Select Committee on Corruption. In addition to exposing corruption cases, these committees made recommendations on how corruption could be curbed. Parliament also introduced a number of corruption-related bills aimed at establishing a legal framework to deal more adequately with the crime.

In July 1998, responding to intense international pressure (mainly from the IMF) as well as internal pressure (from the civil society and opposition MPs), the government, through parliament, established the Parliamentary Anti-Corruption Select Committee chaired by Musikari Kombo. The Kombo Committee submitted its report to Parliament in 2000, which led to the publication of the Anti-Corruption and Economic Crimes Bill in 2000. Had the recommendations been adopted, they might have significantly enhanced the fight against corruption. They were not adopted.

Corruption in the judiciary was the result of a complex mixture of institutional weaknesses, poor remuneration, poor administration, institutional dysfunctions and excessive political patronage. Since independence, the judiciary had been the most patronised institution in Kenya. The entire institution was under executive control, which historically patronised key appointees to the judiciary. In the post-1990 period, the judiciary played a key role in maintaining the KANU government in power despite challenges from the opposition. Since the infamous queue-voting elections of 1988, numerous cases against the president and the KANU government were brought to court for determination. In the run-up to the multi-party system and during the first years of its introduction, these cases increased tremendously. In almost all the cases, the judiciary determined cases in favour of the government and pro-KANU politicians. In return, corruption within the judiciary was allowed to continue unchecked. Attempts to reduce corruption by improving remuneration and other perks did not reduce malpractices (Chweya 2005, 35). The problem did not lie in the structure of incentive but in the structure of political patronage. The Parliamentary Select Committee recommended in its report for a change in the way judges were recruited (Republic of Kenya, 2002: 70; ECA, 2003).

The Kombo Committee's 2000 report made 17 recommendations (Republic of Kenya, May 2000: 63). Among the most important were that corruption in all its manifestations could not be handled all at once and required a "permanent watchdog committee of the House" to constantly monitor anti-corruption efforts. The report recommended a multi-pronged approach, including stricter anti-corruption legislations, the establishment of stronger agencies to prosecute corruption cases, civic education as well as reforms in the public service.

Other recommendations included:

- the establishment of an Anti-corruption and Economic Crimes Bill, 2000, which was to repeal the Prevention of Corruption Act (Cap. 65 of the Laws of Kenya)and broaden the KACA powers to prosecute;
- the promotion of civic education towards a culture that does not condone corruption;
- the establishment of an Anti-Corruption and Economic Crimes Court;
- the establishment of Parliamentary Ethics and Integrity Committee to vet appointees to the KACA and its board;

- the formulation of a leadership Code of Ethics and the regular review of Anti-Corruption and Economic Crimes legislation;
- the revival of the Parliamentary Implementation Committee;
- declaration of assets and interests;[19]
- reforms in the Justice Department; and[20]
- reforms in the civil service.[21]

Outcomes of President Moi's Anti-corruption Public Sector Reforms

An evaluation of Moi's anti-corruption measures is provided in an article by Peter Anyang-Nyong'o on the "Political Economy of Corruption in Kenya" (2006). He notes Kenya's legal framework deliberately left too much room for civil servants' discretion – readily exploited for personal gain. It is this discretionary power that allowed for collusion between public servants and politicians that led to the many grand corruption scandals in Kenya. According to Anyang-Nyong'o and Martha Karua, the Moi regime "sanctioned corruption". Anyang-Nyong'o asserts that lawyers dealing with corruption cases were "killed" while arrests of those charged with corruptions "rarely led to conclusive prosecutions". The rich and powerful were quick to file injunctions that delayed and even obstructed corruption cases against them while the poor were punished for receiving or giving small bribes. Anyang-Nyong'o noted that:

"University lecturers were thrown into police cells and detained; students were butchered while demonstrating and violence meted out against their parents as they demanded transparent use of national resources in development of the nation.. lawyers following up witnesses in corruption cases have been bought off or bumped off. Prosecutors have been threatened. Witnesses have disappeared without trace."(Anyang-Nyong'o 2006, 28).

Where corruption has powerful official sanction, law enforcement agents have cause to be afraid of apprehending suspects. Thus, those who should have been spearheading the fight against corruption became "a speed governor, checking people intent on fighting corruption... and joined the chorus of those calling for a 'go-slow' in dealing with corruption cases and investigations". When those meant to hunt the corrupt became the hunted, any fight against corruption in government was hijacked by "a mafia of plutocrats", who in public spoke against the vice but in private urged that the hunters go slow in their job, or abandon it altogether.

The Moi regime turned out to be a complex syndicate of corrupt officials, where "even the judges before whom corruption cases appear engage in the game of filibustering.. adjourning cases endlessly, losing files deliberately and even excusing themselves from hearing a case when many months have gone down the drain as evidence is given and witnesses grilled. Wrong people have been deliberately arrested and brought to court, charged with corruption or drug smuggling, when the law enforcement agencies know exactly what they are doing: pulling the wool over the faces of Kenyans in a make–believe exercise of fighting corruption"(Anyang-Nyong'o 2006, 28).

By the end of the Moi regime, corruption had become so institutionalised that the struggles to oust him from the presidency became an anti-corruption campaign as well. In the words of Uhuru Kenyatta, Moi's chosen successor to the presidency, the failure of Moi's government to curb corruption was responsible for the defeat of KANU in the 2002 elections[22]. Indeed, the overwhelming support for Mwai Kibaki in his successful bid for the presidency was mainly the result of a belief that he would rein in corruption.

Kibaki's Anti-Corruption Initiatives, Outcomes and Challenges (2003–2011)

Initiatives under President Kibaki

Having come to power on a wave of anti-corruption sentiment, and a promise to "firmly deal with corruption", the Kibaki government adopted a "zero tolerance"[23] crusade. A number of legislations started with the establishment of the Kenya Anti-Corruption Commission (KACC), the appointment of a Permanent Secretary in the Office of the President in charge of Ethics, signing of the African Union (AU) Convention on Preventing and Combating Corruption, and ratifying the United Nations (UN) Convention Against Corruption. The Kibaki government appointed the Bosire Commission to investigate the Goldenberg Scandal.[24]

It also passed the Public Officer Ethics Bill (April 16, 2003), which Kibaki signed into law in May. This was a resubmission of the Public Service (Code of Conduct and Ethics) Bill that had been introduced by the Moi government, but which was defeated in parliament just before the dissolution of the last session leading up to the December 2002 elections. After coming to power in January 2003, the Kibaki government had this bill passed in parliament within three months. The Public Officer Ethics Act (2003) compels public servants to declare their wealth (income, assets and liabilities), and sets up a code of conduct and standards of honesty and efficiency (in the provision of services) which each public officer is expected to adhere to. Public officers were to avoid nepotism or favouritism, and were expected to adhere to the general practices of impartiality in their duties. More importantly, the act holds public officers personally responsible for the public property under their care.

The Kibaki administration also signed the following acts into law: a) The Anti-Corruption and Economics Crimes Act (May 2003), establishing the Kenya Anti-Corruption Commission to prevent, detect and prosecute corruption offences; b) The Public Audit Act 2004; c) The Public Procurement and Disposal of Assets Act 2005; and d) The Government Financial Management Act 2007. The administration also introduced Performance Contracting in 2003, and a cabinet committee on anti-corruption, chaired by the Minister for Justice, whose mandate was to oversee the implementation of government policies on corruption and review progress. Government barred state officers from soliciting for *Harambee* funds (voluntary donations to development projects), improved the functional capacity of the police force, encouraged public education against corruption, and put in place the strategic KACA (2005), in which the government brought together stakeholders for input.

As corruption within the judiciary in Kenya is a generally acknowledged fact, Kibaki started by suspending the Chief Justice (who resigned soon after to avoid facing the tribunal appointed to investigate his conduct). A purge in September 2003 suspended 23 High Court and Court of Appeal Judges and 82 magistrates on suspicion of corruption (Wahome 2007, 36). In the end, 70 magistrates were retired "in the public interest" by the Judicial Service Commission. None was ever prosecuted. The purge was not accompanied by underlying structural reforms, and the summary nature of the removals, though popular, endangered the security of tenure of judges and magistrates, which negatively affected the institution's independence. Personnel were changed, but the executive maintained dominance over their replacements.

Under a new Chief Justice, a number of anti-corruption measures were put in place within the judiciary, key among them being the establishment of the Integrity and Anti-Corruption Committee of the Judiciary (2003)[25] (which implicated a large number of High Court and Court of Appeal Judges) and set up the Ethics and Governance Committee of the Judiciary (2005) and another Ethics and Governance Committee in 2007.

Outcomes and Challenges of Kibaki Reforms

The incidence of corruption, especially bribery, decreased significantly over the first few years of the Kibaki regime. General awareness among the people and stakeholders of the need to stand up against corruption increased (Chweya 2005, 140).

The necessary legal and institutional structure to fight corruption is now in better shape and the political playing field has undergone profound changes, but a significant number of the players on that field are the same people with histories and entrenched habits from older regimes. Little wonder that the behaviour of senior politicians within the Kibaki government has "denied the government critical support and slowed down the implementation of anti-corruption programmes". Those facing investigations or cases related to corruption and other economic crimes, though now often the most vocal on the war against corruption, want the fight to be restricted to new cases only and cry foul whenever the government attempts to resurrect old cases. Little wonder that even as the Kibaki regime finally put the perpetrators of Goldenberg in the dock, cronies of the same regime were grabbing public utilities, illegally selling public plots, and excising supposedly sacrosanct forest lands (Chweya 2005, 3). Indeed, some of the biggest corruption scandals – Anglo Leasing (which was far greater in scale than Goldenberg), Triton and Free Primary School Fund – have taken place on Kibaki's watch, with no resignations of suspects to facilitate independent investigation, no charges and no prosecutions.

The purge of judges was not successful in ensuring an effective and corrupt-free judiciary because it was not accompanied by any mechanisms for continuous evaluation and monitoring. The judiciary has since been a substantial hindrance to the fight against corruption - most cases taken to court have been delayed on "unmeritorious constitutional grounds" (Karua 2006). With the second vetting of the judiciary, the establishment of the Supreme Court, and the swearing into office of nine justices in 2011, there is hope delays will be fewer. Other changes that could make the judiciary more functional include restructuring to create the Supreme Court, the introduction of a president to head each court, and the signing of performance contracts that the judiciary had resisted for many years.

In a speech made to the Regional Conference on Corruption and Human Rights held in March 2006 in Nairobi, the then Minister for Justice and Constitutional Affairs, Martha Karua, exhaustively and openly discussed the hindrances to the fight against corruption. She especially cited the transition process following the 2002 elections; the unresolved constitutional review process; and resistance from the corruption networks of the past.

When the Kibaki government came to power, the coalition partners did not establish a common objective: "[T]here were [and still are] many in the [Kibaki] coalition [government] that stood, and stand, to lose from an effective campaign against corruption. Though outwardly supportive of the war against corruption, such persons are not enthusiastic about anti-corruption efforts. Many corrupt individuals have found political comfort among such persons" (Karua 2006, 6-7).

While the Public Officer Ethics Act 2003 demands declaration of wealth, the declaration forms are not available for public scrutiny. There is no mechanism for verification. The Constitution of Kenya (2010) may resolve this through its Freedom of Information provision, but then, the declaration applies to the official only not, for example, to spouse, siblings or children.

Other acts of commission and omission also cast a cloud. The Kibaki government failed to secure the KACC within the constitution. Like its predecessor, it remains a creature of parliament (Chweya, Tuta and Akivaga 2005, 21), subordinate to the Attorney

General and his veto power. Furthermore, the KACC was denied the necessary powers to prosecute. It can only investigate, offer advice, and conduct civic education programmes on the dangers of corruption. Anti-corruption enforcement mechanisms continue to be highly selective.

The Constitution of Kenya (2010) and the Future of War on Corruption

The new constitution demands a higher level of transparency in government and public accountability. It provides for enhanced checks and balances; separates the functional roles of the executive and legislature, and makes the executive more accountable to parliament and to the people.

Closely related to these positives are ongoing institutional reforms. These began with the introduction of the multi-party system in the early 1990s, and have been accelerated in the past eight years. As part of Agenda 4 reforms contained in the Kenya National Dialogue and Reconciliation accords that ended the 2007 post-election violence, parliament was to undertake further reforms, which have been completed, and which have improved its institutional functional capacity as well. With a more functional legislature and a better system of checks and balances parliament has become more assertive. The new constitution has increased the effectiveness of parliament in checking the executive by providing that all major presidential appointments be approved by parliament before they are effected.

The new constitution demands the appointment of a new Attorney General and Chief Justice, the vetting of judges, reduction of executive dominance over the other arms of government (which had been the bedrock of corrupt practices), new institutionalised checks and balances within government, and the new Director of the Kenya Anti-Corruption Commission. Chapter Six of the Constitution of Kenya (2010) also demands a high degree of integrity for leaders to run any public office. Public officers must be people who have not been associated with any scandal or any corruption cases. All these promise to provide the anti-corruption crusade with new muscle. The recent high-level cases the new KACC director has taken to court against three cabinet ministers are indicators of the powers the new constitution provides.

Previously, the fight against corruption in Kenya never had legal foundation underpinned by the constitution, nor was it granted financial or administrative independence. The powers of the Attorney General and the KACA were not harmonised and the two offices acted more as competitors than collaborators.

The hallmark of Kenya's post-colonial state and the fount of corruption was the imperial presidency, which has been at the centre of every political problem the country has faced since independence, including corruption. The pre-2010 constitution granted the president powers to appoint people to almost every important government position and other government bodies without institutional checks and without those appointed being vetted either by the judiciary or the legislature[26]. In addition, the old constitution gave the President unbridled power to hire and fire almost every senior member of the government. In particular, the President's powers to appoint members of the judiciary and the requirement that the cabinet be appointed from among MPs had elevated the executive above all other institutions. This meant that corrupt practices sanctioned by the executive could not be curtailed by either the legislature or the judiciary.

The pre-2010 constitution provided successive presidents with opportunities to patronise MPs and dominate the judiciary. The President has used positions in the cabinet and the judiciary to reward those MPs and judges who cooperated with the executive. Being an avenue for personal enrichment, these cabinet positions have over the years become a coveted prize, encouraging corruption both to get there and stay there.

The new constitution, by preventing the executive from hiring and firing public officials at will, and strengthening the judiciary and the legislature, has strengthened the fight against corruption. The executive is more accountable to the other arms of government, helping to ensure a functional separation of powers. The new constitution has abolished the practice of appointing cabinet ministers only from among parliamentarians as unelected technocrats are now eligible, and has introduced institutional checks on all presidential appointments. Executive excesses, such as the arbitrary firing of "uncooperative" civil servants who refused to do the President's will, are curbed by the new constitution, which has also restricted patronage politics in favour of a more merit-based system of recruitment and promotion.

The new constitution has reconstructed parliament through the establishment of a second chamber (the senate), and has expanded the institution while parliamentary committees have been revitalised. Parliament's oversight role on the executive has been enhanced by a mandate to vet every important presidential appointment. All these measures effectively bring the era of the imperial president to an end.

Since the introduction of the multi-party system and the introduction of public sector reforms in the 1990s, parliament has become increasingly assertive (Barkan 2010), a trend that has improved during the Kibaki era, particularly after the formation of the Grand Coalition Government in 2008. The legislature has also embraced the ongoing institutional reforms[27] and regained some of its lost independence. The new constitution has further enhanced parliament's oversight role over the executive by granting members of parliament the authority to demand the dismissal of non-performing government officials. The fact that a member of parliament can compel the President to dismiss a Cabinet Secretary or other government officer further reduces the President's ability to influence or protect anyone involved in corruption. This is likely to curb nepotism, patronage-based appointments and the culture of impunity in public service that has been the bedrock of high level corruption. In addition, the new constitution demands a new crop of leadership with more integrity and ethical standards that will facilitate more and better service to the people.

As part of removing or reducing the dominance of the Attorney General's office in prosecutions, the new constitution has established an independent Office of Director of Public Prosecutions (ODPP). Since the ODPP is controlled neither by the Attorney General nor by the executive in general, it has the potential to improve the delivery of justice in Kenya. The Director of Public Prosecutions will have powers to direct the Inspector General of the National Police Service to investigate any case. This is a major departure from the current practice, where the Attorney General, a presidential surrogate, heads all public prosecutions. With an independent and non-political ODPP and a non-political Kenya Anti-Corruption Commission

(KACC), it is anticipated that the two institutions will work more closely with each other and with less political interference.

The judiciary has been the weakest, least-trusted and the most dysfunctional of the three arms of government. It has lacked either operational or financial independence and has grossly failed in its core mandate of dispensing justice. Indeed, the people of Kenya had lost faith in the institution of the judiciary, recognising its weaknesses made it a channel for, not a check on, corruption. Although earlier attempts in 2003 to reform the judiciary did not succeed, the new constitution makes very significant changes in the structure and design of the judiciary. The newly established Supreme Court will have powers of original jurisdiction to determine its own jurisprudence. The expectation is that the Supreme Court will steer Kenya away from the bad laws and rulings that have hitherto given corrupt suspects immunity. The new constitution has created the position of presiding judge to head each division of the courts. The Supreme Court will have the Chief Justice and the Deputy Chief Justice as President and Vice President of the Court, respectively. The Court of Appeal will be headed by an elected President (elected by fellow judges of the Court of Appeal), while the High Court will be headed by an elected Principal Judge (elected by fellow judges of the High Court). This will bring about accountability in the institution, essential if corruption is to be eliminated.

The judiciary has been accorded financial independence and the powers of "the" President over the institution, exercised through appointments of judges and the financing of the judiciary, have been curtailed. Although the President will continue to appoint the Chief Justice, the Deputy Chief Justice, and other Judges, these appointments will be in accordance with the recommendations of the Judicial Service Commission, and the choice of Chief Justice and the Deputy Chief Justice will be vetted by parliament. The independence of the Judicial Service Commission has been ensured by removing the president's role in the selection of the Judicial Service Commissioners (JSC). Of the 11 or so members of the JSC, only two members, representing the public, will be appointed by the President, and even this will require the approval of the National Assembly.

In a bid to restructure the government to facilitate better provision of services and better systems of accountability, the Constitution of Kenya (2010) seems to have created a fourth arm of the government — that of constitutional office holders and commissions — which, collectively, have far-reaching functions and mandates. The senate will also strengthen the administration of justice and demand for accountability from government officers.

Conclusion

Complete eradication of corruption borders on impossibility in human terms (Kibwana *et al.* 2001, 18). However, to reduce corruption to levels that do not seriously challenge the government's ability to provide services to the people at an acceptable cost, an holistic and multi-pronged approach which combines a number of approaches is required. Key among them are:

- anti-corruption legislations;
- a zero-tolerance approach on the side of the government;
- more integrity in the conduct of governmental affairs; and
- increasing the penalties for corruption that would turn low-risk/high-gain into a high-risk/low gain activity.

If and when the costs of corruption far outweigh the benefits, many will be deterred and desist. Extensive civic education that will socialise the people into refusing to give or accept bribes will also be necessary. In sum, concerted efforts that combine preventive and punitive anti-corruption strategies as well as public awareness and civic education measures are required if corruption is to be eradicated. Public awareness and civic education exercises are also given prominence by The Constitution of Kenya (2010), reflected in the Devolved Government Bill (2011) which provides for "sustained", "systematised" and "orderly" civic education programmes to be undertaken at all levels of government to ensure that the people are engaged in the implementation of the new constitution.

The government has put in place many of the necessary anti-corruption mechanisms, institutions and the necessary legal framework to make the war on corruption winnable. Today, the entire governmental machinery has accepted and has undertaken public sector reform. Sustained demands by civil society for more reforms and better governance have seen tremendous improvement in structures and systems. As a World Bank expert on corruption recommended, corruption needs to be viewed within a broader governance context such as the rule of law, protection of property rights, freedom of the press, political competition, transparent campaigns, financing and other things that change the environment in which corruption exists.

The Kibaki government has improved the governance systems, including greater respect for human rights, poverty eradication programmes, and enhanced rule of law. Since 2010, the coalition government has put in place the new constitution, which sets very high standards for those who work in the public sector, and better systems for ensuring public accountability, better mechanisms for running elections, more checks and balances, and generally introduced more transparent and accountable governance structures.

Clearly, corruption and the corrupt will not go down without a fight. However, after two decades of public sector reforms and the anti-corruption war, especially in the past eight years, the necessary critical mass to fight the vice seems to have been created.

Chapter Six of Kenya's new constitution demands that the recruitment of public servants be done openly to ensure that only competent and persons of integrity are recruited. The new constitution has also legislated for easier access to information held by the state. This is reinforced by Article 35 (3) of the Devolved Governments Bill (2011) that requires the state to publish and publicise any important information affecting the nation. Indeed, the Devolved Government's Bill (2011) requires every county agency to designate an officer for the purpose of ensuring that citizens have access to information held by the government. County governments are also required to develop and pass laws and regulations to ensure expeditious access to information (Article 102). This, together with the changing political environment, and the checks imposed on the executive and executive excesses have made the fight against corruption winnable. The optimism and the high hopes brought about by the new constitution will, however, face a first acid test: whether the Devolved Government Bill, in substantive whole, is passed as an act. At the same time the fight against corruption will also be slowed down by corrupt officials of the old order who still occupy senior positions in government.

Notes

1. Transparency International's CPI, 2001-2008; available at http://www. transparency.org/policy_research/surveys_indices/cpi.

2. As Mugambi Kiai notes for Kenya, corruption has its roots "in colonial Kenya" (Kiai 2003). Chweya, Tuta and Akivaga view the entire "colonial project" in Kenya as having been in itself "a single, but comprehensive act of corruption" (See Chweya, Tuta and Akivaga 2005, 8).

3. Kenya was not among the original African countries that were, through the World Bank, undertaking the CSRP, and hence, when Kenya accepted the CSRP, there were already 25 African countries undertaking them. Thus, when in 1992 Kenya accepted the CSRP as part of the SAPs package, Kenya joined other African countries that were already implementing the CSRP of the SAPs (Oyugi 2006: 45).

4. Nigeria passed a bill in 1999 that outlawed and punishes bribery and corruption by public officials. Similarly, in 2001, Ethiopia created an Anti-Corruption Commission to stem out corruption (ECA 2003: 35).

5. The 1988 elections were manipulated to ensure that only supporters of Moi got re-elected. The queue voting procedures were aimed at ensuring this outcome, which it succeeded in achieving.

6. Prior to the re-introduction of the multi-party system in the 1990s, any cases of corruption were dealt with administratively, through existing codes of conduct within the civil service. Existing codes of conduct in the civil service did not specifically address issues of corruption and, hence, even the few cases that were punished administratively were not essentially those engaged in corruption. Thus, this system was not an effective deterrence to those bent on engaging in corruption.

7. The failure by the Attorney General to prosecute those involved in the Goldenberg Scandal forced the Law Society of Kenya (LSK) to institute private prosecutions. Interestingly, the Attorney General objected to this, leading to the case by the LSK being thrown out. The court ruled that only the Attorney General could institute criminal prosecutions in the public interest. Later, attempts by Raila Odinga, then a leading opposition figure, also met the same fate with the Attorney General terminating Odinga's private prosecution. The Goldenberg Scandal has not been completely resolved to date.

8. KANU, the Manifesto of the Kenya African National Union, at http:/ www.Kanu-kenya.org/governance.htm.

9. For a comprehensive study of the Goldenberg Scandal, please see Kivuva and Odhiambo, (eds.), 2010.

10. See Republic of Kenya, Public Procurement Reform and Enhancement Capacity Project (Ministry of Finance), Record of the Deliberations and Recommendations of the Project Launch Workshop, KCCT-Mbagathi, November 25, 1998.

11. See, for example, two technical reports made by these teams: The first was the Republic of Kenya, Report on Strengthening Government Finance and Accounting Functions (Prepared by Accountant General's Department and KPMG), Vol. 2 main Report, June 1997: 1-2. The second was the Republic of Kenya, Report on Strengthening Government Finance and Accounting Functions (prepared by Accountant General's Department and KPMG), Vol. 2 Main Report, June 1997: 23.

12. The KACA was established in December 1997, when parliament amended the Prevention of Corruption Act that had created the Anti-Corruption Squad with the Kenya Anti-Corruption Authority (KACA).

13. See, for example, Ng'weno, Hillary "Toothless: Mwau's Anti-Corruption Authority comes under fire", The Weekly Review, May 15, 1998.

14. Suspicions on the sources of his wealth had been rife even before he was appointed. Recently he was named in parliament as a major drug dealer, prompting his resignation from government in December 2010.

15. Those charged included the Commissioner General of the Kenya Revenue Authority, the Financial Secretary and the Director of Fiscal and Monetary Affairs.

16. With this ruling, all cases that the KACA had taken to court were in jeopardy.

17. The Attorney General published The Anti-Corruption and Economics Crimes Bill 2000, which re-established the KACA, an Anti-Corruption and Economic Crimes Board and an Economic Crimes Court.

18. The Mbogua Committee, for example, investigated corruption in the Nairobi City Council and the council's failure to provide adequate services to the people. (Although the report of the Mbogua Committee was never made public, CLARION 2001: Kenya: State of Corruption Report, Issue 2, Claripress: Section 5 has described the Reports major findings. The Daily Nation also serialised the report. See The Daily Nation 26 October, 2000).

19. The Report also recommended that public office holders, including MPs and civil servants declare their wealth and assets.

20. The Committee recommended that reforms be undertaken in the Justice Department, particularly, in the administration of the entire justice system as well as in the appointment of judicial officers, with a view to ending the executive dominance in their appointment. The report recommended the involvement of the Law Society of Kenya and the Judicial Service Commission in doing this.

21. The report made recommendations covering many areas of the civil service to eliminate nepotism and cronyism (by encouraging meritocracy), dismissing civil servants who have been mentioned in corruption, recruiting police officers with at least university degrees, making government departments, especially revenue collection and tendering more transparent. Other recommendations included the establishment of a proper legal framework to regulate Harambees, instituting economic and land reforms; and, the establishment of the office of the Ombudsman.

22. Uhuru Kenyatta, Leader of official opposition in Kenya in a speech he gave to a seminar for the African Parliamentarians Network Against Corruption (APNAC) held at the Grand Regency Hotel on November 3-4, 2003. In this speech, Kenyatta admitted that the failure to reign in on corruption, and the perception that his party (KANU) was either not serious in its fight against corruption or was unable to fight the vice was the major reason why the party lost the presidency after almost 40 years in power.(see Daily Nation, November 4, 2003.)

23. See the National Rainbow Coalition (NARC), 2002. Democracy and Empowerment: Manifesto of the National Rainbow Coalition (NARC). Nairobi: November 2002.

24. The Goldenberg Scandal was by then Kenya's grandest corruption scandal since independence through which the country lost over US $493 million in less than three years.

25. This is also known as the Ringera Committee, named after its Chairman, Aaron Ringera. It is the Ringera Committee that led to the "radical surgery" in the judiciary that led to the purging of corrupt judges from the institution.

26. Since the 2007 post-election violence, the National Accord that was signed in February 2008 establishing the Grand Coalition Government created the position of Prime Minister who has to be consulted in the appointment and firing of key government officials. Before the accord, the President held unchecked powers to hire and fire at will.

27. According to reports by South Consulting, the legislature has reviewed its standing orders, opened up parliamentary committee deliberations to the public, revitalised key committees and acquired professional staff to help in drafting and budgeting. Parliament has also started live broadcasts of its deliberations. These reforms have made the institutions more transparent and assertive.

References

Achebe, C. 1984. *The trouble with Nigeria*. Lagos: Heinemann Publishers.

Barkan, J. 2009. African legislatures and the "Third Wave" of Democratization. In Barkan, J. (ed.), 2009. *Legislative power in emerging African democracies*. Bouder, London: Lynne Rienner Publishers.

Centre for Law and Research International (CLARION). 2000 and 2001. *Kenya state of corruption report, Issues 1, 2, 3 and 4*. Nairobi: CLARION.

Chweya L. 2005. The government anti-corruption programs, 2001–2004. In Chweya, L. Tuta, K., and Akivaga K, (eds.), *Control of corruption in Kenya: Legal-political dimensions 2001–2004*. Nairobi: Claripress.

——.2010, Corruption and the limits of bureaucratic rationality. In Kivuva, J and Morris Odhiambo (eds.), *Integrity in Kenya's public service: Illustrations from Goldenberg and Anglo-leasing scandals*. Nairobi: CLARION.

——.Tuta, K., and Akivaga K, (eds.), 2005. *Control of corruption in Kenya: Legal-political dimensions 2001–2004*. Nairobi: Claripress.

Economic Commission for Africa (ECA). 2003. *Public sector management reforms in Africa: Lessons learned*. Addis Ababa, Ethiopia: Development Policy Management Division, ECA.

Huntington, S P. 1991. *The third wave: Democratization in the late 20th century*. Norman and London: University of Oklahoma Press.

IMF. 1997. A decade of civil service reforms in Sub-Saharan Africa. IMF Working Papers.

KACA. 2005. *National anti-corruption plan: Implementation proposal*. Nairobi: National Printer.

Kagwanja, P. 2009. Corrupting power-sharing: Kenya's democratic recession and the stalled war on Corruption. Nairobi, The East Africa Policy Series, March 2009.

KANU. 2002 Manifesto of the Kenya African National Union. Available at Http://www.kanukenya.org/governance.htm (accessed on March, 2006)

Karua, M. 2006. Tackling corruption after a transition. In KNCHR, the human rights dimensions of corruption: Proceedings of a Regional Conference on Corruption and Human Rights held in Nairobi, Kenya, in March 2006.

Kaul, M. 1995. Civil service reform: Learning from Commonwealth Experiences. In Langseth, P. et al, (eds.), Civil service reform in anglophone Africa: Report on the proceedings of a Workshop on Civil service Reform in Anglophone Africa, held at the Lord Charles Hotel Somerset West, South Africa, 24–28 April 1995. Washington DC: World Bank.

Kiai, M. 2003. Changing the face of the judiciary—What criteria shall we use? *The Lawyer*. Nairobi: Oakland Media Services Ltd., December 2003.

——.2003. The social-political dimensions of corruption in Kenya. In *KHRC, human rights as politics*. Nairobi: KHRC.

Kibaki, M. Zero tolerance for corruption: New culture sought. A speech read during the National Anti-Corruption Workshop: Achievements and Challenges after the Transition, held on 23rd July 2003 at the Hotel Intercontinental, Nairobi.. See Adili, Issue No.41, July 28, 2003, p. 1.

Kibwana, K., Akivaga K, Mute L., and Odhiambo, M. (eds.). 2001. *Initiatives against corruption in Kenya: Legal and policy interventions 1995–2001*. Nairobi: Claripress.

——.Wanjala S., and Oketch-Awiti, eds. 1996. *The anatomy of corruption in Kenya: Legal, political and socio-economic perspectives*. Nairobi: Claripress.

Kiragu, K. 2002. Wave of public service reform and impact on service delivery. In Kiragu, K & J. Clerke (eds.) 2002, *Public service reform impact on service delivery in Sub-Saharan Africa: Lesson of experience from five selected countries*. Nairobi: Donors Working Group on PSR Country Engagement Initiative.

Kiragu, K and Mutahaba, G. (eds.), 2006. *Public service reforms in eastern and southern Africa: Issues and challenges*. Dar es Salaam: Mkuki na Nyota Publishers.

Kivuva, J., and Odhiambo, M. (eds.). 2010. *Integrity in Kenya's public service: Illustrations from Goldenberg and Anglo-leasing scandals*. Nairobi: Claripress.

Mbaku, J. M. 1998. Corruption as an important post-independence institution in Africa. In J. M. Mbaku (ed.),. *Corruption and the crisis of institutional reforms in Africa*. Lewiston: E. Mellen.

McCormack, R. 1997. International corruption: A global concern. Paper presented to the International Anti-Corruption Conference, Peru 1997.

Mullei, A. (ed). 2000. *The link between corruption and poverty: Lessons from Kenya case studies*. Nairobi: African Centre for Economic Growth.

Ng'weno, H. 1998. Toothless: Mwau's Anti-Corruption Authority comes under fire. *The Weekly Review*, May 15, 1998.

Nzioka, G. L.M. 2002. Kenya: Towards a comprehensive program. In Kiragu, K &J. Clarke, J. (eds.), *Public service reform impact on service delivery in Sub-Saharan Africa; Lessons of experience from five selected countries*. Nairobi: Donors Working Group on PSR County Engagement Initiative.

Odhiambo, M. 2010. Corruption and regime consolidation in a neo-patrimonial state system. In Kivuva, J. and Odhiambo, M. (eds.), *Integrity in Kenya's public service: Illustrations from Goldenberg and Anglo-leasing scandals*. Nairobi: CLARION.

Oyugi, W. 1996. The performance of the higher civil service on policy management. Addis Ababa: DPMF Working Paper No. 5.

Republic of Kenya. 1980. Report of the Civil Service Review Committee, 1979–80 (also known as the Waruhiu Report after its Chairman, S. N. Waruhiu). Nairobi: Government Printer.

——.1982. Working Party on government expenditures. Report and recommendations of the Working Party. Nairobi: Government Printer.

——.1992. *Economic survey 1992 Issue.* Nairobi: Government Printer.

——.2000. *The constitution of Kenya (2010).* Nairobi: Government Printer.

——.2003. Gazette Notice No,1238. The Commissions of Inquiry Act, Cap 102: Judicial Commission of Inquiry. *The Kenya Gazette, Vol. CV-No. 22, 24th February 2003.* Nairobi: Government Printer.

Republic of Kenya Central Bureau of Statistics, Ministry of Planning and National Development. 2003. *Republic of Kenya: Statistical abstract 2003.* Nairobi: Government Printer.

Republic of Kenya Directorate of Personnel Management (DPM)/Kenya Anti-Corruption Commission (KACC). 2003. *Public service integrity program: Sourcebook for corruption prevention in the public service.* Nairobi, May 2003.

Republic of Kenya Judiciary Committee on the Administration of Justice. 1998. Report of the Committee on the Administration of Justice. Chairman, Justice R O Kwach.

Republic of Kenya National Assembly, Eighth Parliament, Fourth Session. 2000. *Report of the parliamentary anti-corruption select committee, Vol. 1 and 2.* Nairobi: Kenya Parliament, May 2000.

——.2002. *Report of the parliamentary anti-corruption select committee.* Nairobi: Government Printer.

Republic of Kenya Ministry of Justice and Constitutional Affairs. *Draft terms of reference of the National Anti-Corruption Campaign Steering Committee (NACCSC).* Nairobi: Government Printer.

Ross, H. (ed.). 2004. Portraits of graft in the Moi era. *E-Africa: The Electronic Journal of Governance and Innovation, Vol. 2,* February 2004. Johannesburg: South African Institute of International Affairs (SAIIA): 2. (See also http://www.wits.ac.za/saiia.).

Throup, D. and C. Hornsby. 1992. *Multiparty politics in Kenya: The Kenyatta and Moi states and the triumph of the system in 1992 elections.* Oxford: James Currey Press.

Transparency International — the Global Coalition Against Corruption. 2001–2008. Corruption Perceptions Indices (CPIs) 2001–2008. Available at http://www.transparency.org/policy_research/surveys_ indices/cpi (accessed on Feberuary, 2011)

Wahome, G. (ed.). 2007. *Kenya: The state of corruption report (Issue No. 15).* Nairobi: Claripress.

Chapter 3

Public Sector Reform amid Adversity and Uncertainty: The Zimbabwean Experience

Claudious Chikozho

Abstract

Zimbabwe has gone through three different phases of public sector reform. All aim to increase the efficiency of government operations and the effectiveness of service delivery. This chapter assesses the process and outcomes of the civil service and state-owned enterprise reforms in Zimbabwe during the last three decades. Based on the findings, the chapter argues that reforms should not be treated as once-off technical events expected to yield positive results within a short space of time but as long-term experiential processes demanding serious and consistent commitment from all stakeholders to implement the reforms, learn from the process and make necessary adjustments along the way. It suggests that strong political will to implement the reforms consistently is crucial. It also predicts that introduction of the latest reform — Results-Based Management — is promising for Zimbabwe.

Introduction

In Africa's first post-colonial decade, the state was seen as the only organisation with the capacity to engineer socio-economic development. The creation and subsequent phenomenal expansion of the public sector reflects this orthodoxy (Zhou 2001). It was assumed that the state would deliver macro-economic stability, stimulate growth, redistribute incomes, provide social welfare, and develop physical infrastructure and infant industries (Bangura 1999;

Nellis 2006). By the late 1980s, however, the consensus was that the public sector's contribution to economic development was far below expectations and needed to be reformed (World Bank 1994; Killick 1995; Rammanadham 1989; Cook and Kirkpatrick 1988). State-owned companies that were expected to provide investible surplus to the government often required massive subsidy, imposing a fiscal burden (Nellis and Kikeri 1989). The civil service was characterised by poor service delivery, rampant corruption and patronage. There was overwhelming pressure to reduce the role of the state by restructuring public agencies and re-orientating them towards efficiency and effectiveness (Keyter 2007).

In more recent years, public sector reforms have been guided by the New Public Management (NPM) doctrine, which suggests enhancing the performance of the public sector by creating a framework for the delivery of public services which puts customers (citizens) first and enables them to hold public servants to account for the service they receive (Brignall and Modell 2000). It also proposes that the key to implementing responsiveness lies in being able to identify, quickly and accurately, when services are falling below the promised standards, and having remedial procedures in place (Ohemeng 2010).

The literature on the recent wave of public sector reforms in sub-Saharan Africa indicates that implementation is strongly influenced by a variety of international and local agendas and circumstances that lead to significant differences in outcomes across different countries with very mixed results. While reforms help to generally improve the performance of the public sector, it seems many have failed to sufficiently address local priorities and are based on a misreading of Africa's geographic, political, and socio-economic context (Mamdani 1991; Gibbon *et al.* 1992; Stein 1992; Mosley and Weeks 1993; Polidano and Hulme1997). The success of reforms is compromised when introduced as top-down initiatives in which those directly affected or expected to play a key implementation role are not consulted in advance, thus generating strong resistance (Makumbe 1997; Larbi 1999; Andrews 2009).

In the past two decades, Zimbabwe has gone through three different phases of public sector reform, all aiming to increase the efficiency of government operations and the effectiveness of service delivery. Core objectives have been the reduction of the role of the state by restructuring the civil service and the parastatals, withdrawing subsidies, and sub-contracting some government functions. This paper seeks to critically assess the process and outcomes of civil service and state-owned enterprise reforms in Zimbabwe during the past three decades, as well as to identify their strengths and weaknesses and draw relevant lessons. The paper reviews secondary data, published and grey literature and government policy documents, to explore the efficiency and effectiveness of reforms from the early 1990s until 2011.

Public Sector Reforms in Zimbabwe – The Background, Phases and Implications

As a result of socialist policies adopted soon after independence, the public sector in Zimbabwe expanded rapidly from 45,000 employees at independence in 1980 to 192,000 by 1990 (Chimhowu 2010). This resulted in a bloated bureaucracy characterised by red-tape, corruption, inefficiency and other administrative malpractices typical of the newly-independent era. The Public Service Review Commission of 1987 cited the most prominent obstacles as lack of direction, leadership and supervision; lack of measurable targets or standards; poor work ethic; duplication of roles; lack of control over resource use; high staff turn-over; and poor decision-making (Gordon-Somers and Khosa 2006; Berejena 2011).

The number of Public Enterprises rose from 20 in 1980 to more than 40 by the 1990s, operating in almost all sectors of the economy. The majority were monopoly corporations in which the state had 100 per cent ownership (Godana and Hlatshwayo 1998; Zhou 2001). Subsidies and grants from government led to unacceptably high budget deficits which, by 1990, averaged 10 per cent of the Gross Domestic Product (GoZ 1991). The irony is that despite the massive injection of subsidies, most of the large PEs almost always realised negative returns on investment and ended up depending either on more subsidies from government or on domestic and offshore borrowing, further worsening their deficits (Herbst 1989; Masunungure and Chimanikire 2007). A Commission of Inquiry into the Administration of Parastatals set up in 1987 concluded that the inability of most PEs to conduct their business operations efficiently stemmed mainly from political interference in appointments for top managerial positions; politically-determined pricing structures designed to address the government's social objectives; sheer incompetence; and a general passiveness about the need to become profitable - undoubtedly because of the widespread presumption that the government would always fund their deficits (Herbst 1989; GOZ 1989; Masunungure and Chimanikire 2007; Keyter 2007). While it had been possible to write off PE losses with huge subsidies in the 1980s, socio-economic and political challenges constrained the capacity of the national treasury in the early 1990s and beyond.

In addition to these internal pressures, the World Bank and the International Monetary Fund (IMF) were pressing for public sector reform across the entire developing world and made adoption of 'economic liberalisation' a pre-condition for balance of payments support.

First Phase of the Reforms in the Civil Service (1991–1996)

The Zimbabwe 'Framework for Economic Reform (1991–1995)' outlines the main objectives of the first phase as:

- improvements in policy formulation and implementation processes;
- re-defining ministries' mission statements, functions and client charters to make them focus on efficiency and effectiveness and to eliminate duplication;
- reducing the size of the civil service by at least 25 per cent through retrenchments;
- improving management of resources;
- reducing the national budget deficit;
- introducing sound performance management systems;
- improving conditions of service through job evaluations and review of compensation packages;
- improving public service regulations and procedures; and
- developing a civil service training policy (Berejena 2011; Gordon-Somers and Khosa 2006).

A voluntary retrenchment scheme with financial compensation packages was launched in 1990 and opportunities for re-training were provided to reintegrate retrenched workers into the mainstream economy (Berejena 2011). Some 23,000 workers (12 per cent) came off the civil service payroll almost immediately and the number of ministries fell from 27 to 16 by 1995 (Moyo 1998; Bangura 2000). Existing Public Service Commission regulations and procedures were also reviewed and re-designed to support performance management (*Ibid*).

Impact of the First Phase of Civil Service Reforms

Retrenchments caused increasing resentment among civil servants; severance package costs were high; and implementation was corrupt. The programme was abandoned in 1995 (Makumbe 1997). Real wages fell by about 14 per cent between 1990 and 1996, according to IMF estimates, but by more than 50 per cent according to official government statistics (Moyo 1998). Overall public sector employment was reduced by not more than 12 per cent (Bangura 1999). There were also numerous strikes over wages and other socio-economic issues in the early 1990s.

A performance management system was introduced in 1994, initially aimed at top management and later intended to cascade through the entire service. The system required ministry heads to prepare work plans specifying outputs and targets. These were to be reviewed by the respective minister and the Office of the President and Cabinet (Moyo 1998). Training to introduce performance-related pay, which would link job ratings to pay increments and bonuses at the individual level, was also introduced. This supposedly key element of reform was also abandoned in 1996 when it was recognised that more groundwork still needed to be done (Makumbe, 1997). In the end, the *status quo* prevailed. Control of the civil service remained in the hands of the Public Service Commission and only the most mundane of administrative activities relating to recruitment, training and staff promotion were decentralised to ministries (*Ibid*).

According to Botchwey *et al.* (1998), the fiscal aspects of the first phase pre-supposed an astonishing contraction of non-interest expenditures, which, as the economy declined (contrary to IMF projections), led to a massive under-estimation of the social cost of the programme. In addition, the programme was manifestly unsustainable politically, because it required the government to dismantle its social sector achievements of the 1980s, particularly in health and education (UNDP 1998; Masunungure and Chimanikire 2007). Both the economic down-turn and the efforts to meet fiscal targets led to a significant reduction in government funding and support for these two sectors.

Just a few services, in cleaning and catering only, were sub-contracted by various ministries. For example, some 1,000 retrenched lower-level staff from the Ministry of Defence were sub-contracted as "business entrepreneurs" to do cleaning/catering work they had been previously employed to do (Makumbe 1997). By 1998, sub-contracting had not resulted in any significant reductions in middle and senior-level employment (Moyo 1998; Davies and Rattsø 1999; Bangura 2000). A considerable number of skilled staff left the service as real ages in the public sector rapidly declined (Moyo 1998).

The quality of and access to public services declined significantly in the health, education and other social sectors (Botchwey *et al.* 1998; UNDP 1998). In addition, the reform programme itself remained very slow and, in some ministries, was not implemented at all (Makumbe 1997). Batley (2004) states that the first and second generation of reforms in Zimbabwe were slow and became conflated. Key factors included weak policy commitment to reforms imposed by donors, fear of disturbing existing patron-client relationships, and concern over losing important sources of public revenue (Makumbe 1997). Because the government negotiated and implemented the reform programme, by both fair and foul means, 'business-as-usual' was perpetuated.

For the most part, the government did not encourage the participation of important constituencies such as private businesses and NGOs, choosing instead a top-down approach (Kherallah *et al.* 2000). At the same time, the government itself did not feel the sense of ownership necessary to sustain the reform effort (Stein 1992; Masunungure and Chimanikire 2007). Chimhou (2010), who carried out an extensive review of progress during all the phases, points out that effective and efficient public services did not materialise; indeed, there was general decline in service provision and staff morale, and hence, poor staff performance. A customer satisfaction survey in 1996 depicted public servants as arrogant, impolite and self-serving, behaving as if the people had no right to demand or enjoy a better service (Public Service Commission of Zimbabwe 1998).

The Reform of Public Enterprises during the First Phase

PE reform set out in the Framework for Economic Reform (1991-95) had similar objectives to the civil service reforms. They expressly sought to remove restrictions within the policy environment and at enterprise levels (Zhou 2001); eliminate financial losses; make parastatals more efficient in their operations; promote foreign investment, technology and know-how; harness and encourage local entrepreneurial skills; and generate revenue from sales and leases (GoZ 1991; Zhou 2000). Various options and reform models were considered, including outright sale of shares and assets (privatisation); commercialisation; leasing and management contracts; sub-contracting services; removal of government subsidies; and offering incentives for voluntary retrenchments (GoZ 1991; Stein, 1992; Usman 1993).

The PE reform envisaged government relaxing its direct control and giving more autonomy to parastatal boards and management in micro decision-making - such as price-setting, investment, and hiring of top management (Godana and Hlatshwayo 1998). An enterprise earmarked for reform would be subjected to the stimulus of competition so that it operated as a commercial entity and set its own prices in order to realise profits (Keyter 2007). The idea was that the enterprise's balance sheet should be healthy enough to be attractive to private investors before it was privatised (Stein 1992; Pandey and Moynihan 2005).

Impact of the First Phase of Reforms on the PE Sector

The disposal of state shares and the revenue raised became the accepted measure of success or failure of the programme (Godana and Hlatshwayo 1998). PEs which undertook earlier restructuring included the National Railways of Zimbabwe (NRZ) and the Zimbabwe Electricity Supply Authority (ZESA). NRZ's restructuring concentrated on its core business and shed non-core activities such as the Road Motor Services, now a private company. A 3 per cent reduction in staff was also targeted, alongside tightening of staff supervision, improvement of management information systems, filling crucial job vacancies, and increasing security to reduce cases of theft *(Ibid)*.

Zhou (2001) argues that while the World Bank Report of 1995 was quick to declare this restructuring exercise a "success story", PE performance in the ensuing years did not support this judgment. For instance, by 1998 the restructured NRZ was among state companies contributing most heavily to PE losses (GoZ, 1998). The Financial Gazette of 21st August, 1997 notes that, in the 1995/96 financial year, the NRZ incurred a deficit of USD 192 million — well over twice as bad as the previous year.

ZESA was turned into a top-heavy holding company with four subsidiaries - ZESA Enterprises, Zimbabwe Electricity Distribution Company, Powertel, and Zimbabwe Power Company. A USD6 billion agreement with a Malaysian company, YTL Corporation Berhad, was signed for a joint venture in which ZESA would have 49 per cent equity while the majority shareholding of 51 per cent would be held by the Malaysian company (World Bank 1995).

Meanwhile the Cotton Marketing Board (CMB), Cold Storage Commission (CSC), Dairy Marketing Board (DMB), and Grain Marketing Board (GMB) were fast-tracked towards more profound reforms. They were converted from statutory corporations to private companies, although 100 per cent share capital was still owned by the government (GoZ 1998; Zhou, 2001; Jayne *et al.* 2002). Their core business and products were liberalised and were now subject to competition from private manufacturers and service providers.

Several diagnostic studies aimed at effectively restructuring and commercialising all major PEs by the end of the first phase did not sufficiently address the fundamental causes of PE inefficiency and ineffectiveness (GoZ 1998; Sadza 2002). The government continued to exercise direct controls on pricing, investment, and hiring and firing of top management. By the end of 1995, none of the PEs was ready for privatisation (Zhou 2000). Creating sound financial systems also proved difficult and the PE sector's privileged access to government subsidies was not significantly curtailed (Zhou 2001; Keyter 2007).

The legal framework around PE reforms remained largely unchanged. Most PEs continued to operate under their traditional pre-reform enabling acts, and parent ministries continued to view PEs as government departments to whom they could give directives (Commonwealth Secretariat 1994; GOZ 1998). Even enterprises such as the Dairiboard Zimbabwe Limited (DZL), Cotton Company of Zimbabwe (COTTCO) and Cold Storage Commission (CSC), which had been allowed to commercialise, continued to be tied by government dictates (Godana and Hlatshwayo 1998; Zhou 2001; Jayne *et al.* 2002). The absence of employee participation in preparations for PE reform made the process non-transparent and generated worker hostility to the whole exercise (Keyter 2007). The government prevaricated on reforms to retain some of its social obligations (Masunungure and Chimanikire 2007). For instance, price controls on maize-meal were eliminated in 1993 as part of trade liberalisation, but subsequently re-imposed in 1998 (Durevall and Mabugu 2000; Jayne *et al.* 2002).

Second Phase of the Reforms (1998 – 2003)

The second phase coincided with implementation of the Zimbabwe Programme for Economic and Social Transformation (ZIMPREST) and with the rapid deterioration of the Zimbabwean economy and public service delivery system (GoZ 1998; Chimhou 2010). It concentrated on enhancing performance and service delivery, putting citizens first and promoting good governance (GoZ 1998; Kiragu 1998). Berejena (2011) describes the second phase as essentially a continuation of unfinished business.

Civil Service Reforms During the Second Phase

In the civil service, the main objectives of the second phase included re-focusing the government on its core-business by sub-contracting, commercialising and privatising non-core business functions (Kiragu 1998; Chimhou 2010). The change agenda also embraced improved quality of service delivery, effectiveness and efficiency through strategic planning and management, staff motivation, performance management, budget reforms, and decentralisation (Public Service Commission of Zimbabwe 1998; Gordon-Somers and Khosa 2006; Berejena 2011).

The Public Service Commission committed itself to transforming the public service into a highly focused and motivated vehicle of national development working in accordance with well-articulated mission statements, organisational goals and objectives, and striving to achieve set targets which were SMART - specific, measurable, appropriate, results-oriented and time-framed (Public Service Commission of Zimbabwe 1998; Kiragu 1998; Sadza 2002). Key features of the new approach included adoption of client charters; regular service delivery surveys; establishing citizens' complaints units; decentralisation with substantial devolution; and contract employment for civil servants (Kiragu 1998).

In 1997/98, arrangements were made to ensure every civil servant attended workshops on Performance Management (Madambi 2011). Some government departments were commercialised. These included the Customs and Excise Department, which was re-designated as the Zimbabwe Revenue Authority; the Printing and Stationery Department, which is now known as Printflow; and the Department of Water, which was re-designated as the Zimbabwe Water Authority (Chimhou 2010). The net result of the commercialisation and privatisation of public services was to reduce the number of posts in the public service by 15,595 and to make administrative structures flatter. Shorter reporting lines were expected to result in quicker decision-making (*Ibid*).

On-going reforms continued to outsource non-essential services such as cleaning and catering to the private sector. Functions were streamlined to reduce duplication, and decision-making was to be expedited by compressing the top level grades from six to three (Gordon-Somers and Khosa 2006; Chimhou 2010). However, efforts to sub-contract met with limited success, mainly owing to lack of skills in contract management and also the award of contracts to private providers who did not necessarily have the required capacity (Sadza 2002; Madambi 2011).

A new Public Financial Management System was introduced in 1999, reducing financial indiscipline among line ministries and achieving significant reductions in unauthorised expenditures and fraud (Madambi 2011). To ensure fiscal rationalisation and discipline across government departments, by the end of 2000, about 265 internal auditors in the civil service had been trained in value-for-money and performance-based auditing practices to enforce control systems (Gordon-Somers and Khosa 2006). Another key aspect of the second phase was that all administrative offices were to be manned by professionally qualified personnel (technocrats) with at least a diploma in the relevant field (Chimhou 2010). Management posts were supposed to be manned by those with at least a first degree or a higher diploma in the area concerned. Officers without the minimum qualifications were given a grace period of three years to get them (Musingafi 2007; Aziz 2010).

Impact of the Second Phase on Public Service Delivery Efficiency and Effectiveness

The cumulative effect of the first and second phases was the down-sizing of the civil service from 192,000 in 1990 to 161,101 by December 2007. Of these, 144,015 posts were filled while 17,086 vacancies existed (Chimhou 2010). A job evaluation was carried out to reduce categories of job grades (Moyo 1998; Musingafi 2007). However, the fiscal position did not necessarily improve and the successes of the reform measures were limited in scope as the acute economic crisis which began in the 1990s forced government priorities and attention away from the reform process (Sadza 2002; Berejena 2011).

A study by Musingafi (2005) established that during the second phase, there were serious financial and skilled personnel shortages in the civil service. The brain-drain and/or high staff turn-over were so severe that government institutions were often run by under-qualified and inexperienced people. A study by the Scientific and Industrial Research and Development Centre in 2006 revealed that skills shortages were widespread throughout the civil service (Chimhou 2010). There were gaps in everything from high level technical specialists and managerial expertise to lower-level frontline grades in agriculture, construction and mining, education (science and maths teachers), transport, commerce, finance and insurance, legal and health (*Ibid*). In addition, civil servants did not sufficiently understand the concept of performance management, and yet this was a cornerstone of the reforms. Staff members claimed that performance management was just a formality and no one really believed in it (Sadza 2002; Musingafi 2007).

Staff morale nose-dived as civil servants' remuneration remained far below market rates. Poor communication and lack of transparency, especially with regard to retrenchments, career progression and promotion, compounded the challenge (Aziz 2010; Madambi 2011). For instance, when the reform programme started, the Public Service Commission was tasked with reducing the size of the civil service and was responsible for retrenchments. Civil servants became suspicious when the commission introduced new performance management and performance appraisal systems. Better communication with civil servants might have averted some of these concerns (see Moyo 1998; Sadza 2002; Gordon-Somers and Khosa 2006).

Reform of the PE Sector during the Second Phase

During the second phase, a few more PEs were commercialised and then subsequently privatised. Notable cases include the then Cotton Marketing Board, Dairy Marketing Board and the Commercial Bank of Zimbabwe. These were the success stories of Zimbabwe's PE reform through privatisation in 1997/98 (Berejena 2011). With the successful launching of the first privatisation exercise, government seemed determined to move faster than ever before. For example, the Post and Telecommunications Corporation (PTC) was unbundled into three separate and fully commercialised entities - Tel-One, Net-One and ZIMPOST. Its regulatory functions were transferred to other bodies. Major changes were also effected in the structure and operations of the Zimbabwe Broadcasting Corporation (ZBC), including unbundling into several stand-alone public companies (Zhou 2001).

A major milestone was the establishment of the Privatisation Agency of Zimbabwe *(PAZ)* towards the end of 1998 with a USD 120 million cash injection from the British Government (Mdlongwa 1999). The PAZ was established as an autonomous and professionally-run body responsible for evaluating PEs earmarked for sale, deciding how best the disposal should be handled, assessing the legal environment and other aspects of privatisation (Zhou 2001). The PAZ also took over the responsibilities previously undertaken by more than ten separate state institutions. This was expected to eliminate delays (The Zimbabwe Herald, 22 October, 1998). While the establishment of PAZ was a welcome development, the agency's operational effectiveness was constrained from the onset by the absence of a privatisation law. Without such a legal instrument, the PAZ could not make binding decisions on the implementation process (Zhou 2001). The chronology of reforms carried out on a handful of PEs in Zimbabwe during the first and second phases shows that progress in that sub-sector was significantly more consistent than in the civil service reform. The commercialisation and subsequent privatisation of PEs such as the Dairy Marketing Board (DMB) and the Cotton Marketing Board (CMB) are typical cases. The unbundling of the Zimbabwe Broadcasting Corporation (ZBC), Post and Telecom Corporation (PTC) and Zimbabwe Electricity Supply Authority (ZESA) into smaller companies and profit-focused business units also illustrates progress in the PE reform process, even though the overall reform of PEs remains a challenge and not more than 20 PEs out of a total of 72 have been restructured significantly (Berejena 2011).

Third Phase: New Frontiers of Reform - 2004 Onwards

The third phase gave and continues to give greatest emphasis to wide-spread implementation of Results-Based Management (RBM) (Makochekanwa and Kwaramba 2009). In 2005, the government approved the introduction and implementation of RBM in both the civil service and PE sector. Key components include systems for Results-Based Budgeting; Personnel Performance; Results-Based Monitoring and Evaluation; Management Information; and Results-Based e-Government (Madambi 2011). A complete set of the RBM guidelines and training manuals for capacity-building were developed and made available to trainers and the RBM implementing agencies (Gordon-Somers and Khosa 2006). The targets have been to do more with less, cost-recovery, cost-sharing, securing value-for-money, setting performance standards, targets and indicators, as well as monitoring and evaluation of public sector performance in order to achieve pre-determined results at various levels (Berejena 2011).

To coordinate the reform process, change management units were established in each ministry and coordinated at the Public Service Commission by a national coordinator linked to the Office of the President and Cabinet Reform Unit (Gordon-Somers and Khosa 2006; Aziz 2010). A Monitoring and Evaluation Unit in the Office of the President and Cabinet was set up to coordinate, direct and give some control and oversight to the reform initiatives (Berejena 2011). An electronic financial management system was introduced to improve accountability and expenditure control (Gordon-Somers and Khosa 2006). A computerised human resources information management system was introduced, initially at the Public Service Commission and subsequently cascaded to line ministries, to facilitate appropriate staffing levels, career planning, promotion, staff appraisal and disciplinary action, incentives and time management (Chimhou 2010; Madambi 2011). Other initiatives included job evaluation and job profiling to match skills to tasks, and institutionalisation of cost-benefit audits (Musingafi 2005).

Guidelines for performance appraisal, and separate appraisal forms for Heads of Departments and for members in different salary bands, have been widely circulated (Berejena 2011). The new appraisal system has been pilot-tested in several ministries and departments; an e-enabled customised version was introduced to track work distribution and deliverables at individual unit, section, department, ministry and national levels (Gordon-Somers and Khosa 2006). Assessment centres have been set up to administer examinations and other forms of assessment for recruitment and promotion of potential candidates into various positions, with a view to matching skills to jobs. Accompanying performance appraisals and reward systems are being put in place (Chimhou 2010; Berejena 2011).

It was quickly realised that in order to have high-performing civil servants, specific capacity-building programmes would be essential. Training of trainers for implementation of the performance appraisal system was completed in August 2006 (Madambi 2011). A steering committee and an agency programme management unit was established by the Public Service Commission to coordinate modular training, which is integral to effective implementation of various components of the RBM (Berejena 2011). An executive management development programme was introduced at the Zimbabwe Institute of Public Administration and Management (ZIPAM), targeted at civil service middle managers and above, to enhance management skills (Chimhou 2010). Specialist courses for economists, accountants and pension mangers were also negotiated and conducted at tertiary institutions on behalf of the Public Service Commission (*Ibid*).

However, civil service employees continue to be under-paid and de-motivated (Gordon-Somers and Khosa 2006). Moyo (1998) argues that civil servants cannot be expected to be impressed by calls to be more efficient and effective if the value of their salaries and allowances deteriorates below certain basic standards. The IMF (2005) concurs that the major reason for the exodus of professionals from the civil service has been inadequate remuneration. Real wages declined substantially and wage indexation lagged behind high inflation. For instance, the average wage for December 2009 of USD180 per month is 64 per cent lower than the poverty datum line of USD500 per month.

By 2005, the public sector had only 687 of the 1,530 medical doctors it needed, and fewer than 7,000 nurses against an established need of more than 11,000 (*Ibid*). According to Makochekanwa and Kwaramba (2009), between 2000 and 2008, more than 25,000 teachers are estimated to have left Zimbabwe. The same trend was also observed at universities, technical and teachers' colleges, where more than 80 per cent of lecturers have left since 2000. This picture is echoed in other government ministries and departments and generally affects service delivery throughout the civil service (*Ibid*).

Performance appraisal does not correlate with the poor quality of services delivered to the public (Musingafi 2005). A clear communication strategy still needs to be put in place to inform all staff on the objectives and progress of the reforms. Clear, reliable and frequent messages anchored on policies that engender widespread stakeholder consultations, transparency and accountability at all levels of decision-making are missing (Gordon-Somers and Khosa 2006).

Impact of the Third Phase of Reforms on Public Sector Performance

It is difficult to assess or attribute the impact of the third phase on service delivery, since problems related to the overall economy worsened during the same period in ways that affected all sectors and governmental operations (Zwizwai 2007). Implementation of the

RBM is on-going and impacts are not yet manifest. Under-investment and hyper-inflation have certainly depleted the physical and human capital of the civil service and this has seriously undermined the capacity to deliver quality public services (Chimhou 2010).Gordon-Somers and Khosa (2006) argue that introducing a new initiative in a hyper-inflationary environment in which budgets rapidly evaporate, sometimes within a month, threatens the RBM credibility, even before it is fully installed.

Nevertheless, the introduction of the RBM in the public sector has brought new operational systems and efforts in that direction continue. Gordon-Somers and Khosa (2006) outline a number of preliminary achievements:

- A team of the RBM trainers was established to promote and cascade the RBM concepts and skills throughout government departments. This has resulted in increased awareness and appreciation of the RBM as a management tool (*Ibid*).

- An electronic Monitoring and Evaluation System, known as the Zimbabwe Integrated Performance Management Solution, is now in place and has significantly enhanced the monitoring and evaluation function (Madambi 2011).

- Under the RBM module, the new performance appraisal system comprising different appraisal forms for different staff categories has replaced the old 'one-size-fits-all' form (*Ibid*).

Forty senior officials participated in Training of Trainers workshops in June and July 2005, covering all RBM components (Gordon-Somers and Khosa 2006). These trainers subsequently carried out extensive downline training with participants from all ministries and departments. By the end of 2006, at least 1,478 civil servants had been trained in the RBM (*Ibid*). Thus, most ministries and departments are now in a position to produce the RBM-compliant documents in the form of Ministry Integrated Performance Agreements; Departmental Performance Agreements; Departmental Work and Performance Monitoring Plans; and Departmental Quarterly Performance Reports. In addition, ministries are also required to produce and adhere to Client Service Charters (Berejena 2011).

Heads of Ministries are now required to sign Performance Contracts with the Chief Secretary to the President and Cabinet for the major outputs they plan to implement during the budget year. All these instruments are designed to bring ministries to account through managing their performance - to improve service delivery. RBM awareness-raising workshops have also been carried out in Local Authorities such as Rural District Councils and Provincial Government offices since 2006 (Chimhou 2010; Madambi 2011).

A few 'quick wins' have been realised. For example, Gordon-Somers and Khosa (2006) concluded that the time taken to effect payments for pensioners has been reduced from six months to 45 days; the speed with which passports and birth certificates are now issued has improved from six months to one week; the Zimbabwe Revenue Authority has witnessed a 40 per cent increase in revenue collection since its commercialisation; the Zimbabwe Tourism Authority improved inflows by 15 per cent; the Cabinet secretariat has managed to set up an effective Management Information System; and the Ministry of Youth Development and Employment Creation established a functional National Youth Data Bank (also see Berejena 2011). The fact that the third phase was mainly driven by the government suggests considerable political buy-in, which is crucial for effective reform implementation (Aziz 2010; Clarke and Wood 2010).

Under the RBM initiatives, there is a renewed focus and thrust for extensive PE reforms. To facilitate this, the government launched the new Corporate Governance Framework for State Enterprises and Parastatals in November 2010, which is designed to provide the government, parastatals and stakeholders with a common framework of reference on corporate governance issues while promoting the efficient use of resources (Zhou 2007; GoZ 2010). The framework clearly specifies the roles of shareholders, board of governors, and PE management, thereby helping to avoid overlaps and political interference that used to hamper effective management of the PEs (Zhou 2007). It further seeks to provide for performance agreements, monitoring and evaluation.

Every PE is now expected to adhere to and implement sound corporate governance policies, procedures and practices, as required by Section 50 of the Public Finance Management Act (GoZ 2010). The framework also expressly acknowledges that there is a need for PEs to reach a balance between provision of commercial services on a cost-recovery basis, and services that are of a non-commercial and social nature (*Ibid*). A further 10 PEs have been scheduled for privatisation and an elaborate programme of action is now in place to introduce the RBM in the PE sector (Madambi 2011).

Throughout all three main phases of reform, the state has remained the majority shareholder in most PEs, either having 100 per cent ownership in the case of a commercialised entity such as ZIMRA, or 51 per cent in the case of a joint venture such as the Zimbabwe Passenger Company which provides bus services in urban areas (Zhou 2000). Even in PEs that were eventually privatised, government equity is still considerable through allocation of shares to some state-owned enterprises such as the National Social Security Authority (NSSA) and the National Investment Trust (Godana and Hlatshwayo 1998; The Zimbabwe Herald Online, February 2011). Thus, while the declared policy is to shift from interventionism to application of market-orientated approaches, interventionist intentions and practices remain a core part of the PE management regime (Zhou 2001; Masunungure and Chimanikire 2007).

Conclusion

From a purely comparative perspective, more noticeable gains were achieved in the reform of parastatals than in the civil service, perhaps because parastatal reform has been more consistent - a slow but on-going effort since the early 1990s, with clear attempts to re-structure, unbundle, commercialise or privatise. An important lesson is that public sector reform programmes cannot be treated as once-off technical events expected to yield positive results within a short space of time. It is better to implement them as long-term experiential processes in which the government demonstrates serious and consistent commitment to implementing the reforms as well as learning from the process and making necessary adjustments along the way (see Bienen and Herbst 1996).

The government of Zimbabwe has tried and continues to try to address contradictory social and economic policies and objectives/ priorities that pull an enterprise in opposite directions. On the one hand, they want to implement reforms and arrest the budgetary deficit through adoption of market-orientated approaches to public management. On the other hand, they still want to satisfy sociopolitical goals such as suppressing the price of certain goods and services. This cannot be easily reconciled with the market orientation that the NPM emphasises (Mohan 2009).

During the first and second phases, retrenchment was a painful and expensive process. While thousands of civil servants were laid off during the 1990s, the overall impact on the performance of the civil service institutions and government expenditure in the sector was insignificant. That is why more recent efforts to inculcate the RBM culture have become very important (see Moyo 1998; Bangura 1999). The salary bill, for instance, was not reduced significantly while real wages have been declining (Sadza 2002; IMF 2005). Those retrenched have not necessarily been re-integrated into the mainstream economy and have become worse off (Makumbe 1997; Zwizwai 2007). In PEs such as the Dairyboard Zimbabwe Limited (DZL) and the Cotton Company of Zimbabwe (COTTCO) where down-sizing was implemented in a more systematic fashion, the results have been relatively positive and they are now self-sustaining business entities. But even there, success is the outcome of a more comprehensive package of mutually reinforcing reform components than just down-sizing for its own sake (Zhou 2001; Andrews and Shah 2003).

Implementation of public sector reforms involves change management and clear communication - on the need to change and the main objectives to inculcate new values, attitudes and a performance culture in line with the reforms (Larbi 2001). For instance, during the phase one reform in Zimbabwe, there were sustained protests by workers against down-sizing but these gradually tapered off as unions began to understand and accommodate the logic of retrenchment and privatisation in exchange for severance pay (Makumbe 1997; Sadza 2002). Had the reform process been more transparent from the beginning, the protests might have been avoided (Chimhou 2010). There was very little effort made during the first phase to counteract the perceptions of key stakeholders that they were mere spectators to the reform process and that the reforms required little on their part other than "getting out of the way" (Masunungure and Chimanikire 2007). Resources should be mobilised to educate the public, politicians and the bureaucracy on how the reforms will work and what kind of supportive actions are required from all stakeholders for benefits to be realised (Clements 1994; Nellis 2005; Chang 2007). The need to systematically foster greater local ownership and commitment cannot be over-emphasised.

Efforts to instil a performance ethos in the public sector have been difficult to implement. Performance monitoring and evaluation systems have had to be abandoned in the civil service following strong resistance, and because performance targets may be difficult to quantify when individuals are given a wide range of fixed and *ad hoc* duties (Bhalla *et al.* 1999). The foregoing resonates with Hulme and Wright (2010), who posit that the system of performance evaluation with targets and goals is not always the best way to ensure performance progress in the public sector because "you don't make a pig fatter by weighing it". In other words, it is not necessarily the robustness of the performance monitoring and evaluation system that will make the public sector perform better. What matters is how you structure the reform mechanisms and processes to achieve better service delivery. The RBM initiative, which focuses more on performance targets and results, is the cornerstone of reforms in Zimbabwe in the third phase. It is expected to bring a better and more sustained implementation and outcomes. As time goes on and implementation unfolds, it will become clearer how effective the RBM is in enabling the delivery of better public services to citizens. Zimbabwe, however, should learn from the first and second phases of reforms and needs to understand that reform is not just a technical matter of finding the best technical design solution and applying it. It entails restructuring policies, institutions and organisational arrangements, taking into account the local socio-economic and political environment.

References

Andrews, M. 2009. Isomorphism and the limits to African public financial management reform. *Harvard Kennedy School Faculty Research Working Paper Series RWP09-012.* Cambridge.

——.2010. How far have public financial management reforms come in Africa? *Harvard Kennedy School Faculty Research Working Paper Series RWP10-018.* Cambridge

——.and Shah, A. 2003. Citizen-centered governance: A new approach to public sector reform. In: Shah, A. (ed.) *Bringing Civility in Governance, Vol. 3 of Handbook on Public Sector Performance Reviews.* Washington, D.C: The World Bank.

Aziz, N. 2010. *Zimbabwe AGI HRM instrument application analysis.* Washington D.C: World Bank.

Bangura, Y. 1999. New directions in state reform: Implications for civil society in Africa. *UNRISD Discussion Paper* No. 113, Oct. 1999, Geneva.

——.2000. Public sector restructuring: The institutional and social effects of fiscal, managerial and capacity-building reforms. *UNRISD Occasional Paper* No. 3, Feb. 2000, Geneva.

Batley, R. 2004. The politics of service delivery reform. *Development and Change, 35 (1),* pp 31–56.

Berejena, S. 2011. An overview of public sector reforms in Zimbabwe. Paper presented at the OSSREA Regional Conference on Three Decades of Public Sector Reform in Sub-Saharan Africa, Cresta Oasis Hotel, Harare, Zimbabwe, 4–6 July 2011.

Bhalla, A., Davies, R., Mabugu, M.C. and Mabugu, R. 1999. Globalization and sustainable human development: Progress and challenges for Zimbabwe. *UNCTAD/EDM/Misc.128.*

Bienen, H. and Herbst, J. 1996. The relationship between political and economic reform in Africa. *Comparative Politics, Vol. 29, No. 1 (Oct., 1996),* pp23–42.

Botchwey, K., Collier, P., Gunning, J.W. and Hamada, K. 1998. Report of the group of independent persons appointed to conduct an evaluation of certain aspects of the enhanced Structural Adjustment Facility. Washington, D.C.: IMF.

Brignall, S. and Modell, S. 2000. An institutional perspective on performance measurement and management in the 'new public sector'. *Management Accounting Research, 2000,* 11, pp281–306

Chang, H. 2007. *State-owned enterprise reform. Reader in the political economy of development.* Cambridge: Faculty of Economics, University of Cambridge.

Chimhowu, A. 2010. *Moving forward in Zimbabwe - Reducing poverty and promoting growth.* Manchester: Brooks World Poverty Institute.

Clarke, J. and Wood, D. 2010. New public management and development: The case of public service reform in Tanzania and Uganda. In McCourt, W. and Minogue, M. (eds.), *The internationalization of public management: Reinventing the Third World state.*, Cheltenham: Edward Elgar.

Clements, L. 1994. Privatization American style: The grand illusion. In Thomas Clarke (ed.), *International privatization: Strategies and practices.* Berlin: Walter de Gruyter and Co., pp87–104.

Commonwealth Secretariat. 1994. *Management of the privatization process: A guide to policy-making and implementation.* London: Commonwealth Secretariat.

Cook, P. and Kirkpatrick, C. 1988. *Privatization in less developed countries.* New York: St. Martin's Press.

Davies, R. and Rattsø, J. 1999. Zimbabwe: Economic adjustment, income distribution and trade liberalization. Paper prepared for the project 'Globalization and Social Policy'. Center for Economic Policy Analysis, London.

Durevall, D., and Mabugu, R. 2000. *Maize markets in Zimbabwe. Country Economic Report 2000.* Stockholm: SIDA.

Gibbon, P., Bangura, Y. and Ofstad, A. (eds.). 1992. *Authoritarianism, democracy and adjustment: The politics of economic reform in Africa.* Uppsala: SIAS.

Godana, T. and Hlatshwayo, B. 1998. Public enterprise reform and privatization in Zimbabwe: Economic, legal and institutional aspects. *Zambezia (1998), XXV(i).*

Gordon-Somers, T. and Khosa, M. 2006. Zimbabwe civil service reform and results-based management: Lessons learned. Harare: Consultancy Report.

Government of Zimbabwe. 1989. *General report of the committee of inquiry into the administration of parastatals* [Chairman: L. G. Smith]. Harare: Government Printers.

——.1989. Public Service Review Commission report. Harare: Government Printers.

——.1991. *Zimbabwe: A framework for economic reforms, 1991–95.* Harare: Government Printers.

——.1998. *Programme for economic and social transformation [ZIMPREST],* Harare: Government Printers.

——.2010. *Corporate governance framework for state enterprises and parastatals.* Harare: Government Printers.

Herbst, J. 1989. Political impediments to economic rationality: Explaining Zimbabwe's failure to reform its public sector. *The Journal of Modern African Studies, Vol. 27, No. 1 (Mar., 1989),* pp67–84.

Hulme, C. and Wright, C. 2006. You don't make a pig fatter by weighing it—Performance management: The experience of the Youth Justice Board. *Public Money and Management, Vol. 26, No. 3,* pp189–192.

International Monetary Fund (IMF). 2005. Zimbabwe: Selected issues and statistical appendix. *IMF country report No. 05/359, October 2005.* Washington, D.C.

Jayne, T. S., Govereh, J., Mwanaumo, A., Nyoro, J. K., and Chapoto, A. 2002. False promise or false premise? The experience of food and input market reform in Eastern and Southern Africa. *World Development Vol. 30, No. 11,* pp. 1967–1985.

Keyter, C. 2007. Factors, triggers and measures of public sector reform within transitional countries. In *ASSADPAM conference proceedings.* Windhoek, Namibia.

Kherallah, M., Delgado, C., Gabre-madhin E., Minot, N. and Johnson, M. 2000. The road half-travelled: Agricultural market reform in Sub-Saharan Africa. *IFPRI food policy report, Oct. 2000,* Washington, D.C. IFPRI.

Killick, T. 1995. *IMF programmes in developing countries—Design and impact.* London: Routledge.

Kiragu, K. (ed.). 1998. Civil service reform in Southern and Eastern Africa: Lessons of experience. Report on proceedings of a consultative workshop held on March 4 – 6, 1998, Arusha.

Larbi, G. A. 1999. The new public management approach and crisis states. *UNRISD Discussion Paper No. 112,* September 1999.

Larbi, G. A. 2001. *Administrative reform in core civil services: Application and applicability of the new public management.* Geneva: UNRISD.

Madambi, F. 2011. *Zimbabwe public service reforms — 1980 to-date.* Ministry of Public Service: Harare.

Makochekanwa, A. and Kwaramba, M. 2009. State fragility: Zimbabwe's horrific journey in the new millennium. Research paper presented at the European report on New Faces for African Development, ERD Conference, 21 – 23 May 2009, Accra.

Makumbe, J. M. 1997. The Zimbabwe civil service reform programme: A critical perspective. *Paper No. 16, The role of government in adjusting economies series.* Birmingham: Development Administration Group, University of Birmingham.

Mamdani, M. 1991. Uganda: Contradictions in the IMF Program and Perspective. In D. Ghai (ed.), *IMF and the South: Social impact of crisis and adjustment.* London: Zed Books.

Masunungure, E. and Chimanikire, D.P. 2007. Policy paradigm shifts in Zimbabwe: From statism to rolling back the state to policy vacillations. In Maphosa F., Kujinga K. and Chingarande, S.D. (eds.), *Zimbabwe's development experiences since 1980: Challenges and prospects for the future.* Harare: OSSREA.

Mdlongwa, F. 1999. "Zimbabwe's Parastatal Reforms Dancing out of Tune." *Financial Gazette*, Sept 16-22, Harare.

Mohan, J. 2009. Visions of privatization under new labour. In Jonathan Gabe and Michael Calnan (eds.) *The New Sociology of the Health Service*, Routledge: London, pp79–98..

Mosley, P. and Weeks, J. 1993. Has recovery begun? Africa's adjustment in the 1980s revisited. *World Development, Vol. 21, No. 10*, pp1583–1606.

Moyo, J. 1998. Civil service reform in Zimbabwe. Paper presented at the Eastern and Southern Africa Consultative Workshop on Civil Service Reform, Arusha, 4–6 March 1998.

Musingafi, M. 2005. An evaluation of the acceptance and implementation of the Zimbabwean Civil Service Performance Management Programme at Gweru Polytechnic. Unpublished Higher Diploma in Human Resources Management Dissertation. Institute of Personnel Management, Zimbabwe.

——.2007. *Improving performance: The case of the Zimbabwean civil service.* Harare: Zimbabwe Open University.

Nellis, J. 2006. Back to the future for African infrastructure? Why state-ownership is no more promising the second time around. *Working Paper Number 84*, February 2006.

——.J. 2005. Enterprise reform in Sub-Saharan Africa. *ESMAP Technical Paper 084*. Washington, World Bank.

——.and Kikeri, S. 1989. Public enterprise reform: Privatization and the World Bank. *World Development,17*, pp659–672.

Ohemeng, F. 2010. The dangers of internationalization and "one-size-fits-all" in public sector management: Lessons from performance management policies in Ontario and Ghana. *International Journal of Public Sector Management, Vol. 23 Issue 5*, pp.456 – 478.

Pandey, D. and Moynihan, S.K. 2005. Testing how management matters in an era of government by performance management. *Journal of Public Administration Research and Theory, Vol. 15, no. 3*, pp421–439.

Polidano, C. and Hulme, D. 1997. No magic wands: Accountability and governance in developing countries. *Regional Development Dialogue, 18(2)*, pp1–16.

Public Service Commission of Zimbabwe. 1998. *Performance-based management*. Harare: Public Service Commission.

Rammanadham, V. V. 1989. *Privatization in developing countries*. London: Routledge.

Sadza, H. 2002. Civil service reform in a developing country: A critique of the management and administration of the Zimbabwe reform programme. In Farazmand A. (ed.), *Administrative reform in developing nations*. Westport: Praeger Publishers, pp202–271.

Scientific and Industrial Research and Development Centre. 2006. An analysis of the cause and effect of the brain drain in Zimbabwe. SIRDC, Harare

Stein, H. 1992. Deindustrialization, adjustment, the World Bank and the IMF in Africa. World Development Volume 20, Issue 1, *January 1992*, pp83–95.

The Zimbabwe Herald Online, February 2011. Cited at http://www.zimpapers. co.zw (accessed on 2nd February, 2011).

The Zimbabwe Herald, 22nd October, 1998

UNDP. 1998. *Zimbabwe human development report*. New York: UNDP.

Usman, S. 1993. Monitoring and regulatory aspects of the privatization and commercialization programme in Nigeria. Paper presented at UNDP Regional Taskforce, Oxford, UK, 19th –23rd July.

World Bank. 1994. *Adjustment in Africa: Reforms, results and the road ahead. A World Bank Policy Research Report:* London: Oxford University Press.

——.1995. *Bureaucrats in business – The economics and politics of government ownership.* New York: Oxford University Press.

Zhou, G. 2000. Public enterprise sector reforms in Zimbabwe: A macro analytical approach. *Zambezia (2000), XXVII (ii)*, Harare.

——.2001. From interventionism to market-based management approaches: The Zimbabwean experience. *Zambezia* (2001), XXVIII (ii), Harare.

——.2007. The corporate governance question in Zimbabwe. *Zambezia* (2007), XXXIV (i/ii), Harare.

Zwizwai, B. 2007. Zimbabwe, missing SADC macroeconomic targets— Deepening integration in SADC. *Regional Integration in Southern Africa* - Vol. 10. Friedrich Ebert Foundation/ IDS, Gaborone.

Chapter 4

The Privatisation and Deregulation of Dar es Salaam's Public Transport, 1983–2010: Outcomes and Dilemmas

Matteo Rizzo

Abstract

Attempts to reform Dar es Salaam's public transport system are seeking an elusive balance between free enterprise and fair practice. This chapter traces the decline of the government-owned transport system, the opening of the market to private companies in 1983, and its deregulation. The quality of the service is critically assessed as competition trampled safety, and tensions arose between the transport workforce and both owners and consumers. The chapter investigates labour relations and shows their centrality in explaining the inefficient performance by the private sector following reform. Focusing on the shortcomings of public transport privatisation and deregulations, the chapter analyses government's attempts to reintroduce some degree of regulation to the sector and reflects on the wider lessons that can be learned.

Introduction

In colonial Tanzania, and for nearly a decade after independence, the bus service in Dar es Salaam was provided by a British company called Dar es Salaam Motor Transport (DMT) through a highly regulated but monopolistic franchise. There was no commercial competition, but service quality was subject to stringent performance conditions (such as compulsory coverage of non-profitable routes in return for exclusivity on profitable ones).

The DMT was nationalised in 1970 (in line with the 1967 Arusha Declaration) and in 1974 it was split into two companies: the Kampuni ya Mabasi ya Taifa (KAMATA) which plied up-country routes, and the Shirika la Usafiri Dar es Salaam (UDA) which retained the "exclusive licence to operate public omnibuses in Dar es Salaam" (URT 1974).[1]

The UDA's performance was disappointing from the outset, and it progressed downwards. By 1983 its performance was so bad, and the consequences to city mobility so dire, that the government allowed multiple private operators into the sector. What happened to bus services in Dar es Salaam over the next two decades reflects the issues and outcomes of most other public sector reforms in Tanzania. Initially, government combined private entry with regulation. From the early 1990s, following intense pressure from donors, the pace and depth of truer liberalisation dramatically increased.

This chapter has two main objectives: to critically assess the impact of privatisation and economic deregulation on passenger transport in Dar es Salaam; and to investigate the state's capacity to design and implement such reform. It draws on four spells of fieldwork: in 1998, from 2001 to 2002, in 2009 and in 2010. Sources include Tanzanian newspapers (from library archives) to reconstruct the chronology of change and follow the debate among policy makers and the general public. Grey literature and discussion with policy makers deepened analysis of the process of policy making. When it became evident that labour relations were a central issue of privatisation and deregulation, in particular the non-compliance of private operators with road safety rules, a standardised questionnaire was randomly administered and answered by 688 respondents.

This chapter explores general remarks on the arguments for privatisation in sub-Saharan Africa; it discusses the two main phases of deregulation and privatisation reforms in Tanzania's public transport system; and it analyses the impact of the reforms, especially the different forms of inefficiency, the class stratification between bus owners and transport workers, and the tensions between transport workers and students.[2]

The Case of Privatisation in Sub-Saharan Africa

The Berg Report in 1981 (World Bank 1981) — urging governments to enable rather than participate in economic activity — has shaped subsequent strategy for economic growth and development in sub-Saharan Africa. Excessive state interference with market forces was squarely blamed for the lack of development. Neo-liberal ideology, which has been central to policy-making in Africa ever since, espouses the virtues of the market and the unrestrained activities of the private sector. Structural Adjustment Programmes have been implemented in every African country on that basis.

Privatisation of public companies and public utilities has been pushed by the World Bank and the International Monetary Fund as a pillar of economic reform. This was expected to reduce public deficits through the sale of loss-making public companies, and to increase productivity and efficiency. Those in favour of economic deregulation usually contrast the image of bloated bureaucracies, riddled with corrupt vested interests against the professional and competitive (and thus inherently efficient) private enterprise.

However, nearly three decades of privatisation reform have yielded less than wholly impressive results. The World Bank itself has shifted its message to states from "get off" to "get better" through reforms of governance (World Bank 1989). Mkandawire (2001) and Sender and Smith (1986) took issue with the Bretton Woods' negative assessment of state-led development. It has been also argued that an effective and interventionist state, managing economic growth and directing the process of development, lay behind virtually every success story in development - Asia's "late developers", for example (Chang 2002; Mkandawire 2001). Specifically on privatisation, some authors stressed the contrast between the high expectations placed on its benefits and how little we actually know about its impact (Bennell 1997; Berg 1996; Cramer 2000). Case studies in Africa illustrate that privatisation does not necessarily result in the creation of highly efficient services, driven by the growth-enhancing competition that many had hoped for (Cramer 2000; Temu and Due 2000). Even a report sponsored by the World Bank suggested that 'competition is more important than privatisation, *per se'* (Campbell-White and Batia 1998:24).

State regulation has consequently made its way back into the debate. If public interests and private sector interests do not coincide, and the private sector's behaviour leads to forms of perverse and anti-social competition, the state must regulate its activities (Adam, Cavendish and Mistry 1992). At the same time, an important point has been raised that a state's capacity to regulate should not be taken as a given. If anything, decades of freezing wages in the public sector, and of shrinking its size, have undermined states' regulatory capacity in Africa (Mkandawire 2001). This sets up a major impasse in development, as weakened states and a less-dynamic-than-expected private sector are unlikely to drive the process well.

Given the strategic importance of passenger transport to urban and national economies, little attention has been given by social scientists to the study of urban transport in Africa under privatisation and economic liberalisation. A handful of studies exist, focused on Kenya and South Africa, but those few do throw light on the impact of urban transport reform, and the key characteristics of private sector performance. Mutongi's study of private buses (known as *matatu*) in Nairobi, the capital and largest city in Kenya, documents the U-turn in public perception. *Matatus* were heroes back in the 1970s, as they invaded the routes of an officially franchised monopoly. By the end of the 1990s, their popularity was replaced by the catchphrase "*matatu* menace" as they obstructed and disrupted all traffic flows, disregarded speed limits and most other rules, grossly overloaded their vehicles and caused lethal accidents on an astonishing scale (Mutongi 2006). Khayesi (2001) documented systematic violation of road safety rules by *matatu* drivers, and attributes their behaviour to very harsh conditions of work, and to exploitative employment relations with *matatu* owners. Khayesi stresses that the employment relationship is central to understanding the conduct of the private sector and to successfully tackling urban passenger transport problems.

Work by Xhosa (1992) on South African cities presents a remarkably similar picture. He identifies the context of market saturation and documents speeding, overloading, chronic aggression (to the point of active violence) as trademarks of private bus operators. The industry is controlled by gangs, not unlike the structures of organised crime, ousting operators who do not have or do not pay for criminal muscle. Rival gangs fight over territory (routes).

The universality of the "*matatu* menace" outcome calls into question the superior efficiency of an unfettered private sector that has been so touted by advocates of deregulation. The case studies of South Africa and Kenya reveal the importance of context. Xhosa's work shows the importance of understanding the history of each urban economy. In Kenya, gangster-style control is now operating in the *matatu* sector, but in South Africa organised crime was more developed and more entrenched even before "pirate" transport became an officially recognised form of public transport. This contextualises the understanding of why and how criminal groups took control of private passenger transport, once the opening to invest in the sector materialised. The analysis of Dar es Salaam must start with how passenger transport was provided before privatisation, and the factors that made reform imperative.

Background to Passenger Transport in Dar es Salaam

Two decades of state monopoly, which ended in 1983, were characterised by two trends which negatively impacted public transport.

Firstly, Dar es Salaam experienced dramatic growth. In 1967, Dar es Salaam's population was 273,000. The National Census of 1978 saw its population nearly triple to 769,000 (O' Connor 1988:136). By 1988 the population had nearly doubled again to 1,360,850 (Bureau of Statistics 1989). Secondly, the UDA was not able to increase its supply to meet demand. As Table 1 shows, UDA's fleet, from a total of 130 buses in 1974, increased to 254 in 1975 but thereafter steadily declined. In 1983/84 UDA could put only 141 buses on the road. Set against massive population increase, this was a shortfall of crisis proportions which in many respects mirrored the harsh economic conditions experienced by the Tanzanian state since the mid-1970s.

To critically assess the "intrinsic inefficiency" of the public sector, it is important to make sense of the factors which prevented the UDA from stepping up its transport supply and ultimately led the government to liberalise and privatise the sector.

Table 1: **Public buses in service 1974–1998**

Year	Operating buses	Year	Operating Buses
1974	130	1986/87	101
1975	257	1987/88	109
1976	245	1988/89	70
1977/78	221	1989/90	59
1978/79	172	1990/91	32
1979/80	142	1991/92	25
1980/81	141	1992/93	36
1981/82	139	1993/94	54
1982/83	164	1994/95	40
1983/84	141	1995/96	32
1984/85	139	1996/97	24
1985/86	108	1997/98	12

Sources: Shirika la Usafiri Dar es Salaam (UDA) 1995, 6; UDA, 'Fleet performance Files' (1994/95–1997/98).

Inefficient management of the company was partly responsible. UDA's own reports mention under-qualified personnel and absenteeism by the early 1990s (UDA 1994, 31–2). But there were other, more structural, problems.

Foremost, the oil crisis in 1974, later compounded by Tanzania's involvement in the war on Amin's Uganda in 1978–1980, resulted in a dramatic shortage of foreign exchange. For the period 1974 to 1983 the UDA received only 35 per cent of the forex/finance it requested (Stren 1989, 52). The degree of under-funding must be qualified: all parastatal companies reacted to the forex/finance squeeze by pushing up their estimates of operating costs by overbidding for forex/finance allocations (Mamuya 1993, 110). Nonetheless, the UDA simply and certainly did not have the means to purchase the number of buses necessary to meet demand in a rapidly growing city (Kulaba 1989, 240). The shortage of foreign exchange also prevented the purchase of spare parts and the repair of existing vehicles, taking its toll on service provision.[3] Moreover, the operating life of the increasingly inadequate number of serviceable buses was shortened by the deterioration of roads to appalling conditions.

In parallel, the government prioritised the welfare function of public transport by keeping fares low. UDA's licence was to operate on a commercial basis, but state-controlled fares made public subsidies essential. Once the capacity to subsidise disappeared, so did the sustainability of UDA as a passenger transport provider.

Government had little choice but to open passenger transport to private operators, but it simultaneously refused to give up Tanzania's *ujamaa* model of state-led development. So, from 1972 to 1974, the government did briefly tolerate the activities of private sector operators alongside the UDA, but then banned private buses again in 1975 (Stren 1989, 52).

Important to context here, Tanzania had formally set a "classless society" as the ultimate goal of its development strategy; systematic increases in minimum wages and a progressive tax system were reducing income disparity in the formal sector. The gap between top-level and minimum wages fell dramatically from a ratio of 1:50 in 1961 to 1:7 in the early 1980s (Maliyamkono and Bagachwa 1991, 300). The informal economy, of which private transport operators were part, was outside the tax net, so individuals could enrich themselves at the expense of others. That was perceived by the leadership as a significant threat to a more egalitarian society.

The ban on private transport operators was thus part of a broader issue – the brief window of private entry was an attempt by the Tanzanian government to weather the economic storm without dismantling the centrality of the state in development.

Such a stance became less and less tenable as the decline of the state's economic capacity persisted and intensified. Taking advantage of the transport crisis, from 1982, a number of private buses started to operate without licences. At that time, the UDA could satisfy only about 60 per cent of the demand for transport in Dar es Salaam (Mamuya 1993, 111). Rather than cracking down on 'illegal' private buses, in 1983, the government re-admitted private transport operators – known as *daladala* - in Dar es Salaam.[4]

Privatisation and Deregulation in Tanzania's Transport Sector

Government regulation of the transport sector in the period 1983 – 2010 reflects policy-making in Tanzania at a more general level. For much of the 1980s and early 1990s, commitment to privatisation and deregulation of public transport was coy. Then, pressured by donors who were dissatisfied with Tanzania's reform progress, the pace and depth of liberalisation dramatically increased. Such a momentous change was reflected in policy changes in the transport sector, and in a more pronounced withdrawal of the regulatory state.

Phase 1, 1983 – 1990: Private Sector's Initiative and State Control

Firstly, the emphasis of regulation shifted. In parallel with authorising private buses in 1983, government issued a directive requiring all public institutions, including parastatals, to deploy their staff buses as public transport. This increased the number of buses on the road by 61, belonging to 27 different institutions – complementing the 141 operated by UDA (*Daily News* 31st March, 1983).

The UDA's passenger transport licence, issued in 1974, was still exclusive in Dar es Salaam (URT 1974), giving them sole authority to register or reject private operators under sub-licence, and to charge a management fee (Mamuya 1993, 111–112). Applications for sub-licences were presented through the Ministry for Communication and Transport, and operators had to satisfy the safety requirements of the Traffic Police Department. Successful applicants were then allocated a route by UDA, with service of that route being compulsory. Private operators' responsibility to provide service included less busy and unprofitable routes - not only the busiest and more profitable ones which free market forces would have determined.

The government also retained the power to set fares. Since the UDA licence stated that 'the fares to be charged by the company shall not exceed those approved by the government or any other authority responsible for setting fare rates' (URT 1974,2), private operators, as sub-contractors of the UDA licence, were also compelled to operate at set tariffs.

So, the monopoly of the public sector company was formally retained and private sector players had to pay fees to and obey the prescriptions of their largest direct competitor. Furthermore, the fact that licence fees were monthly meant government could prohibit them again at very short notice. Clearly, government saw the private sector as a temporary solution rather than as a new long-term partner in the provision of transport in Dar es Salaam. The 1987 'Proposed National Transport Policy' by the Ministry of Communication and Planning (MCT 1987, 49–50) stipulated that 'other (bus) operators, including private operators, can also be incorporated, but under the co-ordination of one institution' (*Ibid.*, 50-1). The unavoidable acceptance of private transport operators was therefore agreed while anchoring the state's continued control and dominance.

State-led strategy was reinforced with fixed fare levels which protected low-income groups rather than fostering operating profit. As Table 2 shows, although fares registered a 600 per cent increase from 1983 to 1991, in the same period the domestic currency experienced a devaluation of 1,836 per cent. Thus, a ride cost/netted 0.31 USD in 1983, but only 0.10 USD in 1991. The fare review process was so slow that even when fare reviews were finally agreed upon, the increase had been substantially off-set by inflation before it came into effect. Mamuya (1993, 117) reports that in 1988 the government rejected a proposal from the UDA to increase fares from Tshs 8 to 22 on the grounds that this was 'politically unacceptable'.

Table 2: **Fares and devaluation trends 1983–1991**

Year	1983	1984	1985	1986	1987	1988	1989	1990	1991
Tshs/ US$	16.34	17.21	38.16	68.65	108.25	154.68	197	230	300
Fare (Tshs)	5	5	5	6	6	8	15	15	15
Fare (US$)	0.31	0.29	0.13	0.087	0.055	0.052	0.076	0.065	0.10

Source: UDA (1994, 22–23).

Table 3 shows the response of private operators to this new investment opportunity was modest. The number of registered buses fluctuated – in 1983 there were 178 private buses in service; by 1985 this had climbed to 294, only to fall back again by 1989 to 175. Inflation, currency devaluation, fare controls and short-term licensing conspired to discourage private operators. Major investment in a new bus on a venture that could be ended in a month was unrealistic. The majority of private buses were over 10 years old (Mamuya 1993, 112).

Table 3: **Trends in registered private buses, 1983-1991**

Year	Buses
1983	178
1984	271
1985	294
1986	300
1987	300
1988	300
1989	175
1990	175
1991 (March)	355

Source: UDA (1994, 26)

It would be rash to over-play the reliability of official statistics on registered buses. A significant number were operating without a licence, so, "the apparent declining trend of new applications for private bus registration does not necessarily imply a decline in the actual number of private buses in operation" (Mamuya 1993, 115). The state's limited capacity to enforce transport regulation and prosecute non-compliance, and the lack of alternatives the state could command to mobilise the capital city's population, acted as a disincentive to formal registration.

The first phase achieved enough to prevent complete melt-down of mobility in the city, but it did not achieve adequate mass transport. Government did not let go of its state-led development concept in general, nor did it establish a positive design or relationship that would enable full privatisation with effective regulation.

Phase 2, 1990–1999: Private Sector's Initiative with Decreasing State Control

The final tranche of 1986–89 structural adjustment support agreed by Tanzania and the IMF was initially withheld on the grounds that liberalisation policy had to be 'faster and steeper' (Baregu 1993, 111). The government responded with the adoption of the Investment Promotion and Protection Act in 1990, which gave new investors, among other things, full exemption from import taxes, and a five-year moratorium on other taxes *(Ibid)*.

This 'investor friendly' climate extended to the transport sector, with a more profit-based fares policy and the abolition of state control on the number of licences issued to private operators. From 1991 to 1996, *daladala* tariffs increased five-fold, gaining substantially on devaluation. While a ride cost/netted 0.10 USD in 1991, it cost/ netted 0.25 USD 5 years later. The general manager of UDA reported that the number of *daladala* trebled in six months after the doubling of fares from Tshs 15 to 30 (*Daily News*, 25th November, 1991).

Table 4:   **Fares and devaluation trends, 1991 to 2010**

Date of fare review	3.2.1991	11.2.1993	9.10.93	7.1.1995	20.12.96	2007	2008	2009
Tshs/ US$	300	437	530	574	580	1,255	1,178	1,300
Fare (Tshs)	30	50	70	100	150	250	300	250
Fare (US$)	0.10	0.114	0.132	0.174	0.258	0.19	0.25	0.19

Source: UDA 1994, 24; *Africa South of Sahara 1999, Daily News* 8.1.1995, 31.12.1996.

Tariff regulation was progressively removed altogether. The transition began in 1996 when the general secretary in the Ministry for Communication and Transport publicised that while transport operators could not charge fares above the fixed limit, they could charge less (*Daily News*, 31.12.1996), and was completed in 1997 when the minister declared that bus fares would in future be determined solely by market forces (*Daily News* 25.7.1997).

In 1991, the UDA was relieved of its authority to sub-contract licences. The Central Transport Licensing Authority (CTLA) became the sole agency responsible for handling registration applications (UDA 1994, 28), but had no powers to reject any application except on the basis of non-compliance with road worthiness rules.

The number of registered *daladala* rose from 600 in 1991 to 3,301 in 1998 (see Table 5). Still the numbers of "pirate" buses remained high – unofficial surveys indicated roughly a 50-50 split between registered and non-registered (UDA 1994, 26–7). In 1998, according to the president of the *daladala* owners' association, there were as many as 7,648 vehicles in operation (Ndaombwa 1998, Interview).

An article published in *The East African* in July 1999 estimated '6,300 plus' buses, generally corroborating the 50-50 rule of thumb and suggesting a "matching" pirate population of between 3,000 and 4,000.

Table 5: **Trends in registered private buses, 1991 to 2009**

Year	Buses
1991 (Aug)	600
1991/92	824
1992/93	1,440
1993/94	1,484
1994/95	1,484
1995/96	1,897
1996/97	2,342
1997/98	2,798
1998/99	3,301
2005 (May)	6,500
2009	5,188 (a)

Source: UDA (1994:27); Central Transport Licensing Authority 'Microbuses Files' (1994– 98), Mhina (2010, Interview note).

The decrease in the total number of registered buses in 2009 does not reflect a decline in transport supply. In 2005, small buses constituted the majority of transport supply while in 2009 more than half of buses were medium to large size buses. The promotion of larger passenger buses began in 2008.

While this general impression is probably a fair reflection of the situation, monitoring was far from precise. Data was collected in 1998 on *daladala* registered with the City Commission (to which private operators have to pay a fee for the maintenance of the road system), with the Tanzania Revenue Authority (to which operators pay income tax), and with the Central Transport Licensing Authority (which issues the licences for passenger transport). While the Dar es Salaam City Commission (1998) reported a total of 4,012 compliant vehicles, only 3,029 private operators were registered as paying income tax, and only 3,301 *daladala* were recorded as having been issued a licence by the CTLA (1998). These divergent figures suggest operators comply with some state regulations while ignoring others. The choice between formality and informality seems to depend on entrepreneurs' individual evaluation of the comparative costs of legality and illegality, rather than on their perception of the legitimacy, equity or wisdom of the government prescription. If, for instance, a newspaper publicises that the Traffic Police have been given the order to impound vehicles not paying income tax, as in fact happened (*Daily News*, 12.3.1996), then the potential cost of illegality will be perceived to have increased and more operators will elect to comply with this requirement.

By the end of the 1990s, the Dar es Salaam passenger transport system was almost entirely supplied by private operators under a free market regime. Fares, which since 1991 increasingly supported the interests of investors rather than the income of passengers, were liberalised in 1996. The dramatic increase in the number of registered and unregistered buses supplying the market shows the positive response of the private sector to the 'investor-friendly' climate that drove policy since 1991.

Privatisation, Economic Deregulation, and the Social Contract between the State and Its Citizens

While trends in supply and demand of transport are important, it is crucial also to assess the quality of the services and their broader impact on people, and on the social contract between the Tanzanian state and its citizens. It is necessary to recognise the socio-economic stratification in the transport sector, between bus owners and bus workers.

The Unruly Behaviour by Transport Private Operators

Beyond differences in the payment of registration fees and taxes, private and pirate operators share a general disregard for safety regulations. Over-loading, divergence from allocated routes and speeding were the hallmarks of private bus operators from the outset, and Kenya's "*matatu* menace" has become Tanzania's "*daladala* war" (*Daily News*, 27.7.1991). This behaviour appears to be commercially necessary to maintain a competitive edge in a very congested market. Data from the Ministry of Communication and Transport in 1989 (quoted in Mamuya 1993: 113) and from the UDA in 1994 (UDA 1994, 48), concur that most bus owners have a fleet of not more than two. Thus no group of entrepreneurs is able to take advantage of a market share to squeeze out less competitive operators.

By contrast, in a study of the taxi industry in three South African townships, Xhosa (1992) has shown that saturation of the market, over-speeding and the over-loading of vehicles were the outcome of deregulation. Xhosa reports that mafia-type gangs divided up and controlled access to taxi routes in these townships, using guns and violence to effectively enforce restrictions on other operators. While no such pattern of serious criminality is evident in Dar es Salaam, metaphorically cut-throat competition among private operators does have other social costs. In 1992, 93 per cent of all fatal accidents in Dar es Salaam involved *daladala* (*Daily News*, 17.5.1994). In 1996, according to the Ministry of Home Affairs (cited in *Nipashe*, 21.12.1997) data, 3,454 lethal accidents involved a private bus. The use of the word 'accident' seems inadequate because it implies mistake or misfortune (bad luck). In fact, luck has almost nothing to do with the behaviour of *daladala* drivers or the lethal consequences. The (mis)conduct is purposeful, and the outcomes are inevitable.

Many *daladala* vehicles have names or slogans emblazoned upon them. Examples include *Zig-Zag*; another is *Dawa ya moto ni moto* ['If you speed I speed', but more literally 'the medicine for fire is fire']; another is named *Usipotambaa mswaki* ['If you do not run you will be a brush'], brush being the slang word identifying a bus which only 'sweeps the road'... because it has no passengers inside. Another bus has a drawing of two wrestlers face-to-face with the words: 'Warning: no ring, no rules, no referee'. Another is named *Mbele kwa mbele* ['Always ahead'], echoing the daily challenge in the race track that is Dar es Salaam's municipal road system. A final example is a bus named *Utamaliza kuni kwa kuchemsha mawe* [literally 'You will burn the whole log to boil stones'], meaning that there is no point in trying to overtake me.

At the Roots of the Unruly Transport Private Sector: Bus Owners, Bus Workers and the Unregulated Employment Relationship

The approximate number of buses can be well estimated; the number of *daladala* employees is more difficult to quantify. Neither the Ministry of Communication and Transport nor the Ministry of Labour holds any statistical information on that workforce. However, a working figure can be extrapolated at 17,800 (from this study's questionnaire, 44 per cent of buses are of the smaller 'two-man' type, while 56 per cent are the larger 'three-man' type. The mean estimate of vehicle numbers is 6,974).

The sample of 668 workers who responded to the questionnaire represents about 3.75 per cent of the total workforce. The *daladala* employees were asked about the characteristics of the working day (that is, hours per day, days per week, pay per day or per month), and the nature of the relationship between employers and employees (that is, the use of contracts, kinship or other links). Surprisingly, given the emphasis often placed upon the role of kinship in urban labour recruitment in eastern Africa, the results show that 90.7 per cent of workers sampled had an exclusively professional relationship with their employer, while only 7.6 per cent defined the employer as a 'relative', and 1.7 per cent as a 'friend'. Less surprisingly, 82.9 per cent were employed without contract. Taken together, these findings strongly suggest that a large majority of workers in the transport system are employed on a casual basis, and that market relations predominate in defining terms of employment, which are insecure. This confounds the orthodox view of the informal sector as firms where there is 'little or no division between labour and capital' (ILO 1993, 43), or 'as home-based or individual enterprises with few or no employees' (UNDP undated, 5).

The distinctive feature of the *daladala* labour market is a class of bus owners whose interests are distinct from the class of casual workers they employ. This poses analytical difficulties for those, such as Tripp (1997, 136), who write about 'the conflict between the government and those involved in the informal economy', as it overlooks power relations within the informal sector itself. Conflicts of interest between workers and their employers in the distribution of income from passenger transport are a crucial dynamic in understanding why private buses systematically avoid compliance with road safety regulations.

The relative ease of entry into the urban transport labour market has a significant impact on terms of employment. The low level of educational requirements for *daladala* workers is common knowledge in Dar es Salaam, as indicated in an ironic advert quoted from a whimsical Swahili article by a local journalist: '*Daladala* conductor wanted. He has to have studied until the seventh level, if not until the fourth level. If not provided with a fourth level class, he has to be able to count money and to give back to the passengers the right change' (*Majira* 18.1.1998).

The qualifications necessary to become a *daladala* driver apparently present a greater challenge, with an initial capital of Tshs 50,000 shillings being needed to acquire a driving licence through tuition and test.[5] However, fake driving licences can be easily bought in Dar es Salaam for one-tenth of this sum. Ease of access results in over-supply, and this in turn weakens employees' bargaining position. Of those workers questioned, 82.9 per cent were employed not only without a written contract, but without a fixed wage. They operate the bus each day as a kind of franchise, for which they must pay a fixed daily fee. The fee they pay is irrespective of the fare revenue they earn, and is set at a level that would leave no margin (the driver's income) if the bus was operated in a law-abiding manner. The exploitative nature of employer/ employee relations is, therefore, not formalised in any 'agreement' on the workers' wages or conditions of service in the workplace, but lies in the cost set upon the franchise each day. In theory, this fee is negotiable. In practice, the scope that employees have to bargain is severely curtailed by the nature of the labour market. A driver temporarily 'on the bench' explained the predicament in graphic terms (Mashaka 1998, Interview note):

"Us too many of us are jobless, if for instance a bus owner is looking for a driver, he will find more than fifty people just at this station [Mwenge station]. That is why they can ask you whatever they want and you have to accept it. I worked on the same bus for two years. He used to ask me for 50,000 shillings every day. Since then the buses have become too many and the chance of making money has decreased. I went to my employer and I told him 50,000 was not possible any more. He could not understand me and he wanted his bus keys back. He gave the bus to somebody else and he is still working with it. I do not know if he manages to give him back 50,000 every day."

In these circumstances, bus owners can 'squeeze' the fees charged to employees upwards, so drivers and conductors are pressed to make a greater number of journeys and to carry more passengers. The worker's daily return must inevitably depend on these two factors. The number of journeys per day is determined by the speed of the driver in negotiating the city traffic, and the number of hours of daily work. Conductors contribute to maximise the margin by cramming in as many passengers as possible. This strategy implies that the vehicles will be systematically over-loaded and that allocated routes will be ignored if passenger volumes are too low (or the traffic too slow). So, many of the road accidents and discipline problems are directly attributable to employment conditions.

Social Fares vs. Anti-social Employment Conditions: The Tensions between Students and Transport Workers

There is also daily conflict between *daladala* workers and beneficiaries of the welfare state – their passengers. From 1983, when private operators entered the transport system, until 1996, government maintained control over fares levels and students retained the privilege of a 'social' fare on all *daladala* routes in the city. Over this period, the ratio of student to ordinary adult tariffs fluctuated from 1:8 in 1989 to 1:2 in 1992. Even at their lowest level of social protection, students were accordingly paying half the normal fare. For *daladala* workers, that meant in their race/battle to collect enough fares to pay the daily franchise and have something left over for their own income, they were expected to carry some passengers at half price. They, (the *daladala* workers) were personally subsidising the state welfare system.

The state has at no time subsidised the economic loss incurred by bus owners for the transportation of students; nor do workers receive a discount from owners on the amount of money they are asked for at the end of the working day, in relation to the numbers of students transported. The arena of conflict between the two parties is clearly defined: students are entitled to concessionary tariffs on any *daladala* journey, but conductors can only grant those concessions at a cost to their own income. Not surprisingly, clashes between *daladala* workers and students have become a common feature of the Dar es Salaam transport system, with incidents frequently being reported in the press. During the 'Day of the African Child' in 1991, for example, a delegation of children urged President Mwinyi 'to offer them protection against *daladala* bus operators' (*Daily News* 18.6.1991). As local reports reiterate, it is a conflict with victims on both sides. *Daladala* workers have been taken before the courts and fined (*Daily News* 25.7.1992; *Uhuru* 11.6.1994; *Majira* 24.9.1994), while in 1992 a delegation of workers met with the Minister of Home Affairs to find a solution to the abuses suffered by drivers and conductors as a result of the student action (*Daily News* 10.3.1992). Government officials have threatened to withdraw licences from operators for failure to comply with student tariffs, and the actual withdrawal of licences has been reported (*Daily News* 27.7.1991, 6.3.1992, 23.03.1993, 24.3.1995; *Nipashe*, 30.3.1995). Police have also been called to defend students from harassment by bus crews, when they had protested over fares (*Daily News* 11.08.1992, 14.08.1996).

Attempts have been made to reconcile this conflict by imposing limits on the number of students that may be carried by buses on each journey. Until 1993, government regulations stipulated that small buses should carry up to five students per trip, and larger buses up to ten students. But on 26th May, 1993, the Minister of Home Affairs announced that this was insufficient to meet demand, and that *daladala* would be compelled to transport an unlimited number of students until 7.30 a.m. each morning, so that they could attend school on time (*Uhuru* 27.5.1993). In response to this decree, no private buses appeared on the roads of Dar es Salaam the following day until after 7.30 a.m. (*Daily News* 28.5. 1993), vividly demonstrating the incapacity of the state to enforce its own regulatory devices. It is also apparent that the state itself is divided over policy in this area. In November 1998, for example, a press release from the Ministry of Communication and Transport sought to better protect *daladala* workers and reverse the intentions of the Minister of Home affairs, by prescribing that 'small buses should carry three students per trip, big buses five'. In practice, none of these interventions has proved effective.

Public perception is that the government lacks the capacity to intervene. As one *daladala* worker joked: 'they [the government] are strong like Coca-cola' (Airi 1998, interview note); as everyone knows, Coca-cola is a *soft* drink.

Bringing the State Back into Passenger Transport Matters: Coy Attempts to Reclaim Some Policy Space

Government has attempted to reclaim some policy space over transport matters. In July 1999, the CTLA relinquished its licensing mandate in the capital city to the newly established Dar es Salaam Transport Licensing Authority (DRTLA), triggered by the Dar es Salaam Regional Commissioner who needed an institution through which to address the problems faced by passengers (Mhina 2010, interview note).

This allowed a more proactive approach to the management of transport problems. As Mr. Mhina, secretary of DRTLA from its establishment, recalled: 'We looked at *daladala* (licensed buses), and we asked the CTLA how many there were. They had no statistics. How many per route, they did not know. What is the procedure to give them a licence? We discovered that if a businessman comes, he bought his vehicle, he passed the inspection from the traffic police, he paid the Tanzania Revenue Authority, that was it, and they would issue a licence to him' (*Ibid*). DRTLA leaders began by assessing how many routes were needed and by establishing the beginning and the end of each route. By drawing on existing population statistics, they estimated trends in population movements throughout the day, so a target number of vehicles operating on each route could be established. Congested routes were declared "sold out". Owners who could not be issued a licence to operate on their first-choice route were allocated less well serviced routes. The rationale was to ease congestion in some areas and avoid shortages in others. With this measure, DRTLA was asserting public regulation of private transport.

Late in 1999, the DRTLA chairman required buses to have a coloured stripe corresponding to their licensed route (Mwaibula 2010, interview). While this helped solve one problem, there were other contentious issues (such as the tense relationship between students and bus workers, and the unregulated nature of employment relations in the urban transport sector) which the state's weak capacity in both finance and human resources left unattended. The fragmented ownership of buses was a further hindrance to effective policy-making. As Mr. Mhina recalls, any liaison required a meeting with thousands of separate owners. It was not possible to convene such a gathering.

To rationalise the private sector element, the DRTLA proposed a tender system for a maximum of two or three organisations to provide transport services in Dar es Salaam (Mhina 2010, interview note). The idea was logistically feasible but politically unacceptable because such a move would have penalised the many "original Tanzanians" who had already invested in the sector *(Ibid)*.

In 2001, the Surface and Marine Transport Regulatory Authority (SUMATRA) was established by Act of Parliament (URT 2001). It subsumed the DRTLA. This was followed by reclaiming state authority to set fares "to protect both investor and consumer interests." The guidelines were: "the Authority shall have regard to a) the cost of making, producing and supplying goods or services; b) the desire to promote (sic) competitive rates and attract the market; c) the financial implications of the determination; and e) the consumer and investor interest" (URT 2001: 16).

In practice, the SUMATRA kept fares at Tshs 150 until 2007, then raised them to Tshs 250 to partly reflect rising operating costs (especially fuel prices) faced by private operators. In 2008, a further rise to Tshs 300 shillings was agreed, taking into account the further rise in oil prices. Since March 2009, fares have been regressed to Tshs 250 as the price of oil had dropped. For passengers and owners, this meant that the value of a ride was either at its historical peak since privatisation at 0.25 USD in 2008, or slightly below it at 0.19 USD both in 2007 and 2009 (Sulemani 2010, interview).

Set against these regulatory efforts, direct rush-hour observation in both 2009 and 2010 found many buses, often operating obviously without a licence or on a route away from their allocation and demanding fares ranging from Tshs 500 to 1,000. This anomaly applies to many other instances of the SUMATRA's attempts to improve the standards of service provision. For example, the SUMATRA attempted to decrease pollution and to increase the service life of private buses, by regulating that no vehicle would be given a license if it was more than five years old (URT 2007, 66). However, the SUMATRA discovered owners could not afford to purchase vehicles of that age (Sulemani 2010, interview). Special financing schemes for prospective buyers were considered, but in the end the age limit was withdrawn (Sulemani 2010, interview). In a similar but less ambitious effort, the SUMATRA prescribed that no car could be imported to Tanzania if it was more than 15 years old. This was equally unsuccessful. Owners simply falsified documents indicating vehicle age (Sulemani 2010, interview).

More successfully, in 2008 the SUMATRA announced that small buses, known in Tanzania as *vipanya* (small mice), would not be allowed to operate in the city centre, and that licences would be issued only to transport companies, not individuals. While the companies-only condition, clearly a reformulation of the DRTLA's idea a decade back, was dropped (*Mwananchi* 11 July 2008), the phasing out of small buses (technically up to 24 passengers, but in practice 14) from the city centre has progressed rapidly.

Table 6:   **Licensed Buses (*Daladala*) by Size - Dar es Salaam, March 2008 – June 2009**

Date	Large Buses (25 + passengers)	Small Buses (Up to 24 passengers)
March 2008	1,773	3,011
August 2008	2,002	2,978
April 2009	2,617	2,474
June 2009	2,765	2,423

Source: SUMATRA (2009)

In sum, nearly three decades of policy-making over passenger transport in Dar es Salaam has brought about transition from public to private, and progressive (but never total) deregulation. At the same time, a number of initiatives adopted by the state on passenger transport matters, including *ad hoc* regulation as well as the establishment of new transport institutions, suggest attempts by Tanzanian authorities to reclaim some policy space. Overall, reform efforts reveal a gap between the major transport problems of Dar es Salaam and the state's limited capacity to intervene.

Conclusion

The rationale behind widespread privatisation and economic liberalisation in Africa has been the superior efficiency of the private sector as an economic actor. The findings of this chapter, however, question that reasoning. Privatisation with control did not solve the transport shortage in Dar es Salaam; privatisation without control created over-supply and other problems. In either case, how efficient was the performance of the private sector as the main passenger transport provider in Dar es Salaam? The answers question unconditional belief in the virtues of 'free markets'; point to many inefficiencies, and tensions; and outright danger. In sum, persisting problems and new problems have outweighed the capacity of the state to effectively intervene.

There are two broad policy implications for public sector reform in sub-Saharan Africa that can be derived from this case study. One is the need to move away from reflex assumptions about the superior efficiency of the private sector as an economic actor. Private sector initiatives without effective regulation might well result in outcomes that are not desirable, either economically or socially. A second, and related, implication is the strategic importance of developing the capacity of African states to regulate and support private sector growth. The view that the private sector should be the primary driver of development, with the public sector playing a minimalist role, is incomplete and may be short-sighted.

Notes

1. Kampuni ya Mabasi ya Taifa (KAMATA) is the Swahili for 'National Bus Company'. Shirika la Usafiri Dar es Salaam (UDA) is the Swahili for 'Dar es Salaam Transport Corporation'.

2. This chapter builds on Rizzo (2002) and expands the time period and the themes under analysis.

3. The fact that UDA's fleet consisted of four different makes of buses arguably did not help the management of its fleet. Such a heterogeneous fleet was the outcome of four different aid programmes funded by Hungary, Japan, the United Kingdom and the Federal Republic of Germany (Wilburn Smith Associates 1991, 3–4).

4. The name *daladala* comes from the name of the 5 shilling coin *dala* — the cost of one ride in 1983. Conductors used to ask passengers for *dala, dala.*

5. The figure given for the cost of acquiring a driving licence dates back to 1998, the year in which the first fieldwork spell was carried out.

References

Adam, C., W. Cavendish and P. S. Mistry. 1992. *Adjusting privatization: Case studies from developing countries.* London: James Currey.

Baregu, M. 1993. The economic origins of political liberalization and future prospects. In *Economic policy under a multiparty system in Tanzania*, edited by M. S. D. Bagachwa and A. V. Y. Mbelle, pp 105–23. Dar es Salaam: Dar es Salaam University Press.

Bennell, P. 1997. Privatization in Sub-Saharan Africa: Progress and prospects during the 1990s.*World Development* 25, no. 2: 1785-1803.

Berg, E. 1996. Privatization in Sub-Saharan Africa: Results, prospects and new approaches. In *The transition from African socialism*, edited by P. Paulson. London: Macmillan.

Bureau of Statistics. 1989. 1988 population census: Preliminary report. Dar es Salaam: Ministry of Finance, Planning and Economic Affairs.

Campbell-White, O. and A. Bhatia. 1998. *Privatization in Africa.* Washington, DC: World Bank.

Central Transport Licensing Authority (CTLA). 1998. Various years. 'Microbuses file' (files from 1994/95 to 1997/98 accessed on UDA).

Chang, H.J. 2002. *Kicking away the ladder: Development strategy in historical perspective.* London: Anthem Press.

Cramer, C. 2000. Privatization and adjustment in Mozambique: A 'hospital pass'? *Journal of Southern African Studies* 27, no. 1: 79–104.

Dar es Salaam City Commission. 1998. '1998 Microbuses file'.

International Labour Organisation (ILO). 1993. International conference of labour statisticians: Resolution II'. In *The ILO and the informal sector: An institutional history*, edited by P. E. Bangasser, pp41–55. Geneva: ILO (2000).

Khayesi, M. 2001. *Matatu* workers in Nairobi, Thika and Ruiru: Career patterns and conditions of work. In *Negotiating social space: East African micro enterprises*, edited by P. O. Alila and P. O. Pedersen, pp 69–96. Trenton and Asmara: Africa World Press.

Kulaba, S. 1989. Local government and the management of urban services. In *African cities in crisis: Managing rapid urban growth*, edited by R. Stren and R. R. White, pp 203–46. Boulder, CO: Westview.

Maliyamkono, T. L. and M. S. D. Bagachwa. 1990. *The second economy in Tanzania.* London: James Currey.

Mamuya, Ian. 1993. *Structural adjustment and the reform of the public sector control system in Tanzania.* Hamburg: Institut fuir Afrika-Kunde.

Ministry of Communication and Transport (MCT). 1987. *Proposed national transport policy:* Dar es Salaam.

Mkandawire, T. 2001. Thinking about developmental states in Africa. *Cambridge Journal of Economics*, 25: 289–313.

Mutongi, Kenda. 2006. Thugs or entrepreneurs? Perceptions of *matatu* operators in Nairobi, 1970 to the present. *Africa* 76, no. 4: 549–568.

O' Connor, A. 1988. The rate of urbanisation in Tanzania in the 1970s. In *Tanzania after Nyerere*, edited by M. Hood, 136–42. London: Pinter.

Rizzo, M. 2002. Being taken for a ride: Privatisation of the Dar es Salaam transport system 1983–1998. *Journal of Modern African Studies* 40, no. 1: 133–157.

Sender, J. and S. Smith. 1986. *The development of capitalism in Africa*. London and New York: Methuen.

Shirika la Usafiri Dar es Salaam (UDA). 1994. Five year development plan. (Unpublished document in author's possession).

——.1995. Maelezo mafupi kuhusu UDA na shuguli zake yasiyowasolishwa kwa mheshimiwa Dr. Maua Daftari Mbunge Naibu Waziri wa Mawasiliano na Uchukuzi alipotembelea UDA 21.12.1995. (A short report on the performance of UDA, presented by Dr Maua, Vice-Minister of Communication and Transport, on the occasion of his visit to UDA). (Unpublished document in author's possession).

——.Various years. 'Fleet performance files' (files from 1994/95 to 1997/98).

Stren, R. 1989. The administration of urban services. In *African cities in crisis: Managing rapid urban growth*, edited by R. Stren and R. R.White, pp37–68. Boulder, CO: Westview.

SUMATRA. 2009. *Daladala* information. Print out of trends in licenses issued from 2008 to 2009. Handed to the author in SUMATRA Regional Office, Mwalimu House, Dar es Salaam.

Temu, A. E. & J. M. Due. 2000. The business environment in Tanzania after socialism: Challenges of reforming banks, parastatals, taxation and the civil service. *Journal of Modern African Studies* 38, no. 4: 683–712.

Tripp, A. M. 1997. *Changing the rules: The politics of liberalization and the urban informal economy in Tanzania*. Berkeley, CA: University of California Press.

UDA 1994 & 1995., see Shirika la Usafiri Dar es Salaam above.

United Nation Development Programme (UNDP). [Undated]. *Supporting informal sector activities*. New York, quoted in United Nations; 1996.

United Republic of Tanzania (URT). 1974. Exclusive licence granted to Shirika la Usafiri Dar es Salaam to operate passenger services in Dar es Salaam. Unpublished licence, 19 January 1974.

——.2001. The surface and marine transport regulatory act, 2001. Act No. 9 of 2001, 20 June 2001.

——.2007. The transport licensing (Road passenger vehicles) regulations 2007. Government Notice no. 218, published on 26/10/2007.

Xhosa, M. 1992. Routes, ranks and rebels: Feuding in the taxi revolution. *Journal of Southern African Studies* 18, no. 1: 232–51.

Wilbur Smith Associates. 1991. Dar es Salaam urban passenger transport study. Unpublished consultancy report.

World Bank. 1981. *Accelerated development in Sub-Saharan Africa: An agenda for action*. Washington, D.C.: World Bank.

——.1989. *Sub-Saharan Africa: From crisis to Sustainable Growth: A long-term perspective*. Washington, D.C.: World Bank.

Interviews cited:

Airi. 1998. A bus driver, Masaki, 18th December, 1998.

Mashaka. 1998. A bus driver, Mwenge Station, Dar es Salaam, 10th December, 1998.

Mhina, Tambo. 2010. Former Secretary of DRTLA (1999–2005), Ilala, 9th August, 2010.

Mwaibula, David. 2010. Former Chairman of DRTLA (1999–2005), Sinza, 11th August 2010.

Ndaombwa, George. 1998. Former Chairman of MUWADA, the association of *daladala* owners. Kisutu, Dar es Salaam, 20th December, 1998.

Sulemani. 2010. SUMATRA Director of Operations, Kisutu, September 2010.

Newspapers (all published in Dar es Salaam):

The African; Alasiri; Daily News; Dar Leo; The Guardian; Majira; Mtanzania; Mwananchi; Nipashe; Uhuru.

Chapter 5

Integrating All Stakeholders: Health Service Governance in Addis Ababa

Kassa T. Alemu and Shawel A. Yosef

Abstract

The Ethiopian capital of Addis Ababa has made considerable efforts to improve health service delivery, but the system still has much room and urgent needs for improvement. This chapter assesses the link between the health sector governance reform and the status of health service delivery outcomes in Addis Ababa city. Data were collected using questionnaires and interviews with officials, experts, and service providers as well as patients from sample health institutions from the public, private and NGO sectors. The data was analysed using the Brinkerhoff and Bossert (2008) health governance framework and the UNDP good governance principles. The health governance status index in Addis is fair (56 out of 100), but the city's health service system has not achieved adequate participation, transparency, accountability, responsiveness, equity and inclusiveness, efficiency and effectiveness – all of which are of extreme importance to target the poor in health service delivery. There is a need to improve the interaction and collaborative efforts of stakeholders in the system.

Introduction and Approach

Ethiopia is one of the least-developed countries in the world with low development indicators even by sub-Saharan Africa standards. Ethiopia's Human Development Index is 0.414 – ranking the country 171st out of 182; 44.2 per cent of the population lives below the poverty line of $1.25 per capita per day (UNDP 2009); the country's healthcare system is characterised by severe, long-lasting financial and human resource shortages and weak infrastructure (Wamai 2009); and Ethiopia has one of the worst health outcomes in the world, where under-five mortality is 166 per 1,000 live births, and maternal mortality is 850 per 100,000 (WHO 2009).

Addis Ababa, hosting 30 per cent of the country's urban population, is one of the fastest-growing cities on the continent (UN-HABITAT 2008). It attracts hundreds of thousands of migrants from all parts of Ethiopia in search of employment opportunities and better social services. City Governance Needs Assessment (AACG 2006) identified the city's health sector constraints as poor management capacity at all levels, a centralised structure that swamped managers with routine activities to the detriment of policy and strategic issues, concentration on curative services rather than preventive and promotive health service, lack of transparency and accountability, ethical problems among health professionals, poor systems of health information, deficient monitoring and evaluation, input orientation rather than focus on output/outcomes, and lack of integration and co-ordination with development partners and professional associations.

To address these and inter-related challenges, since 2003, Addis Ababa has undertaken healthcare system re-structuring and re-organisation. The health policy developed in 1993 focused on decentralisation, expanding the primary healthcare system, encouraging partnerships, and the participation of non-governmental actors (FDRE 1993). Despite considerable progress, significant obstacles remain. Health institutions suffer from inadequate facilities, shortage of medical equipment and drug supplies, and a limited number of health professionals. Lack of responsiveness and accountability in service delivery also challenged outcomes (Tigist and Yilma 2006; Wamai 2009; AACG 2009).

This chapter examines the extent, opportunities and challenges of health service reforms, especially measures intended to enhance interaction among state and non-state providers as well as citizen/client.

This study adopts six out of nine elements of the good governance report card developed by the Urban Governance Initiative of the UNDP: participation, transparency, responsiveness, equity, effectiveness-and-efficiency, and accountability. For each of the six elements, five indicators were used and graded (1 point for "very poor" to 5 points for "very good"). The overall performance percentage calculated by adding up the score for each core characteristic is interpreted as: 85 per cent -100 per cent "Very good" ; 65 per cent - 84 per cent "Good"; 50 per cent - 64 per cent "Fair"; 35 per cent - 49 per cent "Poor" and below 35 per cent "Very poor".

Primary data was collected from the major stakeholders (state; public, private and NGO providers; and clients) in the healthcare system of 4 of Addis Abeba's 10 sub-cities: Yeka, Gullele, Arada and Kirkos. Four hundred questionnaires were distributed and 358 responses were received. Interviews were conducted with 44 city /sub-city /*woreda* administrators, 22 hospital directors and health centre/clinic heads, and 13 sub-city and *woreda* health office heads in the 4 selected sub-cities. A summary of selected institutions and respondents is given in Table 1.

Table 1: **Sample health institutions and number of respondents**

Sample health institutions (employees)					Number of respondents (for questionnaire)												
Providers					Clients (patients)				Health experts (city, sub city and woreda¹ level)								
	(1)	(2)	(3)	(4)	(1)	(2)	(3)	(4)	(1)	(2)	(3)	(4)	(a)	(b)	(c)	(d)	
Hospital	4	4	2	10	24	24	12	60	32	32	16	80					
HC/Clinics	8	8	8	24	32	32	16	96	32	32	32	96					
Total	**12**	**12**	**10**	**34**	**56**	**56**	**28**	**140**	**64**	**64**	**48**	**176**	**4**	**22**	**16**	**42**	

Note: Column headings are as follows: (1) public; (2) private; (3) NGO and (4) total

(a) city; (b) sub-city; (c) woreda; and (d) total

Secondary data was collected from government policy documents, activity reports, research outputs, donor agency and health project documents as well as relevant published and unpublished literature.

Defining Health Governance

Governance in the context of urban settings is defined by the United Nations Human Settlements Programme (UN-Habitat 2002) as "the sum of the many ways individuals and institutions, public and private, plan and manage the common affairs of the city." Governance in the health sector is defined as:

> ....Competently directing health system resources, performance, and stakeholder participation toward the goal of saving lives, and doing so in ways that are open, transparent, accountable, equitable, and responsive to the needs of the people. For healthcare interventions to work, countries need effective policy-making, transparent rules, open information, and active participation by all stakeholders in the health sector (Islam 2007).

According to USAID (2008), governance in health systems is about developing and putting in place effective rules in the institutional arenas for policies, programmes and activities related to fulfilling public health functions to achieve health sector objectives. As indicated in Figure 1, health governance involves three sets of actors (*Ibid*): government, providers, and beneficiaries/clients. State actors include politicians, policy makers, and other government officials who should be willing and committed to interact with others. Health service providers, depending on the particulars of a given country's health system, mix public, private, and voluntary sector operations. The beneficiaries are service users and the general public – patients. Health governance involves the rules that determine the roles and responsibilities of each of these categories and the relationships and interactions among them.

Figure 1: **Health governance framework**

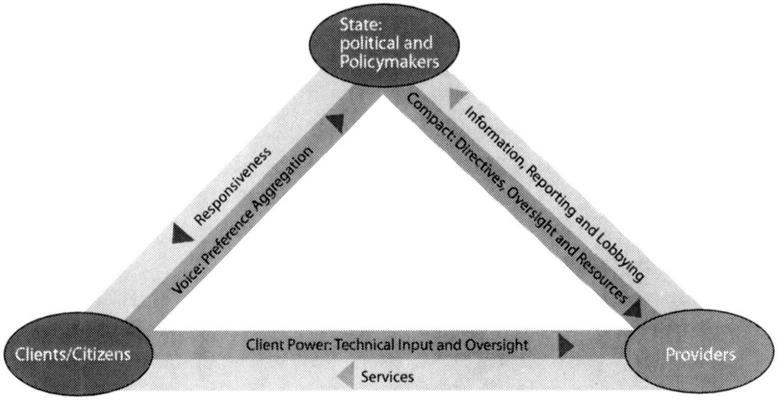

Source: Adapted from World Bank (2004, 2007)

Good governance in health systems promotes effective delivery of health services through: i) improvements in health status through more equitable access to quality health services and prevention and promotion programmes, ii) patient and public satisfaction with the health system, and iii) fair financing that protects against financial risks for those needing health care (WHO 2000; Roberts et al. 2004).

The literature provides different approaches for assessing health system governance in developing countries:

- World Health Organisation's (WHO) domains of stewardship;

- Pan American Health Organisation's (PAHO) essential public health functions (EPHF);

- World Bank's six basic aspects of governance; and

- UNDP's principles of good governance (Siddiqi *et al*, 2009).

The UNDP (1997) principles of governance (which incorporate key aspects of WHO, PAHO and World Bank approaches) are indicated in Box 1:

Box 1: Health system governance principles	
Strategic vision	Leaders should have a broad and long-term perspective on health and human development, along with a sense of strategic directions for such development. There also needs to be an understanding of the historical, cultural and social complexities in which that perspective is grounded.
Participation	All men and women should have a voice in decision-making for health, either directly or through legitimate intermediate institutions that represent their interests. Such broad participation is built on freedom of association and speech, as well as capacities to participate constructively.
Consensus orientation	Good governance of the health system mediates differing interests to reach a broad consensus on what is in the best interests of the group and, where possible, on health policies and procedures.
Rule of law	Legal frameworks pertaining to health should be fair and enforced impartially, particularly on human rights laws related to health.
Transparency	Transparency is built on the free flow of information for all health matters. Processes, institutions and information should be directly accessible to those concerned with them, and enough information should be provided to understand and monitor health matters.

Responsiveness	Institutions and processes should try to serve all stakeholders to ensure that the policies and programmes are responsive to the health and non-health needs of its users.
Equity and inclusiveness	All men and women should have opportunities to improve or maintain their health and well-being.
Effectiveness and efficiency	Processes and institutions should produce results that meet population needs and influence health outcomes while making the best use of resources.
Accountability	Decision makers in government, the private sector and civil society organisations involved in health are accountable to the public, as well as to institutional stakeholders. This accountability differs depending on the organisation and whether the decision is internal or external to an organisation

Source: Siddiqi et al. 2009

Figure 2 sums up these principles and provides the analytical framework used for this study, which builds on the works of Brinkerhoff and Bossert (2008), UNDP (1997) and World Bank (2007). The framework shows how improved health service is attained through the interaction of the three main actors (the state, providers and clients); the facilitating conditions (processes, structure and resources); and elements of governance (participation, equity, effectiveness-and-efficiency, accountability, transparency and responsiveness).

Figure 2: Analytical framework used for the study

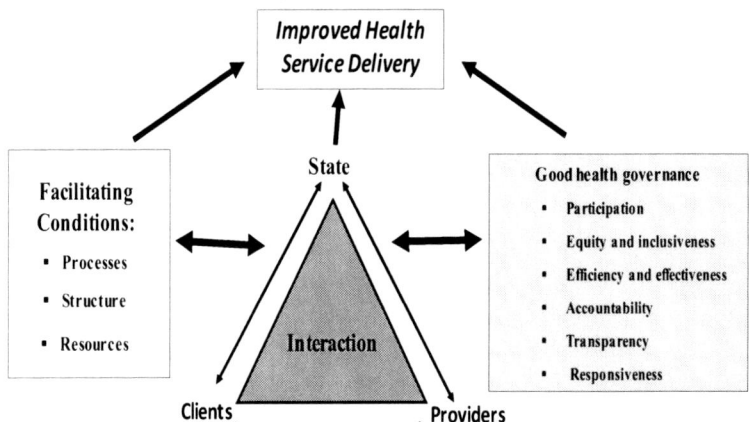

Source: Adapted from Brinkerhoff and Bossert (2008), UNDP (1997), and World Bank (2004, 2007)

Overview of the Addis Ababa City Health Service Delivery System

With a total land area of 540 km², Addis Ababa is the largest city of Ethiopia. It is the Federal Capital and a Chartered City granted administrative and financial autonomy by Proclamation No. 361/2003. According to Addis Ababa Bureau of Finance and Economic Development (AABFED) (2010), between 1994 and 2007 the population of Addis Ababa grew by about 30 per cent to 2.73 million. Addis Ababa city now has three layers of government: The city government at the top, 10 sub-city governments in the middle, and 99 *Kebele* governments at the base. The city is empowered to generate its own revenue from designated sources, to obtain loans from local resources, and to establish its own executive bodies, institutions and enterprises. Priority activities include generation of employment opportunities, construction of residential houses, promotion of neighbourhood upgrading activities, improvement of waste management, reduction of HIV/AIDS prevalence, and providing care for HIV/AIDS victims. The city authorities also strive to create an urban system in which security, social harmony and equitable municipal services are ensured.

In the health sector, the city administration aims to provide equitable preventive and curative health services of good quality and to reduce morbidity and mortality from communicable diseases and other health problems – through active participation of the community and all partners. The Addis Ababa City Administration Health Bureau is authorised to organise, coordinate and regulate public health activities in the city (AACAHB 2008). This Bureau has been developing and implementing various health sector development progammes by working closely with the Ministry of Health, donors, civil society organisations, NGOs, and other community-based organisations.

AACA is currently using a three-tier system - primary healthcare units (PHCUs), general hospitals, and specialised hospitals. The PHCUs are health centres serving 40,000 persons each; general hospitals serve a population of 1-1.5 million, and specialised hospitals serve between 3.5 and 5 million people (FMOH 2010). The city administration espouses decentralisation of the health service delivery system and delegates the authority and accountability for managing health services. Accordingly, the 10 sub-city health departments that manage the city's health centres, clinics and health posts, are directly answerable to their respective sub-city administrations (AACAHB 2008).

The city follows a financing system that allows hospitals and health centres government subsidy, as well as enabling them to collect and utilise revenues from internal and external sources. Cost-sharing is an important element of the system, which involves imposing user fees for some or all health services, thus encouraging clients who pay for services to demand better quality. A waiver system that collects fees from better-off clients and exempts those who cannot afford to pay is also in place, but some studies indicate that this system is not effective. For instance, Barnett and Bekele (2010) stated that "...no differences could be found between the poorest and better-off households, suggesting that the poorest did not receive exemptions or that the exemption did not cover the entire fees." They also found exemptions were accepted by only some health facilities, while other, mostly higher-level facilities, refused to give free treatment despite the exemption (*Ibid*).

Table 2: **Health indicators in Addis Ababa**

Indicators	Type	Figure
Population		2,854,462
Health service coverage based on only public health institutions		35 %
Infant mortality rate per 1000		45
Under-5 mortality rate per 1000		72
Immunisation coverage under 1 year		72 %
Family planning coverage		34.7%
Maternal mortality rate per 100, 000		548
Hospitals	Public	13*
	Private	28
	NGO	2
Health centres	Public	27
	Private	-
	NGO	3
Clinics/Health posts	Public	47
	Private	432
	NGO	31
Doctors	All (public, private and NGO)	648 (1:4226)
	Public only	111 (1:24,668)
Nurses	All (public, private and NGO)	1994 (1:1373)
	Public only	751 (1:3646)
Share of health budget (2009)		4 %
HIV prevalence rate		8.5%

Source: AACG (2009)

*13 public hospitals (5 managed by Addis Ababa Health Bureau, 5 managed by Federal Ministry of Health, 2 by Ministry of Defense and 1 by Federal Police)

The city government has used Business Process Re-engineering with the aim of establishing customer-focused institutions to rapidly scale up and enhance quality. Sub-city heath officials and administrators confirm that, despite city government efforts, major gaps still remain: serious workforce shortages; management issues that cut across city, sub-city and *kebele* levels; poor quality of health services; and a large unfunded gap in estimated budgets. In 2010, in public health institutions, the doctors to population ratio was1:24,668 and the nurses to population ratio was 1:3,646. The infant mortality rate was 71 per 1,000 live births, and under-five mortality was 136 per 1,000 live births. HIV prevalence was 8.5 per cent and the status of health coverage based on the government's total number of health centres was only 35 per cent (AACG 2009; FMOH 2010).

Examination of the Health Governance System in Addis Ababa

The effectiveness of basic healthcare and supporting services, as well as inter-sectoral interventions, rely on the extent of all-stakeholder participation at all stages of equitable health service distribution and access. Bearing in mind that health governance refers to the way in which providers, society and the state - by means of explicit processes and rules - interact to produce and distribute health services in ways that are transparent, accountable, equitable and responsive to the needs of the people, the data collected through the survey instrument - TUGI report card - for Addis Ababa city administration shows the following results:

Participation

All individuals and communities are entitled to active and informed participation in issues bearing on their health. This includes participation in identifying overall strategy, policy-making, implementation and accountability. Technically, government organs working in the health sector have a human rights responsibility to establish institutional arrangements for active participation and to include disadvantaged communities within the stakeholder reach (Hunt and Backman 2008). The health policy of Ethiopia clearly describes the state, the private sector, NGOs, and civil society as key stakeholders, and encourages partnerships and their participation in the health sector, particularly in the scaling-up of HIV/AIDS, TB, malaria and other health services (FMOH 2005; MoFED 2010).

Table 3: **Participation (N=358)**

Indicators	Score	%
1. Existing policies and programmes of the city encourage participation of the private sector and the civil societies for better health service delivery	1,154*	64.5**
2. Situation of the local government and the civil society/private sector partnership programmes for improved health service in the city	1,123	62.7
3. Extent of civil society involvement in the establishment of policies, plans and budgets for health service	1,043	58.3
4. Extent of private sector involvement in the establishment of policies, plans and budgets for health service	973	54.4
5. Extent of community mobilisation to solicit input/views/ideas about their priorities, service efficiency or quality, and resource utilisation	976	54.5
Total (Percentage = [total ÷ 25 (N) x 100])	**5269**	**58.9**

Source: Field Survey (2011)

Note:

$*SCORE = R_1 * 1 + R_2 * 2 + R_3 * 3 + R_4 * 4 + R_5 * 5$

Grade 1-5 represent 5: Very Good; 4: Good; 3: Moderate; 2: Poor; 1: Very Poor

R_1, R_2, R_3, R_4 *and* R_5 *represent the number of respondents who answered very poor, poor, moderate, good and very good respectively.*

$** \% = score /maximum grade * N (358)$

The survey results confirm positive city policy and programmes that encourage stakeholder participation, but the overall result of 58.9 per cent qualifies as "fair", indicating considerable room for improvement. Parallel interviews of city and sub-city administrators shows participation is constrained by capacity, the degree of skills, knowledge, access, political connections, resources and motivation. Officials from private and NGO health institutions noted that participation is largely state-driven, with limited opportunities for civil society and private sectors, as an independent actor, to participate in policies, plans, budgeting and resource allocation. This result correlates with the CRDA research which says NGOs have limited participation in health policy formulation. Banteyerga *et al.* (2006) state that government appears to have realised the value of the private sector and NGOs in scaling-up health services, but so far they have little participation in the policy making process.

Transparency

According to Fernando (2009), transparency means decisions are taken and enforced in a manner that follows rules and regulations; that information is freely and directly accessible to those who will be affected by such decisions and their enforcement; that enough information is provided, and in easily understandable forms and media.

Table 4: **Transparency (N=358)**

Indicators	Score	%
1. The extent to which the allocation and utilisation of resources is regularly tracked, and information on results is available for review by the public and concerned stakeholders	824	46.0
2. The extent to which budget proposals, annual reports and other health-related information are regularly made available to the public	866	48.4
3. The extent to which information is publicly available about quality and cost to help clients make choices as to where they want to go for health services	943	52.7
4. Transparency on health staff recruitment, awarding health project contracts and budget allocation	905	50.6
5. Frequency of communication and information sharing with the public	914	51.1
Total (Percentage = [total ÷ 25 (N) x 100])	**4,452**	**49.7**

Source: Field Survey, 2011

The overall result is a "poor" rating, with quite serious implications. Information is the basis on which the public can form opinions, make decisions, give feedback and – perhaps most crucially – hold government accountable. A poor transparency score erodes all these objectives.

Efficiency and Effectiveness

Efficiency and effectiveness measures whether institutions produce results that meet the needs of society while making the best use of resources at their disposal (Fernando 2009). It also measures the quality of health services, the quality of policy formulation and implementation, and the credibility of the government's commitment to such policies. As indicated in Table 5, the index result shows overall efficiency and effectiveness of the city health sector is fair (57.1 per cent) in terms of the formulation of need-based polices and creating a synergy between stakeholders as well as mobilising internal and external resources for health.

Table 5: **Efficiency and Effectiveness (N=358)**

Indicators	Score	%
1. The extent to which local government officials formulate local policies, plans, regulations, procedures and standards on the basis of clearly identified goals and relevant health-intervention activities	1,046	58.4
2. The extent to which one integrated policy framework for health service exists, creating a synergy between service providers	1,015	56.7
3. Proper utilisation of the scarce municipal resources for better health- related activities (cost effectiveness with no compromise on quality)	1,003	56.0
4. Mobilisation of internal resources from private sector, civil societies and individuals	1,007	56.3
5. Mobilisation of external resources from institutions, individuals and funding organisations	1,035	57.8
Total (Percentage = [total ÷ 25 (N)] x 100])	**5,106**	**57.1**

Source: Field Survey (2011)

City and sub-city administrators and providers from selected public health institutions considered lack of resources, corruption, weak political leadership and a lack of skilled public servants to be the biggest obstacles to improving health service in Addis Ababa. This finding is also supported by the research works Wamai (2009) on Ethiopia, which itemises constraints as a limited number of public health facilities; an ineffective healthcare delivery system which is inefficient and biased towards the curative service; an acute shortage of human and material resources; and little policy involvement/ participation of the private, NGOs sectors and beneficiary communities.

Accountability

Successful services for poor people emerge from institutional relationships in which the actors are accountable to each other (World Bank 2004). Accountability requires that local governments are responsible for delivering health services that are consistent with citizens' needs and preferences (Nuvunga 2007). Not only governmental health institutions, but also the private sector and civil society organisations must be accountable to the public and to their institutional stakeholders.

The overall result with regard to accountability is poor (49 per cent). This is corroborated by sub-city health officers and private providers' officials, who note that in almost all health institutions and sub-city offices, there are no well-established mechanisms for citizens to review the state and private providers' performance and hold them accountable. Worldwide governance indicators on accountability in Ethiopia also show low performance and further decline – from -0.83 in 1998 to -1.30 in 2009[2].

Table 6: **Accountability (N=358)**

Indicators	Score	%
1. The extent to which municipal staff and councillors realise that they are accountable for the consequences of what they do and do not do, in relation to health matters	914	51.1
2. Whether systems exist for reporting, investigating and adjudicating misallocation and misuse of resources	807	45.1
3. Whether civil society organisations and the community provide oversight of public, NGOs and private provider organisations in the way they deliver and finance health services	882	49.3
4. The extent to which a sanctioning mechanism is operational, which penalises misbehaviour by health providers	867	48.4
1) The extent to which a public feedback mechanism related to health service exists (such as complaint offices and procedures, citizen suggestion box and procedures for public petitioning, and so on)	915	51.1
Total (Percentage = [total ÷ 25 (N) x 100])	**4,385**	**49.0**

Source: Field Survey (2011)

Responsiveness

Local government and health service providers must be responsive to citizens' demands and establish mechanisms to hear, address, and act on public complaints and views related to health services (ADB 2007).

Table 7: **Responsiveness (N=358)**

Indicators	Score	%
1. Whether local government officials make decisions about resource allocation for health services on the basis of evidence regarding needs and effectiveness of services and in conformity with policies	1,036	57.9
2. Whether service providers regularly review and update the mix of services they deliver on the basis of evidence about the effectiveness of health services, client needs and health problems	1,014	56.7
3. The existence of mechanisms to ascertain the needs and aspirations of the city on health service's stakeholders	998	55.8
4. The existence of mechanisms to hear, address, and act on public complaints and views related to health service	1,002	56.0
5. The extent to which priority is given to health service in the city	985	55.0
Total (Percentage = [total ÷ 25 (N) x 100])	**5,035**	**56.3**

Source: Field Survey, 2011

The overall responsiveness index is "fair" at 56.3 per cent, suggesting room for improvement. Technically, sub-cities and *woreda* health sectors are responsible for personnel issues, health facility construction, and procurement of drugs and equipment. Sub-cities/*woredas* are also responsible for the mobilisation of community leaders, of the community itself, and of community-based organisations. However, in practice, responsive health service delivery is negatively affected by shortage of trained human resources, high turn-over of existing staff, inadequate office facilities, and limited financial resources within *woredas* and health facilities. Sub-city officials explained that efforts have been made to improve responsiveness through decentralised policy and sector reform, using BPR to pinpoint areas needing improvement. The effort is not matched by result yet.

Equity and Inclusiveness

A state has a legal obligation to ensure that a health system is accessible to all without discrimination, including those living in poverty, minorities, women, children, slum dwellers, people with disabilities, and other disadvantaged individuals and communities (Hunt and Backman 2008). This shows that equity and inclusiveness can be seen from the accessibility of healthcare for all and equitable distribution of health facilities and resources in the city. The survey shows encouraging results as indicated in Table 8.

Table 8: **Equity and Inclusiveness (N=358)**

Indicators	Grade (1-5)	%
1. The extent to which the health service provision is inclusive to everyone in the city – be it the poor, the young or older persons, religious or ethnic minorities or the handicapped	1,277	71.3
2. Extent of gender sensitiveness (how men and women participate equally) in decision-making, priority-setting and resource allocation of health service	1,193	66.6
3. Concern shown by NGOs, CBOs, communities and private sector for health service	1,082	60.4
4. Coverage of the health service and health institutions established in the city	1,321	73.8
5. Level of support provided to health-related workers and institutions	991	55.4
Total (Percentage = [total ÷ 25 (N) x 100])	**5,864**	**65.5**

Source: Field Survey (2011)

The overall result on equity and inclusiveness of health service in the city ranks as "good" by TUGI criteria, though distribution is uneven. Public health institution officials and sub-city administrators note there are many *kebeles* in the city without health facilities. UN-HABITAT (2008) states that the private sector has been playing a substantial role in improving physical coverage, though practical access remains a challenge as private health institutions are not affordable to the majority of the population.

Figure 3: **Overall urban governance indicators**

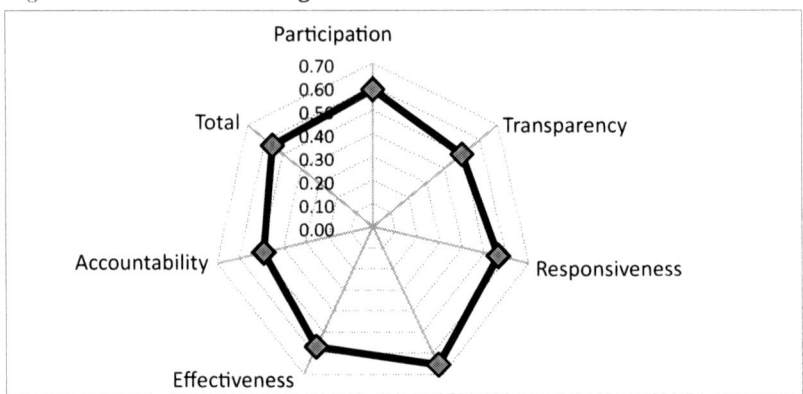

Source: Authors' calculation from the survey data

Figure 3 shows that the overall average score on governance in the health sector in Addis Ababa is 56 out of 100. Most scores on the indicators were fairly close to this average figure with a highest score of 65 ('good") and a lowest of 49 ("poor"). The 56 average ranks as "fair", indicating a degree of achievement but that city government and other stakeholders could and should do much better. Kaufmann, Kraay, and Mastruzzi (2009), in their worldwide governance study, also concluded that Ethiopia exhibits poor performance in governance, with low scores on all six indicators of voice and accountability, government effectiveness, rule of law, regulatory quality, political stability, and control of corruption.

Health Service Improvements

The study for this chapter distributed a questionnaire asking exit clients from public, private and NGO health institutions to assess the extent to which they were satisfied with the health service provision. The response summarised in Table 9 is based on the sample category of clients (public 64, private 64, NGO 48, total 176).

Table 9: **Respondents' perceptions on health service improvement**

Indicators		(5)	(4)	(3)	(2)	(1)
1. I was satisfied with the length of time I had to wait for service.	Public clients (n=64)	4.7	34.4	28.1	26.6	6.3
	Private clients (n=64)	9.4	57.8	17.2	15.6	-
	NGO clients (n=48)	4.2	54.2	22.9	18.8	-
	All (N=176)	6.3	48.3	22.7	20.5	2.3
2. The facility is at a convenient distance from my home.	Public clients (n=64)	7.8	29.7	40.6	15.6	6.3
	Private clients (n=64)	6.3	64.1	20.3	9.4	-
	NGO clients (n=48)	14.6	62.5	16.7	6.3	-
	All (N=176)	9.1	51.1	26.7	10.8	2.3
3. The medical staff were readily available.	Public clients (n=64)	6.3	23.4	54.7	10.9	4.7
	Private clients (n=64)	10.9	50.0	31.3	7.8	-
	NGO clients (n=48)	10.4	37.5	45.8	6.3	-
	All (N=176)	9.1	36.9	43.8	8.5	1.7
4. The facility had all the necessary medicines and supplies.	Public clients (n=64)	14.1	25.0	26.6	25.0	9.4
	Private clients (n=64)	9.4	54.7	20.3	15.6	-
	NGO clients (n=48)	18.8	43.8	35.4	2.1	-
	All (N=176)	13.6	40.9	26.7	15.3	3.4
5. Health service fees and costs of medicine were reasonable.	Public clients (n=64)	15.6	42.2	17.2	18.8	6.3
	Private clients (n=64)	-	20.3	34.4	43.8	1.6
	NGO clients (n=48)	12.5	58.3	22.9	6.3	-
	All (N=176)	11.9	46.6	20.5	18.2	2.8
6. I received any health information I wanted without any difficulties.	Public clients (n=64)	6.3	32.8	42.2	18.8	0
	Private clients (n=64)	6.3	51.6	35.9	6.3	-
	NGO clients (n=48)	-	54.2	37.5	8.3	-
	All (N=176)	4.5	45.5	38.6	11.4	-

7. The medical	Public clients (n=64)	6.3	50.0	29.7	9.4	4.7
staff were	Private clients (n=64)	15.6	62.5	20.3	1.6	-
courteous	NGO clients (n=48)	8.3	62.5	22.9	6.3	-
and helpful to me.	All (N=176)	10.2	58.0	24.4	5.7	1.7
8. The buildings	Public clients (n=64)	4.7	40.6	42.2	7.8	4.7
were in good	Private clients (n=64)	4.7	54.7	35.9	4.7	-
condition	NGO clients (n=48)	8.3	43.8	45.8	2.1	-
and well maintained.	All (N=176)	5.7	46.6	40.9	5.1	1.7
9. I would	Public clients (n=64)	12.5	23.4	39.1	18.8	6.3
get better	Private clients (n=64)	17.2	32.8	34.4	15.6	-
service if I	NGO clients (n=48)	4.2	37.5	41.7	12.5	4.2
paid a small informal fee.	All (N=176)	11.9	30.7	38.1	15.9	3.4
10. I received	Public clients (n=64)	10.9	35.9	43.8	7.8	1.6
good medical	Private clients (n=64)	14.1	62.5	17.2	3.1	3.1
attention	NGO clients (n=48)	8.3	50.0	37.5	4.2	-
by qualified staff.	All (N=176)	11.4	49.4	32.4	5.1	1.7

Source: Field Survey (2011)

Note: *Column headings are as follows: (1) don't know; (2) strongly disagree; (3) disagree; (4) agree; (5) strongly agree*

Table 9 shows that only 54 per cent of clients were satisfied with the waiting time for health services, but results differ widely among the different types of providers: 67 per cent of respondents from private services, 58 per cent from NGO institutions and 39 per cent from public health institutions indicated that waiting time was not a major problem. Public hospital directors and health centre officials interviewed confirmed that there is long waiting time at public institutions. They also stated that in private health institutions, competitiveness and profit motive improved speed of service delivery. It has to be noted, however, 46 per cent of respondents indicated their dissatisfaction with the time it takes to get attention.

The survey result showed that 60 per cent of the clients confirmed the availability of health facilities at a convenient distance from their home. A good number of respondents expressed dissatisfaction on the availability of medical staff, medicines and supplies in public sector health institutions as compared to private and NGO health institutions. About 51.6 per cent of clients who visited public health facilities were dissatisfied because drugs were not consistently available. On the other hand, 56 per cent, 70 per cent, and 78 per cent, respectively, of respondents from public, NGO and private health providers, respectively, found the medical staff courteous and helpful.

Interviewed officials from sampled sub-cities rated private providers superior to public and NGO facilities for promptness, availability during off hours and holidays, and patient handling. However, private providers were considered inferior to large government hospitals in terms of medical infrastructure, laboratory, x-ray and surgical services. Private facilities were cited for expensive tests and drugs. NGO providers were rated favourably on providing quality service at reasonable price.

Hospital directors and health centre/clinic heads from all facility groups were asked to reflect on the challenges in providing health services. One of the major challenges for Addis Ababa was a shortage of health professionals due to doctors' migration to developed countries (especially the USA) and even other developing countries, mainly Botswana (Yifru 2008; FHAPCO 2010). Lack of appropriate monetary and other incentives is among reasons cited for this drain. Very recently, hospitals in Addis Ababa have started private wings as an incentive mechanism for health professionals. This is specific to hospitals and has yet to be expanded to other health institutions.

The second related challenge of the health system is also the poor government budget allocation to the sector. While the Abuja Declaration requires 15 per cent of a country's budget to the health sector, in each year from 1996-1999 (AACG 2009), the Addis Ababa city administration allocated not more than 4 per cent of it total budget for health. At interview, four public hospital directors stated that health institutions, mainly hospitals in the city, are not well maintained. The majority of buildings are old and no major expansion has been carried out.

The interviewees also identified lack of facilities and equipment, lack of essential drugs, and lack of committed, competent, ethical medical staff (mainly in public health institutions) to be the major challenges. Wamai (2009) also indicates the number of healthcare facilities is low and that they are generally ill-equipped, mal-distributed and in a state of disrepair, resulting in an inefficient, ineffective healthcare delivery system biased towards the curative service.

Conclusion

A well-functioning health governance framework is neither straightforward nor, by its mere existence, sufficient. It is a very complex concept and process that must comply with crucial principles and secure the involvement and shared responsibility of many actors and stakeholders to make it fully operational. This study shows that Addis Ababa's health service system has not achieved adequate participation, transparency, accountability, responsiveness, equity and inclusiveness, efficiency and effectiveness – all of which are of extreme importance to target the poor in health service delivery. It can be seen that Addis Ababa's overall health governance requires significant improvement if better outcomes are to be achieved.

The Addis Ababa city government's involvement of public, private and NGOs health sectors is somewhat tokenistic – doing something to inform and consult but little to truly transform. In reality, there is no active involvement of citizens, private sector and NGOs in planning and budgeting processes. A number of fiscal, institutional, technical and political constraints limit state and non-state providers from delivering accountable, transparent, efficient and effective, inclusive and responsive health services to citizens. Power imbalances often prevent citizens from dealing with the state or non-state providers concerning health service delivery issues. It is imperative that the city government strengthens health governance and establishes better interaction of stakeholders regarding the availability, quality, distribution and utilisation of health services.

Political will is pivotal; there should be politically committed and strong leadership to ensure health sector reforms become more pro-poor. Proactive approaches need to emphasise public-private partnership, arrange networks and institutions responsible for implementation of health sector policies, and use new ideas and modern techniques to improve operational issues for better health services. Success will not be achieved by state effort alone – it will be achieved by governance that involves all stakeholders and which harnesses their collective effort.

Notes

1. *Woreda* in Ethiopian context refers to an administrative unit (equivalent to a district) within a sub-city.

2. The units in which governance is measured follow a normal distribution with a mean of zero and a standard deviation of one in each period. This implies that virtually all scores lie between -2.5 and 2.5, with higher scores corresponding to better outcomes.

References

AABFED. 2010. The City Government of Addis Ababa the Public Expenditure and Financial Accountability (PEFA) Assessment Report. Addis Ababa.

AACAHB. 2008. Addis Ababa City Administration Health Bureau Report. Addis Ababa.

AACG. 2009. Addis Ababa City Government Five Year Strategic Plan Draft (2009/10–2013/14). Addis Ababa.

——.2006. Addis Ababa City Government Five Year Strategic Plan draft (2006–2011). Addis Ababa.

ADB. 2007. Improving local governance pro-poor service delivery: Citizen report card learning tool kit. ADB.

Banteyerga Hailom, Aklilu Kidanu and Kate Stillman. 2006. The system-wide effects of the global fund in Ethiopia: Final study report. Bethesda, MD: The Partners for Health Reform Plus Project, Abt Associates Inc.

Barnett, I. and Bekele, T. 2010. *Poor households' experiences and perception of user fees for healthcare: A mixed-method study from Ethiopia*. UK: Young Lives, Department of International Development: University of Oxford.

Brinkerhoff, W. and T. Bossert. 2008. *Health governance: Concepts, experience, and programming options*. Washington, D.C.: US Agency for International Development, Health Systems 20/20: Policy Brief.

FDRE (Federal Democratic Republic of Ethiopia). 1993. *Health policy of the transitional government of Ethiopia*. Addis Ababa: FDRE.

Fernando, A.C. 2009. *Corporate governance: Principles, policies and practices*. India, Delhi: Dorling Kindersler.

FHAPCO. 2010. Report on progress towards implementation of the UN Declaration of Commitment on HIV/AIDS. Addis Ababa: FHAPCO.

FMOH (Federal Ministry of Health). 2010. Health sector development programme (HSDP-IV). Addis Ababa: Planning and Programming Department, Ministry of Health: Addis Ababa.

——.2005. Health sector development programme (HSDP-III). Addis Ababa: Planning and Programming Department, Ministry of Health: Addis Ababa.

Hunt, P. and Backman, G. 2008. Health systems and the right to the highest attainable standard of health. Web: www.swisshumanrightsbook. com/...03.../02_453_Backman_Hunt.pd. (accessed on April, 2010)

Islam, M. 2007. Health systems assessment approach: A how-to manual. Submitted to the U.S. Agency for International Development in Collaboration with Health Systems 20/20, Partners for Health Reformplus, Quality Assurance Project, and Rational Pharmaceutical Management Plus. Arlington, VA: Management Sciences for Health.

Kaufmann D., Kraay, A. and Mastruzzi, M. 2009. Governance matters VIII: Aggregate and individual governance indicators 1996–2008.*World Bank Policy Research Working Paper* No. 4978 web: papers.ssrn.com/sol3/ papers.cfm?abstract_id=1424591(accessed on March, 2010)

MoFED (Ministry of Finance and Economic Development). 2010. The Federal Democratic Republic of Ethiopia, Growth and Transformation Plan (GTP) 2010/11–2014/15, Draft, Addis Ababa.

Nuvunga, A. 2007. Post-war reconstruction in Mozambique: The United Nations Trust Fund to Assist the Former Rebel Movement RENAMO. London. Web: citeseerx.ist.psu.edu/viewdoc/download;jsessionid...?doi... (accessed on March, 2010)

Roberts, M. J., W. Hsiao, P. Berman, and M. R. Reich. 2004. *Getting health reforms right: A guide to improving performance and equity.* London and New York: Oxford University Press.

Siddiqi, S., Masud, T. Nishtar, S. Peters, D. Sabri, B. Bile, K. & Jama, M. 2009. Framework for assessing governance of the health system in developing countries: Gateway to good governance. *Journal of Health Policy,* 90 (13–25): Elsevier.

Tigist, G. and Yilma M. 2008. Quality of reproductive health services at private for-profit institute in Addis Ababa. *Ethiopian Jornal of Reproductive Health* Vol. 2 (1): Addis Ababa.

UNDP. 2009. *Human Development Report 2009 Ethiopia.* Addis Ababa: UNDP.

——.1997. *Governance for sustainable human development. A UNDP policy document.* New York: UNDP.

UN-HABITAT. 2008. *Ethiopia: Addis Ababa urban profile.* Addis Ababa: UN-HABITAT.

——.2002. Global campaign on urban governance: Concept paper. 2nd Edition. Nairobi.

USAID. 2008. Health governance: Concepts, experience, and programming options. (www.HealthSystems2020.org). (accessed on March, 2010)

Wamai, R., 2009. Reviewing Ethiopia's health system development. *Japanese Medical Association Journal* 52.4: 279–86.

WHO (World Health Organisation). 2009. *World health statistics 2009.* Geneva: World Health Organization.

——.2000. *World Health Report 2000.* Geneva: WHO.

World Bank. 2007. *Healthy development: The World Bank strategy for health, nutrition, and population results.* Washington, DC: World Bank.

——.2004. Making services work for poor people. *World development report 2004.* Washington, D.C.: World Bank.

Yifru, B. 2008. Medical doctors profile in Ethiopia: Production, attrition and retention. In Memory of 100 years Ethiopian modern medicine and the new millennium, *Ethio-med J* 46 (1), pp 1–77.

Chapter 6

The Ups and Downs of Business Process Re-Engineering (BPR): A Tale of Two Offices in Bahir Dar Town, Ethiopia

Abebe Walle Menberu

Abstract

Since the early 1990s, Ethiopia has been running reform programmes to improve efficiency, effectiveness and accountability in the delivery of public services. One method has been Business Process Re-engineering (BPR). This chapter analyses two public bodies to examine whether their BPR projects have been appropriately designed and implemented, what has worked, what has not, and why. The finding is that BPR designs have been generally sound, but positive results have been prevented or compromised by a wide range of planning and implementation defects, including failure to institutionalise the new systems; lack of monitoring, measuring, and reviewing; and an inadequate incentive structure.

Introduction

Ethiopia's first Civil Service Reform Programme (CSRP) was launched in 1996 (UNDP 2007), designed to improve the efficiency, effectiveness, and transparency of public institutions. It included sub-programmes to reform top management systems, human resource management, service delivery, government expenditure and control, and ethics. In 2001, the government also launched a comprehensive National Capacity Building Programme (NCBP) to strengthen working systems, improve organisational effectiveness, and rapidly develop human resources in the public sector (*Ibid*). Business Process Re-engineering (BPR) was introduced in 2003 and was applied as part of the CSRP (Gebrekidan 2011).

There are very few studies on the outcomes and impacts of PBR reforms in Ethiopia, and even these provide inconclusive accounts. Some argue that BPR reforms have not brought the desired changes, while others indicate success stories. The World Bank (2011) suggests that effectiveness, efficiency and speed of service delivery in Ethiopian public bodies is much talked about but little achieved. There are studies indicating some improvements in service provision as a result of BPR, and some failures (Tilaye cited in Debela 2009; Debela and Hagos 2011; Teklegiorgis and Amare 2007). Empirical studies on the status of BPR reforms in the Regional Government of Ethiopia are scarce.

Focusing on the Amhara Region, this study explores the design and implementation of BPR programmes in two government offices in Bahir Dar town - Bahir Dar City Services Office (BDC) and Bahir Dar University (BDU). Although the two organisations provide different services, both do so to large numbers of customers, mobilise huge resources, and began re-engineering at the same time.

Conceptualising Business Process Re-Engineering (BPR)

BPR is defined as the analysis and design of work flows and processes within organisations (Davenport and Stanton 1990, cited in Dey 2001). Hammer and Stanton (1995) consider BPR as the fundamental re-thinking and radical re-design of business processes to bring about dramatic improvements in performance such as time reductions in the delivery of goods and services, shorter time to market in product development processes, and enhanced employee capabilities. In some organisations, however, re-engineering has been simultaneously a success and a failure as paradoxical outcomes are commonplace (Eugene *et al.* 1994) and BPR is also regarded as a costly and time-consuming undertaking (Abdolvand *et al.* 2008).

The literature cites success factors for BPR effectiveness as leadership commitment; effective project management systems; adequate financial resources; incentive structure; communication and information technology (Abdolvand *et.al*, 2008; Cheng and Chui, 2008; Hammer and Stanton, 1995; Attaran 2000). McAdam and Donaghy (1999) highlight the importance of ownership of the BPR project by management and employees, understanding the drivers of change and process issues related to design methodology, involvement of internal and external stakeholders, customer-focused process designs, and smooth relationships among members of an organisation.

Lockamy III and Smith (1997) also point out that BPR can be successful if organisations align their core processes with their strategic objectives; that is, if all business and support units of an organisation are aligned and linked to the strategy. Success also comes from making strategic objectives everyone's everyday job (Kaplan and Norton 1999). When organisational changes do align with strategies they may still fail, owing to inadequate measurement systems to track and review on a sustained basis (Hacker and Washington 2004, cited in Jayashree and Hussain 2011). It is often said that 'if you can't measure it you can't manage it'. Thus, if organisations are to successfully implement large organisational change, they must use measurement and management systems derived from their strategies and capabilities' (Kaplan and Norton 1996). Jayashree and Hussain (2011) emphasise that performance management systems can help develop and sustain competencies to facilitate change and continuous feedback processes that monitor and evaluate all stages of the BPR process.

This study collected data using survey and interviews and consulted various documents. The survey respondents were purposively selected from organisational units (processes) which began implementing the re-engineering projects during 2010/2011. At Bahir Dar University (BDU), 15 officers from the teaching/learning process and 15 case-team leaders from the support processes; and at Bahir Dar City services (BDC), 3 case-team coordinators from the head office and 27 officers from the sub-city administrators, known as *kebeles,* responded to the survey questionnaire. Top-level officials from both organisations who were actively engaged in the re-engineering process were interviewed. Design documents, minutes of change management committees, review documents and other secondary information were consulted.

This study adopted a survey instrument, which was developed and used in Botswana by Hacker and Washington (2004)[1] in measuring performance of large-scale projects. The instrument measures the performance of any large-scale change through six areas: result areas and goals; objectives; measurement processes; reviews; responsibilities; and evidence of continuous improvement. The instrument has 39 statements within the six headings. Respondents are asked to rate the level of implementation of the items on a scale from 1 (not implemented at all) to 7 (fully implemented). The reliability of the tool (across time and other variables) is computed using Cronbach's alpha, with a result of 0.965 representing a relatively high estimate (Nunnaly cited in Davis 2000, 180).

The Design and Implementation of BPR in the Two Offices

Pre-BPR

Bahir Dar University (BDU) was established in 1999 by merging the then Bahir Dar Teachers' Education and Bahir Dar Polytechnic institutes. The university now has more than 40,000 students in its regular, evening, distance and summer programmes, which include the humanities, social sciences, natural science, engineering, business and economics, agriculture and environmental sciences, legal studies and medical and health sciences. In 2011, the academic and support staff numbered about 2,500.

Before the BPR, the decision-making power was centrally held by the top management of the university, which included the President (Chief Executive Officer), Academic and Research Vice President, and Business and Development Vice President. Under the Academic and Research Vice President, there were seven Deans running their respective faculties. The support activities were run by the Finance, Administration, and General Services departments all organised under the supervision of the Business and Development Vice President. With the exception of student affairs and some aspects of staff affairs, all the powers relating to financial management and procurement were centralised at the top management level, especially with the President and the Vice Presidents. The Academic Deans of the faculties had little authority on hiring and firing of staff, management of their budget, or administering support staff and physical resources. They were responsible only for the day-to-day teaching/learning activities of their faculties.

Bahir Dar City (BDC), the regional capital of Amhara State, has an estimated 220,000 residents (2007 Ethiopia Statistics Authority census survey). The city has a Mayor as Chief Administrator, different sectoral offices, and the city services office. Its objectives are making the city suitable for living, investment, and provision of social services. Major services include development and provision of land for social services, investments, and residential construction; building of infrastructure, beautification and cleaning of the city; and provision of utilities and municipal services.

Before the BPR, the BDC Services had a centralised structure and different functional departments. The Department Heads reported to the City Manager, who was accountable to the Mayor. There were 17 Sub-City administrators known as *kebele administrators* all reporting to the City Manager. Almost every major decision was centralised; for example, every land lease contract between the city and the citizen/investor had to be signed by the City Manager. Service provision took an inordinate length of time and involved numerous procedures. For acquiring a plot of land and securing an approved site plan for constructing residential or commercial houses, an applicant had to wait for at least twelve months; in the process there were 30 different activities performed by different experts in different offices. *Kebeles* had no power with regard to provision of land, construction permits, collection of fees, transfer of title deeds to different parties, or delivery of utilities. Their authority was limited to minor issues like provision of citizen identity cards and minor dispute resolutions.

BPR Design Process

At BDU, the top management formed a team of experts and officials who identified ten business processes, of which five were selected for re-design based on their relative importance to the success of the mission of the university, the resources they consumed and the magnitude of the problems they faced. These processes were: a) Teaching-Learning; b) Human Resource Development; c) Procurement and Property Administration; d) Planning, Implementation, Monitoring and Evaluation; and e) Information and Strategic Communication.

The university formed a separate team for each business process and gave each team a "Process Owner", who reports to the President of the university as the overall "Business Owner". A Tsar was appointed to facilitate logistics and finance operations. A Steering Committee was formed, comprising the Process Owners and chaired by the Business Owner.

BDU set a six-month deadline for "work units" to complete the new process designs. The sudden removal of the then President and Vice President from office disrupted the timetable and there was an over-run of five months. Various consultation meetings were conducted to refine the draft designs of each process. A national workshop was held to present the new work processes and obtain feedback from senior officials of the Ministry of Education, other university presidents, Amhara region officials and experts.

The top management of the BDC started by conducting consultative meetings with all employees on the need to re-design various processes, and trained all on the principles of the BPR. The city selected five processes for redesign – a) Land Acquisition and Administration; b) Design and Construction; c) Utilities Administration; d) City Beautification and Cleaning Administration; and e) Law Enforcement. Subsequently, the BDC top management decided to re-engineer only one process - Land Acquisition and Administration – warranted by its strategic importance. The re-design process was finalised within the planned period of six months and various consultation forums that brought together the design team and employees were conducted. The Mayor held the position of Business Owner. A Tsar was also assigned.

Both BDU and BDC adopted Linden's (1998) methodology for introducing the BPR, as prescribed by the central government. This method has three fundamental principles: a) challenging assumptions behind the old way of doing business; b) focusing on processes, not along functional lines, programme offices or budget departments'; and c) organising around outcomes.

The general approach followed in both organisations included mapping the old ways of doing work, identifying problems, assessing rules, and verifying assumptions behind the rules. Desired outcomes of each process were articulated after focus-group discussions, interviews and surveys with customers and other internal and external stakeholders. The desired outcomes were converted to stretched objectives.

Post-BPR

The implementation of BPR resulted in some changes at both the university and the city services. Jobs and responsibilities were redefined; the number of activities was reduced; the time for each activity was determined; and positions were reduced.

As a direct result of the BPR, the university made its Course System Knowledge Database (CSKD) permanent. Various graduate and undergraduate programmes may come and go, but the CSKDs from which they are derived will remain. The re-design of courses into end-to-end, holistic systems reduced the previous 800 separate courses to 250 CSKDs. Traditionally, courses were each instructor's property; now CSKDs have their respective managers who manage, renovate, continually update the systems, and make them available for delivery.

On approval of the organisational structure by the board, the university elected five Vice Presidents and Process Owners to lead their respective processes. A Change Management Team comprising Presidents, Institutional Transformation Officers and the Tsar was formed by the President to lead the change. The processes have only case teams reporting to the Process Owners and no other hierarchy was created. To facilitate customers services, case teams were located in different parts of the university campuses. The system re-organised the Deans of colleges as well as faculties and schools and provided them discretionary power on procurement, financial services and maintenance services.

BDU prepared an implementation plan and a human resources placement procedure approved by the University Managing Board. Both the plan and the procedure were communicated to the university community through meetings, notice boards and distribution of the documents to each organisational unit/process. Nomination and placement of employees and officers, took about eighteen months to finalise. The Change Management Committee undertook multiple BPR follow-up meetings, on average once every 20 days, for about 18 months. Some 60 per cent of meeting time and decisions were related to placement of employees, nomination of officials, and handling of grievances. Less than 5 per cent of meeting time focused on review of the implementation plan. No major progress reports were made; no follow up of prior reviews was conducted; and no plan revisions were done. After a year and six months, the implementation plan was not revised or improved. There was, however, a two-day observation of the BPR progress conducted by external consultants.

BDC's redesign of Land Acquisition and Administration reduced the previous 62 activities in the process to just 11. The new process is customer-focused, orientated to results rather than activities, and employees are expected to work with team spirit. Each employee is given the authority to process leasehold bids to finality. The time to complete delivery of land on a lease basis, the preparation of site plans, and the processing of construction permits, is down from 529 days to just 20.

The city services developed the implementation plan of the BPR in line with the general regional government strategic plan. This document was communicated to all City Services Office employees. A team comprising of the Mayor, the Process Owner and the head of the capacity-building office was set up by the regional government to monitor re-engineering.

The new Land Acquisition and Administration process allowed one-stop-shop service delivery – for all activities starting with request for land to the provision of construction permits to residents and investors. The decision points are the case worker/ expert or case manager or process owner, without additional reference to the Mayor's Office or the City Manager's Office. The 17 *kebeles* are re-organised as 9 sub-city administration units which take responsibility for granting construction permits and title deed transfers for buildings and collecting fees from citizens. Time taken for acquisition of construction permits for plots obtained on open bid went down from 12 months to an average of 14 days. The Change Management Committee ran weekly, monthly and quarterly review meetings to assess challenges and remedy legal frameworks in conflict with the BPR designs. However, after nine months the review tempo slowed and performance declined.

The following section presents the results of the survey on the level of implementation of the PBR.

Assessment of the Level of Implementation of BPR in the Two Offices

Respondents from BDU (Bahir Dar University) and BDC (Bahir Dar City) were asked to assess the level of the PBR implementation through five main indicators with 39 sub-indicators. The main indicators were: result areas and goals, objectives, measurement and reviews, responsibilities, continuous improvement (see Annex 1 for the questions and the responses). Table 1 provides the summary of the results.

Table 1: **Summary of survey result**

	Item	Less Favourable BDU (%)	Less Favourable BDC (%)	Favourable BDU (%)	Favourable BDC (%)	Mean BDU	Mean BDC
1	Result areas and goals	19	41	73	34	4.89	3.99
2	Objectives	24	48	61	31	4.87	3.70
3	Measurement processes	75	63	14	17	2.46	3.35
4	Reviews	54	59	26	21	3.46	3.37
5	Responsibilities	39	46	41	23	4.1	3.69
6	Continuous improvement	88	70	6	14	1.96	3.03

Note:

1. *The percentages indicate the proportion of respondents who have positively and negatively assessed the level of the BPR implementation.*
2. *The detailed survey result for each of the items is given in Annex 1.*

   • Result areas and goals: Measureable unit goals linked to the overall vision of the organisation are an indicator of proper implementation. It is essential to have clearly defined and understood goals and result areas (Hacker and Washington 2004). The scores in Table 1 indicate that both the university and city services did well in these respects, and this was re-affirmed by interviews with the top management of the two organisations.

The BDC implementation plan also indicates the major goals, measures, targets and bodies responsible for the different goals, although it does not show the different input requirements crucial for the success of the BPR project. For example, office space, ICT and budget requirements are not indicated.

- Objectives: Another main indicator is when organisational goals guide organisational unit objectives, and unit objectives guide functional tactics or operational plans. The implementation of the BPR is all about the "how", which involves translating strategic goals into annual objectives, cascading them into all organisational units, including to employees, and ensuring resource provision (Hamel and Prahald 2005; Kaplan and Norton 2008). The survey results indicated that both the University and the City services office scored above average results in crafting well-defined objectives. There are, however, no documents to support the survey result. The interviewees at both offices also contended that organisational objectives were not cascaded down across all units; organisational plans were not sufficiently aligned with organisational units and the objectives of each unit were not linked with the overall vision of the organisations. Although cascading helps to pass on organisational accountability to all units for the results they achieve, and to measure and evaluate their performance, this is not done adequately in either organisation.

- Measurement processes: Both the BDU and BDC scored below the benchmark point of 3.5 (the mean score), showing their weakness in designing systems to measure the performance of the implementation process. During interview, an official from the university admitted that the university did not consider the measurement system while preparing the planning documents. As a result, the performance of the implementation plan was not – could not be – measured. Among reasons cited for this omission was that the President, Vice Presidents and Process Owners were preoccupied in daily routines and other priorities like 'emergency' or 'urgent' assignments from higher political bodies and negotiations with service providers. BDC did not have their own measurement plans, but followed a system established by the regional government.

- Review processes: Both BDU and BDC scored below average on the availability of a well-designed review process. The university did conduct occasional reviews, but these were limited to the hearing of progress reports and presentations of challenges faced by the process owners. No organised quarterly reports were produced; no follow-ups from previous reviews were heard; no term plans were prepared; and clear accountability was not mentioned. Most change management meeting time (60 per cent of the agenda for more than eighteen months) was about the placement of employees and handling of employee grievances rather than the performance of the implementation process. The university also struggled for lack of legal frameworks to support the new processes; the financial management and procurement and property administration proclamations enacted by the federal government reduced BDU's autonomy and flexibility in implementing the BPR projects and reviewing the processes.

BDC, however, showed improvement in the delivery of services because it was led by regulations, emanating from the regional government, that supported the new designs and empowered managers at all levels. During the first six months of implementation (in 2008) BDC held daily review meetings at unit level with employees, weekly meetings with management and monthly meetings with the Mayor's office. In those meetings, decisions important for the smooth-functioning of the new design — like amendment of rules, procedures, formats and other matters – were made by management. But this review process was not sustained and the office's delivery of services declined. Reasons for this decline included the office's inability to develop and implement employees' performance measurement and incentive systems, and the frequent turn-over of management before the system was institutionalised. The federal and regional labour laws do not allow for performance-based benefit packages (see, for example, FDRE (2004) proclamation No. 377/2003). The regional government's top political leaders, 'who lacked trust in the middle and lower managers of the city service offices', (interview) took back the discretionary power given to BDC. This situation not only stalled progress but also frustrated regular employees and Process Owners and led to high turn-over of employees.

At BDU, the managing board replaced the President, three Vice Presidents, and four Process Owners during the implementation stage. Similarly, at BDC, the Mayor, the City Manager and other city administration cabinet members were replaced. This turn-over of top functionaries was mainly for political reasons. It disrupted the implementation of BPR projects. Moreover, in the case study offices, there were no continuous review meetings which led to loss of strategic direction while management was immersed in what one interviewee labeled 'irrelevant, minor daily routines'.

- Responsibilities: Both organisations under study scored high in terms of having well-defined responsibilities. This shows that responsibilities were fixed to the persons assigned for the different duties.

- Evidence of continuous improvement: The survey scores and interviews reflect little continuous improvement at either BDU or BDC – because there was no measurement system and sufficient data. It was also impossible to determine whether the organisational activities are achieving desired results and whether new decisions should be made.

Conclusion

Aligning large-scale change initiatives to organisational mission and vision, designing strategic plans accordingly and installing robust measurement systems would greatly improve the effectiveness of these change projects. Since change projects such as the BPR require huge amounts of time, budget and manpower, it is crucial that organisations monitor the performance of strategic initiatives through measurement systems that enable them to continuously learn and improve.

The organisations under study are good at designing, but find execution of those designs a major problem. Shortfalls include leadership commitment and continuity, alignment of organisational objectives to lower-level units, and understanding of employee intentions or resistances, and translating nominal responsibility into practical accountability. The following points indicate the major issues that transpired from the discussion in this chapter:

- While the PBR is perceived by top management as very important tool in enhancing the efficiency and effectiveness of the organisations, failure to have monitoring system, performance measurement and incentive structure leads to poor outcomes of reforms.

- High turn-over of officials, especially at the top level, breaks continuity of the BPR design and implementation process.

- ICT is an essential enabler for the success of the BPR, but it is given little attention while implementing the BPR projects.

- Public offices shy away from change management efforts when there is a perception by management that the change process is a political project.

- Persistent and diverse communication strategies are vital for selling a change agenda; successful change begins with acquiring employees' buy-in to the change process.

Annex 1: **Survey result for each of the factors (own computation)**

1. Well defined goals and result areas

	Bahir Dar University				Bahir Dar City services			
	Min.	Max.	M	SD	Min.	Max.	M	SD
Linked to the organisation vision	3	7	5.33	1.37	2	7	4.4	1.69
Goals defined as appropriate	3	7	5.17	1.27	2	5	3.9	1.02
Cross office result areas identified as needed	2	6	4.60	1.43	2	6	3.9	1.17
Measurable	2	6	4.67	1.56	1	7	4.0	1.50
Targets	2	7	4.67	1.61	2	7	3.9	1.27
Total Mean			**4.89**				**3.99**	

2. Well defined objectives

	Bahir Dar University				Bahir Dar City services			
	Min.	Max.	M	SD	Min.	Max.	M	SD
Linked to specific key result areas	2	7	5.25	1.71	1	7	3.4	1.50
Strategies defined as needed	1	7	4.50	1.98	2	6	4.0	1.43
Prioritised critical few	1	7	3.91	2.07	2	7	3.9	1.39
Measurable	1	7	4.92	2.07	1	6	3.5	1.28
Long term targets	2	7	5.33	1.44	2	6	3.9	1.31
Annual targets	2	7	5.33	1.37	2	6	3.7	1.28
Total Mean			**4.87**				**3.70**	

3. Well defined measurement processes

	Bahir Dar University				Bahir Dar City services			
	Min.	Max.	M	SD	Min.	Max.	M	SD
Accepted measures	1	7	3.58	1.73	1	6	3.2	1.28
Understanding of measures	1	6	3.17	1.53	1	6	3.2	1.24
Reliable data sources	1	5	2.42	1.38	2	5	3.3	1.02
Reliable survey mechanics	1	5	2.17	1.40	1	6	3.4	1.23
Plotted as time series	1	5	1.92	1.38	1	7	3.5	1.50
Control charted	1	6	2.08	1.62	2	7	3.6	1.32
Special causes investigated	1	5	2.18	1.33	1	6	3.2	1.15

Control limits revised as appropriate	1	6	2.09	1.76	2	6	3.3	1.25
Data interpretations accurate	1	7	2.55	2.16	1	7	3.5	1.54
Random variations understood	1	5	2.45	1.63	2	7	3.4	1.39
Total Mean			**2.46**				**3.35**	

4. Well established review processes

	Bahir Dar University				Bahir Dar City services			
	Min.	Max.	M	SD	Min.	Max.	M	SD
Quarterly reviews conducted with PS*	1	7	3.75	1.76	1	6	3.1	1.23
Monthly reviews conducted with department heads	2	5	2.91	.94	1	5	3.2	1.04
Status reports generated	2	6	3.92	1.38	1	6	3.7	1.35
Follow-up from previous reviews	1	7	3.91	1.70	1	6	3.1	1.52
Lessons learned discussed	1	5	3.10	1.60	1	6	3.3	1.29
Discussions include plans for next quarter and longer	1	7	3.17	2.04	1	7	3.5	1.58
Performance accountability exists	1	7	3.50	2.20	2	7	3.9	1.49
Total Mean			**3.46**				**3.37**	

5. Well defined Responsibilities

	Bahir Dar University				Bahir Dar City services			
	Min.	Max.	M	SD	Min.	Max.	M	S
To Vice Presidents*	1	7	4.18	1.72	1	7	3.6	1.79
Process Owners	1	7	4.25	1.76	2	7	3.7	1.35
Deans/ Directors	1	7	4.25	1.86	1	7	3.5	1.47
Case team coordinators	1	7	4.17	1.85	2	7	3.8	1.16
Case team workers	1	6	3.67	1.87	1	7	3.9	1.29
Total Mean			**4.10**				**3.69**	

6. Evidence of continuous improvement

	Bahir Dar University				Bahir Dar City services			
	Min.	Max.	M	SD	Min.	Max.	M	SD
PMS* annually assessed	1	6	2.83	1.85	1	5	3.0	0.92
Change efforts of work units aligned with key result areas	1	5	2.33	1.50	1	6	3.1	1.27
Training on PMS conducted broadly and systematically	1	3	1.67	.89	1	7	2.9	1.54
New employees trained in PMS	1	3	1.50	.85	1	7	2.9	1.59
Communication plans keep organisations aware of the status of PMS	1	4	1.75	.97	1	7	3.1	1.58
Internal PMS benchmarking across all organisational units	1	3	1.67	.98	1	5	3.2	1.08
Total Mean			1.96				3.03	

Note: PMS stands for Performance Measurement Systems

Note

Although the Hacker and Washington (2004) instrument was used by the authors in a sub-Saharan country, Botswana, a focus group discussion about the validity of the questionnaire and practical applicability of the instrument in the Ethiopian context with three middle level officials indicated the need for a few adjustments - like reducing the variables from 42 to 39 and changing the names of organisational units to the current organisational contexts under study. Please see the slightly modified questionnaire in Annex 1. For the original version of the questionnaire developed by Hacker and Washington (2004) please visit Hacker, M. and Washington, M. (2004), "How we measure the implementation of large-scale change", in Measuring Business Excellence, Vol. 8 No. 3 page 56.

References

Abdolvand, N., Albadvi, A. and Ferdowsi, Z. 2008. Assessing readiness for business process re-engineering. *Business Process Management Journal*, Vol. 14 No. 4, pp.497–511.

Attaran, M. 2000. Why does re-engineering fail? A practical guide for successful implementation. *Journal of Management Development*, Vol. 19, No. 9, pp. 794–801.

Cheng, T. and Chiu, I. 2008. Critical success factors of business process re-engineering in the banking industry. *Knowledge and Process Management*, Vol. 15 No. 4, pp. 258–269.

Davis, D. 2000. *Business research for decision making.* 5ᵗʰed. Belmost, CA.: Duxbury Press.

Debela, T. 2009. Business process re-engineering in Ethiopian public organizations: The relationship between theory and practice. *Journal of Business and Administrative Studies*, Vol. 1, No. 2.

Debela, T. and Hagos, A. 2011. *The design and implementation of BPR in the Ethiopian public sector: An assessment of four organizations.* Addis Ababa: OSSREA.

Dey, P. 2001. Re-engineering materials management: A case study on an Indian refinery. *Business Process Management Journal*, Vol. 1, No. 5, pp. 394–408.

Eugene, A. H., Rosenthal J., W. and Judy. 1994. How to make re-engineering really work. *Mckinsey Quarterly*, Issue 2, pp. 107–128.

Gebrekidan, A. 2011. Promoting and strengthening professionalism in the civil service: The Ethiopian case. A paper presented on the workshop on "promoting professionalism in the public service: Strengthening the role of human resource managers in the public sector for the effective implementation of the charter for public Service in Africa, 14–18 March 2011 Addis Ababa, Ethiopia. (accessed on 13th January,2011) at http://www.iss.nl/Media/Website/PUBLIC-Files/Academic-publications/5.-Challenges-and-Prospects-of-Implementing-Public-Service-Delivery-Reform-PSDR-in-Ethiopia

Hacker, M. and Washington, M. 2004. How we measure the implementation of large-scale change. *Measuring Business Excellence*, Vol. 8 No. 3, pp. 52–9.

Hamel, G. and Prahalad, C. 2005. Strategic intent. *Harvard Business Review*, Vol. 83 Issue 7/8, p148–161.

Hammer, M. and Stanton, S. 1995. *The re-engineering revolution.* New York: Harper Collins Publishers.

Jayashree, P., and Hussain, S. J. 2011. Practitioner paper— Aligning change deployment: A balanced scorecard approach. *Measuring Business Excellence*, Vol. *15, No.* 3, pp. 63–85.

152

Kaplan, R. and Norton, D. 1996. *The balanced scorecard: Translating strategy into action.* Boston, MA.: Harvard Business School Press.

——.2008. *The execution premium: Linking strategy to operations for competitive advantage.* Boston, MA.: Harvard Business School Press.

Linden, R.1994. *Seamless government: A practical guide to re-engineering in the public sector.* SanFrancisco, CA.: Josey-Bass Publishers.

——.1998. *Workbook for seamless government: A hands on guide to implementing organizational change.* San Francisco, CA.: Josey-Bass Publishers.

Lockamy III, A. and Smith, W. 1997. A strategic alignment approach for effective business process re-engineering: Linking strategy, processes and customers for competitive advantage. *International Journal of Production Economics*, Vol. 50, pp. 141–153.

McAdam, R., and Donaghy, J. 1999. Business process re-engineering in the public sector: A study of staff perceptions and critical success factors. *Business Process Management Journal*, Vol. 5, No.1, pp. 33–52.

FDRE. 2004. *Negarit Gazzeta (2004), Labor Proclamation, No. 377* Berhanena Selam Printing Enterprise: Addis Ababa, Ethiopia

Tekle Giorgis, H., and Amare, G. 2007. Success stories: Public sector capacity in Ethiopia. A consultancy report to Ministry of Capacity Building, Ethiopia.

United Nations Development Programme (UNDP). 2007. Ethiopia: Final evaluation of UNDP programme.

Washington, M., and Hacker, M. 2005. Why change fails: Knowledge counts. *Leadership & Organization Development Journal*, Vol. 26 No. 5, 2005, pp. 400—411.

World Bank. 2011. Public sector capacity building programme support project: P074020 - Implementation status results report: Sequence 10. (accessed 15th September, 2011) at worldbank.org/external/default/main ?pagePK=64193027&piPK=64187937&theSitePK=523679&menuPK= 64187510&searchMenuPK=64187283&siteName=WDS&entityID=000 0A8056_2011020408394461Ethiopia.

Chapter 7

The Inside Story of Outsourcing: Contract Management Capacity in Tanzania

Leonada Mwagike and Mamkwe Claudia Edward

Abstract

The role of the public sector in many African countries is changing, from core "provider" of goods and services to "facilitator" of private sector-led economic development and growth. A central plank of this transition is Public-Private Partnerships (PPPs) by which governments contract-out important public services to private suppliers. The intention is to transform previously monopolistic public services that were often defective in cost and quality into competitive and efficient private services – thus improving delivery and value, invigorating business activity, and allowing the public sector to focus attention and resources on better overall governance. This paper explores Tanzania's contract management experience, through two case studies on outsourcing at Sokoine University of Agriculture and Morogoro Regional Hospital, to identify what works and what does not, and why.

Introduction

The dominance of the public sector in Africa has been repeatedly blamed for the poor delivery of public services (ECA 2005). State-owned and -operated monopolies lack competition, resulting in low quality, inefficient and unreliable delivery, failure to address consumer demand, and often "below-cost" pricing which drains government's investment resources (*Ibid*). From the mid-1980s, however, many governments have begun to hand over supply of goods and services, through privatisation or contracted out-sourcing to competitive commercial operators as part of private sector-led economic development and growth (Ngowi 2005; Njunwa 2007). There are strong arguments that partnerships between the public and private sectors can enable improved service access, variety, punctuality, reliability; and increased value for money, transparency, and accountability in spending of public money (Mohr and Sperkman 1994; World Bank 1994). There are also frequent warnings that the "right" institutional arrangements for PPPs might be absent or not effective, making the partnerships beneficial to some at the expense of others (Itika and Mwageni 2006).

In the past decade, Tanzania's public sector has contracted out the delivery of some services – in areas of health, education, solid waste collection, revenue collection, information technology, cleaning, security, and infrastructure – to private providers (Nkya 2004). Nonetheless, Tanzania has encountered three main limits to the scope, speed and quality of services delivered through PPPs.

Firstly, the identification of reliable and trustworthy private organisations with which to form partnerships is a challenge – many private operations are not legally registered (Ngowi 2006).

Secondly, government officials have yet to acquire the necessary knowledge and skills to deal with private partners who are often more business savvy (Njunwa 2007).

Thirdly, public institutions in Tanzania are bedevilled by bureaucracy and financial bottlenecks. A study by Ngowi (2006) on public-private partnership in Tanzania reports the bottlenecks as public sector characteristics of bureaucracy; inefficiency and ineffectiveness; lack of incentives, creativity, dynamism and vibrancy; generally slow response; and corruption.

A rigorous analysis of the contract management capacity of both public and private sectors is still missing from the PPP debate in Tanzania. The purpose of this study is to fill that knowledge gap, using two case studies - Sokoine University of Agriculture (SUA) and Morogoro Regional Hospital (MRH) – selected by random ballot from nine public institutions known to be contracting out non-core services. Eight key informants were purposely selected: a procurement manager from SUA, a health secretary, a procurement manager and a regional engineer from MRH, and officials from four service providers. Interview by a checklist of open-ended (divergent) questions was used to collect data. Information from the government institutions included the type of services they outsourced, reasons for contracting out, how services were delivered and how they managed the contracting process. Data from service providers included the type and method of service provision. Observation was used to validate the information, and secondary data were collected through reviewing relevant reports from the case study institutions.

This study examines how contracts have been managed and explores why some services are successful while others fail. It analyses how differences in service delivery arise from how contracts are managed. Indicators of the institutions' contract management capacity include staff knowledge and skills, financial capacity and prior contracting experience.

Insights into Public Sector Reform and Contracting Out Capacity

Since the 1980s, the role and institutional character of the state has been questioned, and the public sector has been under pressure to adopt private-sector orientations. Under the influence of the New Public Management, reforms have been driven by a combination of economic, social, political, and technological factors and by good governance conditions on lending (ECA 2005). For example, Kenya, Ethiopia, Ghana, Mauritius, Senegal, Tanzania and Uganda have embarked on comprehensive programmes aimed at improving the quality of life of their citizens, and creating new government mechanisms for efficient and effective public sector management.

Public sector reforms are based on the principles of market, competition, contracting, transparency and emphasis on incentive structures as a way of giving more "choice and voice" to service users, thereby promoting efficiency in public service delivery (Tolofari 2005). The use of PPPs is increasingly being adopted in most African countries (Ngowi 2006). Cases in point include parastatals in Botswana that have contracted out a number of services in maintenance and security (Hope 2002). In Zimbabwe, non-clinical health services such as cleaning, laundry, catering, security, maintenance and billing are contracted out, and, on a limited scale, even clinical services (Russell *et al.* 1997). In Tanzania, non-core services such as grounds' maintenance, security, revenue collection in local authorities, solid waste collection and disposal, and cafeterias are contracted out to the private sector (Nkya 2004; Ngowi 2006).

Public sector reforms in sub-Saharan Africa reality have both success and failure stories.

In Senegal, for instance, success factors include strong political will and good leadership throughout the reform process, with minimal government interference. The processes themselves were well designed, allowing for flexibility and innovation when necessary. ECA (2005) reports how expansion of water supply in rural Ghana has been successful. Factors included strong political leadership and clear legislation (specifically the acts of parliament from 1998 that defined the policies and roles of most sector agencies). Reform of Public Reporting in Mauritius has been successful through a committee with both the expertise and wide-ranging representation of various groups in formulating standards (UMSAC 2002 cited in ECA 2005).

In some countries, however, reforms have been afflicted by problems of nepotism, inefficiency, poor coordination, poor management and institutional capacity shortfalls, bureaucracy and political interference, and declining public service ethics which result in inappropriate practices such as corruption which undermines merit and increases the cost to public service users (*Ibid*).

Capacity under contracting out arrangements is the ability to manage the entire contracting process, from feasibility to contract design and through implementation to monitoring and evaluation. Brown and Potoski (2003) identified three capacity components: feasibility assessment, implementation and evaluation. Feasibility assessment requires the capacity to determine whether a particular service is appropriate for out-sourcing and whether there are vendors able to provide adequate service. Implementation requires the capacity to bid contracts, assess and select vendors, and negotiate and structure contract terms. Evaluation requires the capacity to monitor and evaluate vendor performance against responsibilities specified in the contract.

Brown and Potoski (2003) noted that experiences with prior contracts shape how public sector institutions approach future contracts. For example, if there have been no major problems with contract performance in the past, there is less incentive to upgrade current management capacity. Governments with some degree of previous dissatisfaction are more likely to take steps to improve contract management capacities (DeHoog 1990). Skilled and knowledgeable staffs are essential – the link between their ability and the performance of contracted services is direct. Sclar (2000) notes insufficient management capacity in any of the contracting parties' functional areas can result in poor service performance. For example, weak feasibility assessment may lead to contracting for services in a market in which there is only one provider. A public sector which lacks capacity to effectively bid, let, and negotiate contracts may become legally obligated to disadvantageous and unscrupulous partners. In the absence of capacity to monitor and audit contracts, the public sector may be unable to determine whether the vendor has delivered the service in accordance with contract specifications (Milward 1996).

Public Service Reform in Tanzania

Tanzania's first public sector reform era was from 1962 to 1970. Driven by the realities of independence and sovereignty, the aim was to meet the raised expectations of the people after independence by replacing the previously repressive colonial state with prudent economic and social development functions of the independent state (URT 2007). This reform assumed all progress would emanate from the state and provided the centralised state all the power to manage the political, economic and social affairs of the society.

The second phase was decentralisation reform from 1972 – 1984. During this era, institutionally the government was heavily involved in direct management of the development process and provision of social services. A number of committees were established in the villages, wards, districts and regions, as vehicles for people's participation. Regional administrations became the primary drivers of rural development planning and implementation. Urban councils merged with neighbouring rural councils; government focus and emphasis was on "Socialism and Self Reliance'. There was a major shift of government authority and control from the central government to village level administration. Nonetheless, the decentralisation reform in Tanzania culminated into deconcentration of power by the central government for all social services and economic development activities (Lukumai 2006)

The third phase has been the Public Sector Reform Programme (PSRP) (1987 – present), which is in line with the global development mantra of "structural adjustment" and the experience of New Public Management reform methods in Organisation for Economic Co-operation and Development (OECD) countries. Tanzania's PSRP aims to streamline government, reduce employment numbers, introduce wage bill control, and improve public service incentives, accountability, skills, delivery and management systems. The goal is a smaller, more affordable, well-compensated public service with the emphasis on results and outcomes. The PSRP promotes meritocracy and decentralisation, including the formation of executive agencies and the out-sourcing of non-core services. The PSRP reform has two phases. PSRP Phase I, which ended in 2007, prioritised Performance Management Systems (PMS). The thrust of Phase II, with a date bracket of 2008 to 2012, is enhanced performance and accountability. The drive of PSRP is spearheaded by the President's Office-Public Service Management (PO-PSM). The PSRP has so far been active in reforming health, education, local government, remunerations and recruitment (URT 2007).

An integral component of the PSRP is Public Private Partnership (PPP), which involves different elements of public service contracting. Tanzania's Public Procurement Act, No 3 of 2004, stipulates that the PPP includes the following forms or combinations of them: service contract, management contract, leasing, joint ventures, partnerships, Build Operate Transfer, Build Own Operate, and concession (URT 2004). Tanzania has several activities under public sector contracting. For instance, the collection of parking fees in urban areas and rubbish collection and disposal in almost all local government authorities are now undertaken by private firms (Nkya 2004), as are general cleanliness in public offices, schools, universities, hospitals and hotels. Provision of security services has largely been contracted out to cover shortfalls in state police capacity. Medical and health services are managed through

Cooperative Public Service Delivery (CPSD), with private operators accounting for 25 per cent (Kavishe 1990).

Contracting Out Services at Sokoine University of Agriculture (SUA)

The core activities of SUA are teaching, research and consultancy. Non-core services include security, catering, cleaning, procurement and supplies management. It was in 2007 that SUA started outsourcing delivery of catering, cleaning and security services. This was mainly in response to government directives which required all public institutions to out-source, but also for cost saving because in-house servicing carried administrative and financial burdens like payroll administration, fringe benefits, overtime, transport and sick leave.

SUA management chose the three activities to be contracted out and specified the service standard. The University's Tender Board approved the process of advertising the bid including postings on the university notice boards stating the services to be contracted and the conditions for bidding. Selection criteria of service providers included experience in the business, financial capacity, knowledge and skills, and availability of equipment. The university responded promptly to follow-up questions on detail of the contracting out process from prospective bidders. An evaluation committee of five was formed to check bidders' ability to perform the tasks and assess rival bids on competitive merit. Committee members for the contracting out activities were the procurement manager, a representative of the user of the service, a technical advisor, a supplies officer and a trade officer. The committee submits recommendations to the Procurement Management Unit (PMU) responsible for all procurements at SUA. The PMU sends its own recommendations to the Tender Board, which has the mandate to award a contract. Brief descriptions of the three outsourced activities at SUA are the following:

Cleaning services are provided by two locally-based companies to student hostels, staff offices (including toilets and bathrooms) and their surroundings, including grass-cutting, tree-planting, pruning and flower gardens. The Estate Department is responsible for managing the services providers (SUA Cleanliness Evaluation

Committee Report 2011). Cleanliness services are monitored by a committee comprising a field officer, two senior estates attendants and two estates attendants (SUA Cleanliness Evaluation Committee Report 2011), who submit a monthly report to the Estates Manager. The report findings trigger a sliding scale which can reduce monthly payments to the supplier. If the rating score falls to 60 per cent, payment is reduced to 85 per cent and a warning is issued. After contracting out, there has been visible improvement in the quality of the outdoor areas (increase in trees and attractive flower gardens) but indoor cleaning has not been consistently performed to the specified standards. Interview with officials revealed that in a certain instance, the contractor was not in a position to buy the required materials for cleaning owing to delays of payments from the university, and lacked skilled and experienced supervisors. The initial service provider scored below the minimum level and was terminated. Currently, cleaning at SUA is conducted by the Estate Department using casual labour.

Catering at SUA is out-sourced not only for efficiency but especially to improve the quality of food and avoid conflicts between students and university management, which often led to strikes. It includes provision of breakfast, lunch, supper, and beverages for both students and staff. Out-sourcing has improved the quality and variety of food and prices have reduced. The university also generates income by renting premises (kitchen/storage) to the caterers. The health committee rating has been moderate. User complaints of any under-performance are reported and the service provider is warned in writing of the shortfalls and is expected to rectify them. An example of complaint is inconsistency in the timing of making the food ready. For the catering service, an SUA health committee (comprising a medical officer, a staff member from the office of the Dean of students, a principle administrative officer, and a representative from SUA's Students Accommodation Bureau) make snap inspection visits on a daily basis to the food premises to assess compliance with contract terms. The committee grade a list of performance indicators on three levels: 1 = unsatisfactory, 2 = moderate, 3 = good.

The 24-hour security services at SUA cover the offices of the Vice Chancellor and two deputies; distinguished visitors such as ambassadors, ministers and other top government officials; moveable university property such as vehicles, office equipment and records; and student hostels and their properties. Methods include patrols of large outdoor areas, reception guards at gates and doors, and investigation services when theft is reported. The service is provided by a private security company with bases in Morogoro, Dodoma, Arusha and Dar es Salaam. While adequate systems are in place, ensuring close supervision is a challenge and a rise in theft of students' belongings is attributed to this shortfall. For security services, the SUA's chief security officer checks contract compliance and submits a monthly evaluation report to the Deputy Vice Chancellor (Administration and Finance) through the Principle Administrative Officer (service). Criteria measured include equipment, attendance and incidents (for example, thefts, in which examples ranged from a cow to a generator set). A significant defect or deterioration in any area leads to overall down-rating, which in turn could lead to termination of contract.

Contracting out Services at Morogoro Regional Hospital (MRH)

The core activity of MRH is health services to patients. The Hospital Management Committee (HMC) identified non-core services as catering, laundry, general cleaning, security, and reception services, and started out-sourcing with catering in 2002 – chosen as the area most in need of improvement. As the meals provided by the hospital were not appetising, patients purchased from vendors or had meals brought in by their families (Massi 2009). As a regional referral centre, and recipient of numerous motor accident victims (often people far from home), it was essential for the hospital to provide a healthy and palatable diet.

After identifying non-core services, the HMC tabled recommendations with justifications for contracting out to the Procurement Management Unit (PMU), which works under the Regional Administrative Secretariat (RAS). The secretariat and PMU conducted a feasibility study, using the experience of Muhimbili National Hospital in Dar-es-salaam which had already contracted out most of its non-core services such as cleaning, reception, security and catering. The feasibility study, conducted by a nursing officer, an assistant nursing officer from MRH and the PMU's regional engineer and assistant procurement manager, identified the type of services to be contracted out, the reasons for contracting out, how the services should be provided, the companies that should provide the services, the methods of monitoring and evaluation, the costs and benefits, and set rewards and penalties for performance. The study team submitted the report to the PMU which presented it to the Regional Tender Board (RTB). Bidders were invited – for all four non-core services - in the same manner used by SUA. The selection process was completed but no immediate contracts were awarded because funding was not available. The following year's funding allocation was sufficient to engage only the catering service. The tender board developed the contract terms, including delivery time, variety of food, cleanliness of food premises and provision of special diet to some patients.

The catering contract was awarded to a company working with Morogoro Municipality and Lushoto District. Services included breakfast, lunch and supper, served to patients in the wards. Staff were offered breakfast and lunch on a purchase basis. Members of the hospital management reported that the improvement in catering was immediate and dramatic – renovated kitchens produced hygienic, healthy and tasty food to the delight and direct medical benefit of patients and their relatives; better-fed patients showed higher tolerance to drugs and made more rapid recoveries. Fewer visitors delivering meals reduced congestion, and the valuable caring time of nurses was liberated from waitress duties. In-house catering had previously used five nursing officers, 15 medical attendants and three technicians – all of whom returned to their core professional duties when catering was out-sourced.

Monitoring of service delivery at MRH included regular interview of patients, sampling of food supplied, and responding to complaints from patients. The service provider produced daily reports on the food produced and the number of patients served. The hospital secretaries believed this system assured a level of quality control. Performance indicators include food quality (taste and nutritional value), food quantity (such as price and unit measurement) and delivery time, measured by the head nurses on a daily basis but marked on only two grade options, "acceptable" or "not acceptable". The overall rating of the catering service has been "good".

However, this emphatic success was jeopardised by the hospital's failure to pay the service providers on time, with corresponding shortfalls in service performance. A physical check by the authors of this paper over five consecutive days found meals which lacked variety, and relatives again bringing food in for patients with attendant congestion in the wards.

Conclusion

There are many factors that determine the successful application of out-sourcing. These include staff capacity (knowledge and skills in feasibility assessment, implementation and evaluation), prior contracting experience and financial capacity. This study endorses those principles, but underlines that the financial capacity is a critical element.

The process for contracting out at both SUA and MRH is similar in services chosen, feasibility study, tendering, selection, monitoring and evaluation. Despite their inexperience, both were thoughtful and thorough in designing and implementing arrangements and process. However, both had problems with funding flows, leading to delayed payments, in turn compromising service performance. This does not appear to have been caused by mis-calculation in feasibility or accounts management issues – it was a direct result of delayed payment of funds from the Treasury, on which both institutions depend. The bureaucratic nature of the public sector and slow speed of decision-making and implementation, especially in financial issues, are a major obstacle to effective PPP. Public sectors usually have to operate in severely resource-constrained environments, which hinder their ability to improve service delivery. The public sector is mainly reliant on central government funds that are often unpredictable or not sustained. The stark conclusion of this chapter is that effective out-sourcing by public sector institution depends, above all, on the contractor's financial capacity.

References

Brown, T. L and Potoski, M. 2003. Contract management capacity in municipal and country governments. *Public Administration Review* 63 (2):153–164.

Dehoog, R. H. 1990. Three models for contracting services. *Administration and Society* 22:3 317–340.

ECA. 2005. Public sector management reforms in Africa. Available at http;// uneca. org. (accessed on 15th October, 2010)

Hope, K.R. 2002. *From crisis to renewal: Development policy management in Africa.* Leiden: Brill Publishers.

Itika, J. and Mwageni, E. 2006. The benefits of public-private partnership in health service delivery: Evidence from selected cases in Tanzania. Paper presented at the 28th AAPAM Annual Roundtable Conference, Arusha, Tanzania 4th – 8th (p. 25).

Kavishe, F. 1990. *Access to free health services in Tanzania.* Washington, D.C: World Bank.

Lukumai, E.C. 2006. The implementation of civil service reforms in Tanzania, 1991–2000. Thesis submitted in partial fulfilment of the requirements for the degree of Master of Philosophy in Public Administration (Unpublished). University of Bergen. Norway, 94pp.

Massi, Z.M. 2009. Private sector participation in Morogoro Regional Hospital. Available at www.districthealthservice.com/cms/upload/innolink

Milward, H. Brinton. 1996. Symposium on the hollow state: Capacity, control and performance in inter-organisational settings. *Journal of Public Administration Research and Theory,* 6 (2).

Mohr, J., and Spekman, R. 1994. Characteristics of partnership success: Partnership attributes, communication, behavior, and conflict resolution techniques. *Strategic Management Journal,* 15(2).

Ngowi, P. 2005. Public-private partnership (PPPs) in the management of municipalities in Tanzania — Issues and lessons of experience. Paper presented at 28th AAPAM Annual Roundtable Conference, Arusha, Tanzania 4th – 8th (41pp).

——.2006. Public-private partnership (PPP) in service delivery: Application, reasons, procedures, results and challenges in Tanzanian Local Government Authorities (LGAs), 41pp.

Njunwa, M. 2007. Cooperative public service delivery in Tanzania: Is it contributing to social and human development? *JOAAG,* 2 (1):1–8.

Nkya, E. 2004. Public-private partnership and institutional arrangements: Constrained improvement of solid waste management in Dar es Salaam. In *Uongozi Journal of Management Development,* (16) 1–21.

Russell, P., Kwaramba, C., Hongoro, P., and Chikandi, S. 1997. Zimbabwe –

Reforming the health sector: Does government have the capacity?*The role of government in adjusting economies,* Paper 14. Birmingham: Development Administration Group, University of Birmingham.

Sclar, E. 2000. *You don't always get what you pay for: The economics of privatization.* Ithaca, NY: Cornell University Press.

Sokoine University of Agriculture (SUA). 2011. A report on how to improve cleaning services at the university for the year 2011/2012. Office of the Chief Planning Officer (unpublished 25pp).

Tolofari, S. 2005. New public management and education. *Journal of Policy Futures in Education,* (3) (1): 75–89.

United Republic of Tanzania (URT). 2007. Prime Minister's Office, Public Service Reform Programme— Phase Two (PSRP II): (2008–2012). Dar es Salaam, Tanzania, p. 48.

——.2004. *Public Procurement Act of 2004.* Dar es Salaam: National Printing Company.

World Bank. 1994. *World development report.* World Bank and Oxford University Press.

Chapter 8

E-Government for Good Governance: The Case of Tanzania

Muhajir Kachwamba

Abstract

The relationship between the state and its people has been a central focus of reforms aiming for better delivery of public services. Alongside hard components like privatisation, outsourcing and the mechanics of structures and systems, New Public Management makes the soft elements of participation, transparency and accountability essential. In the 1990s, communication technology prompted many governments to explore the potential of Information Communication Technology as a prime and interactive "meeting place" between officials and citizens. This development, known as e-government, could provide numerous benefits for state and people alike. But e-government is not emerging as a consistent formula — there are variations in the way it operates and the benefit it generates, even among government agencies within the same country. This chapter asks: 'Do government-to-business (G2B) agencies with regulatory functions implement e-government projects more effectively than government-to-citizen (G2C) agencies? And why?' It reveals that types of service delivered and the relative importance of a sector to enhance government revenue are main reasons for variations.

Introduction

Since the 1990s, major public sector reforms have made 'state-customer' relations a central focus in service delivery. With New Public Management (NPM) demanding accountability and performance management, many countries explored e-government

169

to pursue transparency and efficiency in their reform agenda (Hazlett and Hill 2003; Shahkooh, Fasanghari, and Abdollahi 2008; Shim and Eom 2008; Teicher, Hughes, and Dow 2002). Making e-government an innovative component of public service and administration can reduce corruption and other barriers to quality service delivery. It can also improve the internal performance of the public sector through e-administration (Koh and Prybutok 2003; Heeks 2002). The government's use of Information Communication Technologies (ICT), particularly the internet, offers an efficient and effective way to deliver government information and services with greater transparency (DiRienzo *et al.* 2007; Shim and Eom 2008; Yong Hyo and Byung-Dae 2004).

Based on transaction cost and agency theories, the literature suggests that online government information increases transparency and openness; it reduces opportunism and, hence, lowers transaction costs in terms of bribes and delays (Ojha, Palvia, and Gupta 2008). Online systems can maximise information and minimise costs (Awan 2008; Davidrajuh 2004) – less printing and distribution costs; less time wasted by customers or officials in frequent visits to government offices, moving from one counter to another to plough through bureaucratic procedures. Through e-government, the work of agents will be partially substituted by internet technology (Ojha, Palvia, and Gupta 2008), which is a fast, accurate, impartial, diligent, space efficient, and innovative institutional tool (Jun and Weare 2001).

Irrespective of challenges like limited ICT infrastructure, many countries in sub-Saharan Africa are introducing e-government in their public sector operations. The stated objectives are to improve efficiency and transparency and to promote greater accountability. The Tanzanian government website was launched in 2000 (Menda 2005). In 2003, 95 per cent of ministries had websites in Tanzania (Kaaya 2004). The UN's e-government survey of 2012, however, placed Tanzania on 139th position out of 183 countries, with an e-government development index of 0.3311 (UN 2012).

Reports indicate that there are differences in e-government adoption and utilisation among government agencies in Tanzania. Yonazi *et al* (2010) pointed out that individual organisational characteristics, for example, services offered, may be an important factor in adoption of e-government initiatives. Sein (2011) also suggests some government organisations, for example, Tanzania Investment Centre, are prioritised and better resourced in developing e-government services owing to their importance in economic development. Accordingly, this chapter asks: 'Do government-to-business agencies (G2B) with regulatory functions implement e-government projects better than government-to-citizen agencies (G2C)? If so, why?'

Six government agencies and ministries are studied - three G2B agencies with regulatory functions: Tanzania Revenue Authority (TRA), Tanzania Investment Centre (TIC) and Business Registrations and Licensing Agency (BRELA); and three government agencies focusing more on G2C: Ministry of Land (MoL), Ministry of Health (MoH) and Ministry of Home Affairs (MoHA)). Selection was based on functionality, and the type of customers being served. G2B agencies' core functions and mutual interaction with customers is for business purposes. For example, a tax office is categorised as G2B because its core function is tax collection from incomes earned by enterprises and individuals. G2C agencies help people interact with government agencies and obtain information on rules and procedures.

This study uses an e-government maturity model that is based on content analysis of websites. The model classifies certain attributes which indicate degrees of maturity. The analysis is focused on the actual content of an agency's website (West 2000). Since the back-office services (internal operations) of an organisation are not directly observable on the website (Lau 2005), the analysis is based on front-office services (external operations).

To count the number of services available on a website, two strategies were used.

Firstly, a list of attributes for each stage of the maturity were identified with the help of the existing literature (Howard 2001; Pina, Torres, and Royo 2010; West 2000).

Secondly, the agency's website was analysed for the presence or absence of an attribute. The attribute was a dummy variable recorded 1, if present, and 0, if absent. This technique has been used in previous work of website analysis (Nawaz, Issa, and Hyder 2007; Pina, Torres, and Royo 2010). The websites were assessed between May, 2011 and March, 2012.

In addition, interviews with experts and researchers on e-government and ICT in Tanzania were conducted to get a deeper understanding of any other possible explanatory factors. These experts were selected from the joint research under the Norwegian Programme for Research and Education (NUFU) project which comprises researchers from University of Agder in Norway and Mzumbe University in Tanzania, working on e-government development in Tanzania. The experts were asked to give their opinion on the *explanatory factor* (prime causes) for variations in the maturity stages between G2B and G2C agencies. Verbatim transcription of interview data was used to elicit common and stable themes across respondents.

This paper proceeds as follows: Section 2 conceptualises e-government and the e-government maturity model. Section 3 discusses Tanzania's e-government maturity in six case organisations. Section 4 offers a conclusion and policy recommendations.

Conceptualising E-Government and the E-Government Maturity Model

The term e-government can be defined as the use of technology, especially web-based applications, to enhance public access and efficiently deliver government information and services (Brown and Brudney 2001). Alternatively, it can be defined as use of technology, particularly the internet, to deliver services to citizens, businesses and other customers (Golden, Hughes and Scott 2003). There are two basic organisational theories that underpin the conceptualisation of e-government: the transaction cost theory and principal-agent theory.

In short, the transaction cost theory is based on the premise that organisations and individuals incur some costs in terms of effort, time and various expenditures in order to do any buy-sell deal (Williamson 1985). The higher the uncertainty in a transaction, the more information search is required. The principal-agent theory posits that an organisation is a set of contracts, where the *Principal* (for example, government) employs *agents* (such as bureaucrats) to perform some duties on its behalf. However, since the principal is facing information asymmetry, there is no guarantee that agents will maximise the goals of the principal in either absolute terms or relative to their individual goals.

The implication of these theories on e-governance is that by publishing the rules, guidelines, forms and various contacts online, e-government helps to inform individuals and businesses of their specific rights, responsibilities and liabilities - increased transparency (Bhatnagar 2003). This reduces uncertainty in transactions (Cordella 2006) leading to more certain expectation, less opportunism, and hence lower transaction costs (bribes) (Ojha, Palvia, and Gupta 2008). Electronic transactions may eliminate bureaucrats as middlemen (agents) once the communication path between government and citizens or businesses is mediated by ICT. So, e-government in one way or another controls and monitors employees' behaviour more effectively and efficiently (Shim and Eom 2008), thus enhancing bureaucratic quality and transparency. This discussion is from a customer-centric view which asserts that the goal of e-government is to provide a simple, fast, easy and transparent mechanism for interacting with customers, thereby reducing transaction costs.

Brown and Brudney split e-government efforts into three broad categories of government-to-government (G2G), government-to-citizen (G2C), and government-to-business (G2B). G2C services help people interact with government agencies, obtain information on rules and procedures, and download various forms. G2B services help companies get information, procedures and application forms for business permits and licenses. These services give citizens and businesses faster interactions with government agencies, ultimately reducing transaction time/cost and administrative, regulatory burdens (Lau 2005; Singh 2003) G2G services help governments increase their efficiency through accumulation of data which can be processed and shared across departments and agencies. This leads to faster decision-making and reduced costs related to paperwork and processing time (Bhatnagar 2003). Table 1 below summarises benefits of e-government for government, citizens and businesses.

Table 1: **Costs, benefits and beneficiaries of E-Government**

Beneficiaries Type of Benefit	Government	Non-government (citizens and businesses)
Direct financial costs and benefits	**1. Reducing costs** Freeing resources for public and private innovations; increasing value of products and services	**2. Reducing burden** Administrative simplification; providing higher valued and faster services; saving time and money and improving equity
Direct non-financial costs and benefits	**3. Capturing total benefits of investment** Achieving synergies across service delivery channels; enabling the sharing and re-use of data for more proactive service delivery; promoting access as part of channel management strategy	**4. Increasing user satisfaction** Improving personalisation and service quality; improving access and equity; addressing security and privacy concerns; transparency and choice
Indirect costs and benefits: "Good governance" as a public good	**5. Supporting legitimacy** Supporting security and trust at an aggregate level; modernisation and transformation of the public sector; ensuring equity; increasing responsiveness, accountability, and participation **6. Supporting growth** Improving the business environment; creating an information society; establishing an infrastructure for secure and reliable transactions	

Source: Lau (2005)

Table 1 indicates that there are numerous benefits of e-government. For businesses and citizens, e-government reduces transaction costs, that is, time and money associated with administrative burdens when interacting with the government. E-government also brings citizens and businesses closer in terms of increasing access to services and equity which then increases openness and transparency.

E-Government Maturity Models

Scholars differ on the number of stages of maturity of e-government from raw beginnings to full operation (Irani, Al-Sebie and Elliman 2006) and in the terms they use to describe the phases, but all agree that as e-government matures its value increases. Table 2 summarises various stages of e-government maturity models proposed by several authors:

Table 2: **E-Government maturity models**

Author	Number of Stages
Howard (2001)	**Three stages** *Stage 1*: Publish *Stage 2*: Interact *Stage 3*: Transact
Layne and Lee (2001)	**Four stages** *Stage 1*: Cataloguing *Stage 2*: Transaction *Stage 3*: Vertical integration *Stage 4*: Horizontal integration
Chandler and Emanuels (2002)	**Four stages** *Stage 1*: Information *Stage 2*: Interaction *Stage 3*: Transaction *Stage 4*: Integration
Gartner (2000)	**Four stages** *Stage 1*: Presence *Stage 2*: Interaction *Stage 3*: Transaction *Stage 4*: Transformation
UN and ASPA (2002)	**Five stages** *Stage 1*: Emerging *Stage 2*: Enhanced *Stage 3*: Interactive *Stage 4*: Transaction *Stage 5*: Seamless
World Bank	**Three stages** *Stage 1*: Publish *Stage 2*: Interact *Stage 3*: Transact

Source: Adapted with modification (Irani, Al-Sebie, and Elliman 2006; Shahkooh, Saghafi and Abdollahi 2008).

This study chooses the model proposed by Howard and World Bank; though simple, it does not exclude any attribute found in other models. The description of each stage in this model is as follows:

- **Publish**: The government has an electronic presence, static website and simply publishes information about itself and its activities. Information content may also include the organisation's mission, vision and official contacts such as telephone numbers and e-mails, rules and procedures, search engines and sector statistics.
- **Interact**: The site is made interactive, with downloadable forms, status tracking and provision for e-mail enquiries.
- **Transact**: The site enables transactions over the internet, such as purchasing licences and permits and payment of various bills.

The above three stages can be presented as follows:

Figure 1: **E-Government Maturity Curve**

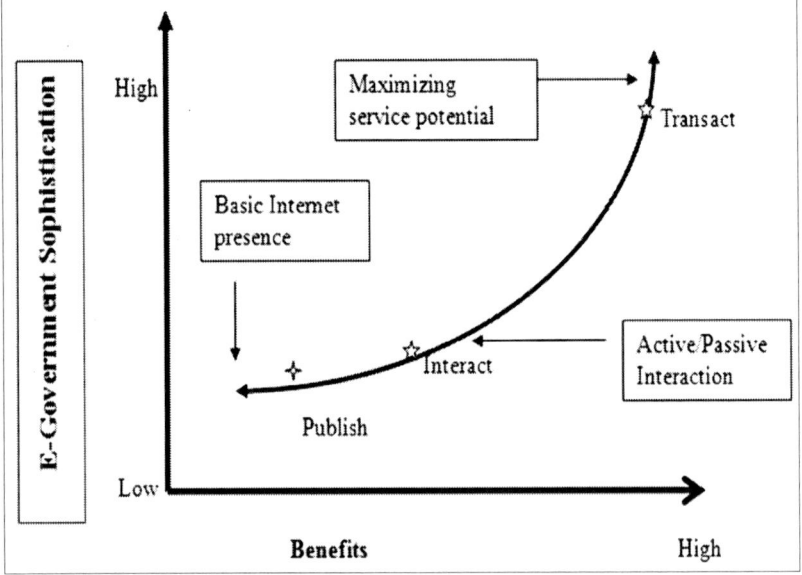

Source: Adapted with modification from Howard (2001)

The presence of an organisational website is positive, but the benefits and sophistication are low. The benefits increase as e-government moves towards the *interact* stage and is then maximised at the final *transact* stage. The higher stages of maturity imply higher utilities from services. This means that the level of maturity will be reflected (Shahkooh, Fasanghari, and Abdollahi 2008) from basic access towards a final stage where users make transactions with government and can track their enquiry or application. The higher the stage of e-government development (maturity) the more transparency is implied. As organisations grow from lower stages to higher stages, managerial and organisational complexity increases, too.

Variations in E-Government Adoption within Government Agencies

The literature provides three possible arguments as to why there are variations in e-government maturity between G2B and G2C agencies. These include: the nature of services, ability to quantify value and revenue generating potential. Bhatnagar (2003) argues that informational content for agencies with regulatory functions, (for example, licences, permits and registrations) is always simple and large which make them more amenable to electronic delivery than service content for welfare agencies/ministries such health and education, which necessarily involve physical delivery of the service such as diagnosis and medicines. In other words, a firm that requires a business licence can easily find information on procedures, instructional processes and submit application forms online without physical contact with officials. Conversely, a sick citizen who needs treatment should inevitably meet the doctor face to face; get diagnosis, medication, instructions and advice. Augmenting this idea, (Buckley 2003) documents that public organisations with regulatory functions, such as revenue authorities and company registrars have a pre-determined, homogeneous group of customers and specific pre-defined tasks an element that increases their potential for online service delivery. The author also argues that expert-driven public services, such as health, tend to have multiple tasks, heterogeneous customer groups and require expert case-by-case input (in this case, a doctor) which limits their potential for online service delivery.

On the second variation factor, organisations, such as revenue authorities, have tasks which can easily be monetised in cash-flow estimates - a necessary input for financial techniques such as Net Present Value (NPV) (Bhatnagar 2003; Kertesz 2003). Value for money in the investment of e-government projects is readily quantified. Normally, benefits of e-government through streamlining back-office and front-office operations are translated into incremental revenue as an ultimate outcome through financial evaluation models (Gupta and Jana 2003). On the other hand, many government agencies in the G2C category have tasks which are broad and difficult to monetise, making financial measures impossible and hence making ITC investment more difficult to justify. This might be the reason why revenue collection agencies have been cited as leaders in e-government maturity (see for example UN and ASPA 2002).

The third variable is the capacity to enhance immediate revenue and economic growth. Business is a key sector for growth of the economy and development of other service sectors such as health and education because of its contribution to government revenue. Of course, health and education can also increase government revenue through a healthy and educated labour force which leads to productivity and growth. However, this value is neither direct nor immediate, since it normally comes through a multiplier effect. One may argue from a public finance perspective that services in which the government earns revenue (for example, business, tax) are likely to be better resourced and more efficient than services that cost the government money (for example, health and education). Arguably, business is more favoured than welfare – one is an income, the other is an expense. Reciprocating the importance of businesses to economic growth, developing countries have prioritised development of e-government systems for agencies such as Investment Centre or Board of Investment (Sein 2011).

Tanzania's E-Governance Maturity in Six Case Organisations

According to the Tanzanian Bureau of Statistics, Tanzania had a population of 12.3 million in 1967 which grew to 34.6 million in 2002 and was projected at 41.9 million by 2010 (http://www.nbs. go.tz/). The country recorded a GNP per capita of $280 in 1982 and declined to $110 in 1990 (Messkoub 1996). In 2010 the GNP per capita was recorded at $530 based on World Bank Development indicators. Tanzania ranks among the countries with highest levels of unemployment and poverty in sub-Saharan Africa; its economy is heavily dependent on agriculture, which accounts for half of the GDP, provides 85 per cent of the country's exports and employs 90 per cent of the workforce.

Towards the end of the 1980s, Tanzania was suffering economic stagnation and significant social problems. Following pressure from international donor agencies, including the World Bank and International Monetary Fund, Tanzania introduced public sector reforms considered essential remedies to poor economic performance, inefficiency in resource use and public sector corruption. Measures from the late 1980s included a reduction in government subsidies of major consumer goods and social services such as education and health; privatisation of the means of production formerly under state ownership; and retrenchment of workers in communal farms, state institutions and organisations (Tripp 1997,8–22). As in many sub-Saharan African countries, however, such reforms did not bring about the expected socio-economic development. Tanzania is still introducing new waves of reforms. One of these is e-government.

Based on the information gathered from six government agencies, Table 3 summarises the major functions of the organisations, web page address and age of the websites.

Table 3: **Case descriptions**

Organisation	Website	Some organisational functions	Approx. Website Age*
TIC	www.tic.co.tz	Coordinate, promote and facilitate investment	9 years
TRA	www.tra.go.tz	Tax collection and promote voluntary tax	9 years
BRELA	www.brela. tz.org	Regulate and facilitate business operations, administer business registrations.	7 years
MoH	www.moh.go.tz	Provision of hospital services, preventive services, reproductive health services.	9 years
MoL	www.ardhi. go.tz	Improve delivery of survey land information systems, create enabling environment for human settlement development	6 years
MoHA	www.moha. go.tz	Save lives and properties, facilitate and control movement of aliens and non-aliens, assist refugees	5 years

Source: for 'Approx. Website Age' http://wayback.archive.org/web/

Key:
TIC *(Tanzania Investment Centre)*
TRA *(Tanzania Revenue Authority)*
BRELA *(Business Registrations and Licensing Agency)*
MoH *(Ministry of Health)*
MoL *(Ministry of Land)*
MoHA *(Ministry of Home Affairs)*

Tables 4 and 5 summarise various e-government services provided by each organisation studied. Table 4 shows services in three stages of the maturity model. Number 1 indicates the presence of the service while 0 means that the service was not found on the website at the time of the study.

Table 4: E-Government maturity in the selected cases

Attributes	TIC	TRA	BRELA	MoH	MoL	MoHA
A) Publish Stage						
Office phone number	1	1	1	1	1	1
Organisational e-mail contact	1	0	1	1	0	1
Organisational mission and objectives	1	1	1	1	1	1
Government policies	1	1	1	1	1	0
Sector statistics	0	1	0	1	0	1
Frequently Asked Questions (FAQ)	1	1	1	0	1	1
Rules and regulations	1	1	1	1	1	0
E-mail contacts of senior officials	1	0	0	0	0	1
Search engine	1	1	1	1	1	1
Downloadable forms	1	1	1	1	0	1
	90%	**80%**	**80%**	**80%**	**60%**	**80%**
B) Interact Stage						
Submit forms online	1	1	0	0	0	0
Feedback forms	0	0	0	0	0	0
Enquiry form	1	1	0	0	1	0
External links to other relevant sites	1	1	1	1	1	1

Tracking application status in process	1	0	1	0	0	0
Online database	0	1	1	1	0	0
	67%	**67%**	**50%**	**33%**	**33%**	**17%**
C) Transact Stage						
Links to online transactional services	0	1	0	0	0	0
Purchasing new or renewal of various documents, e.g.; permits, visa, birth certificates and licences.	0	1	0	0	0	0
Online payment of various application fees, bills, fines and taxes.	0	0	0	0	0	0
	0%	**67%**	**0%**	**0%**	**0%**	**0%**

Source: Author's compilation.

Table 5: **Total number of services in each stage by organisational type**

Agency/ Ministry	Total number of online services						Organisational type
	Publish		*Interact*		*Transact*		
TIC	9	90%	4	67%	0	0%	G2B and regulatory
TRA	8	80%	3	67%	2	67%	G2B and regulatory
BRELA	7	80%	3	50%	0	0%	G2B and regulatory
MoH	8	80%	2	33%	0	0%	G2C and developmental
MoL	4	60%	2	33%	0	0%	G2C and developmental
MoHA	8	80%	1	17%	0	0%	G2C and developmental

Source: Author's compilation.

Three of the organisations — TRA, TIC and BRELA — serve a homogenous group, that is, business people, and perform a regulatory role. Conversely, MoH, MoL and MoHA serve broad heterogeneous groups with different needs and where physical engagement is necessary. For example, saving lives and properties is a task of MoHA which requires direct contact between police forces and customers. Similarly, provision of hospital services is a task of MoH which necessarily requires direct contact between medical staff and patients. Therefore, the type and nature of public services offered can be a determinant of electronic service delivery.

MoL has the lowest percentage score at the "publish stage" (60 per cent) and MoHA has the lowest percentage score at the "interact stage" (17 per cent). Both organisations belong to the G2C category and have the youngest websites. This may imply that apart from the nature of services provided, the age of a website can explain the maturity level. This might explain why TIC and BRELA are not moving to a 100 per cent score at the "transact stage".

Table 5 shows that only one organisation — TRA — offers online transactions such as payment of bills. The others have no services at all at this level; so most customers in most instances still face street bureaucracies instead of system bureaucracies. Street-level bureaucracies are public servants who have direct physical contact with citizens while system-level bureaucracies are information systems that should replace street-level bureaucracies through e-government services (Reddick 2005). TRA also enables online application for a Tax Identification Number (TIN) (though the document is collected from the nearest tax office), VAT registration, application for customs licence and a PAYE calculator. It offers online services through a customs management system for all companies dealing with imports. For example, submissions of important documents for clearing and forwarding agents are processed wholly online.

Table 6 summarises the results of interviewing experts and provides two main reasons for variations in maturity, which are in line with reasons found in the literature, for example, nature of the service (Buckley 2003;Bhatnagar 2003); and prioritisation of the business sector (Sein 2011).

Table 6: **Explanatory factors for variations in E-Government maturity**

Organisational explanatory factor	Transcription from e-government experts
Perceived benefits from the management	It is easy to quantify outcomes of agencies such as TRA and TIC in monetary values. It is difficult to quantify benefits of MoH or MoL in monetary values because their mission is not to generate money. TIC, TRA and BRELA all target the business sector which is important for economic growth and a source of government revenue. CEOs are champions for change and their positive perception is crucial for resource allocation. An e-government investment needs to be justified by the returns.
Nature of the services delivered	Agencies with regulatory roles either G2B or B2C normally have limited and well defined tasks. Normally services delivered include procedures, application forms and payments of fees. These tasks can entirely be provided online without direct contact with officers. Examples include agencies such as TRA, TIC and BRELA. Some Ministries have broader missions which are more than regulatory functions. Some services require face-to-face interactions, for example health services.

Source: Author's compilation.

Conclusion

From the New Public Management point of view, the goal of e-government is to transform the public sector from traditional street-level bureaucracies where services are delivered in face-to-face interaction with bureaucrats towards system-level bureaucracies where e-government services are expected to carry out some works of bureaucrats (Reddick 2005). This shift is expected to create a more transparent, effective, efficient and accountable government.

The discussion in this chapter suggests that there is a promise for the ongoing public sector reforms agendas using e-government to pursue transparency and accountability. It also shows that there is a need for encouraging some of the G2C agencies, like the MoL, to put more effort to implement e-government. Currently there is an increasing use of mobile telephones in all areas. Between 1994 and 2008, the number of cellular mobile telephone subscribers rose from 371 (sic) to 13,006,793 (ITU 2009) and has since risen to 20,983,853 (Tanzania National Bureau of Statistics). Given this increasing use of mobile telephones, partnership between mobile telecommunication companies and the government could bring a type of "online" benefit to people (especially rural) without direct access to the internet. For example, the MoL could send producer prices to farmers.

Finally, it is important to provide the necessary support and incentive for both the G2B and G2C organisations in Tanzania to reach the "interact" and "transact" stages and exploit the potential benefits of e-government. This support will help to raise the status of Tanzania in the worldwide e-government development index.

References

Awan, M. A. 2008. Dubai e-government: An evaluation of G2B websites. *Journal of Internet Commerce* 6(3), 115–129.

Bhatnagar, S. 2003. The economic and social impact of e-government: A background technical paper for the proposed UNDESA publication. E-government, the citizen and the state—debating governance in the information age. www.iimahd.ernet.in/~subhash/pdfs/UNDESAeGovReport.pdf (accessed on April, 2010)

Brown, M. M., and Brudney, J. L. 2001. Achieving advanced electronic government services: An examination of obstacles and implications from an international perspective. Paper presented at the National Public Management Research Conference, Indiana University, Bloomington, IN, October 18-20, 2001

Buckley, J. 2003. E-service quality and the public sector. *Managing Service Quality*, 13(6), 453.

Cordella, A. 2006. Transaction costs and information systems: Does IT add up? *Journal of Information Technology*, 21(3), 195–202.

Davidrajuh. 2004. Planning e-government start-up: A case study on e-Sri Lanka. *Electronic Government, an International Journal*, 1(1), 92.

DiRienzo, C. E., Das, J., Cort, K. T., and Burbridge, J. Jr. 2007. Corruption and the role of information. *Journal of International Business Studies*. 38(2), 320–332.

Golden, W., Hughes, M., and Scott, M. 2003. The role of process evolution in achieving citizen centered E-Government. AMCIS 2003 Proceedings. Paper 100. http://aisel.aisnet.org/amcis2003/100 (accessed on January, 2011)

Gupta, M. P., and Jana, D. 2003. E-government evaluation: A framework and case study. *Government Information Quarterly*, 20(4), 365–387.

Hazlett, S.-A., and Hill, F. 2003. E-government: The realities of using IT to transform the public sector. *Managing Service Quality*, 13(6), 445–452.

Heeks, R. 2002. E-Government in Africa: Promise and practice. Information Polity: The *International Journal of Government and Democracy in the Information Age*, 7(2/3), 97.

Howard, M. 2001. E-Government across the Globe: How will "e" change government? *Government Finance Review* 17(4), 6–9.

International Telecommunication Union (ITU). 2009. World Telecommunication Indicators 2008. Geneva: ITU. Available at http://www.itu.int/ITU-D/ict/publications/world/world.html (accessed on December, 2011)

Irani, Z., Al-Sebie, M., and Elliman, T. 2006. Transaction stage of e-government systems: Identification of its location and importance. Paper presented at the system sciences, 2006. HICSS '06. Proceedings of the 39th Annual Hawaii International Conference on System Sciences, 04-07 Jan. 2006

Jun, K.N., and Weare, C. 2001. Institutional motivations in the adoption of innovations: The case of e-government. *Journal of Public Administration Research and Theory Advance.*

Kaaya, J. 2004. Implementing e-government services in East Africa: Assessing status through content analysis of government websites. *Electronic Journal of e-Government,* 2(1), 39–54.

Kertesz, S. 2003. Cost-benefit analysis of e-government investments. Harvard University. J.F. Kennedy School of Government; www.edemocratie.ro/publicatii/Cost-Benefit.pdf (accessed on May, 2010)

Koh, C. E., and Prybutok, V. R. 2003. The three ring models and development of an instrument for measuring dimensions of e-government functions. *Journal of Computer Information Systems,* 43(3), 34.

Lau, E. 2005. E-government and the drive for growth and equity: Science and international affairs series paper. www.belfercenter.org. (accessed in May, 2010)

Menda, A. 2005. Successes and challenges: e-Governance in Tanzania. http://www.tanzaniagateway.org/news/news/article.asp?ID=76 (accessed on March, 2011).

Messkoub, M. 1996. Impact of adjustment in Tanzania: The crisis of the social sector in the 1980s. *Internet Journal of African Studies,* 1.

Nawaz, M., Issa, M., and Hyder, S. I. 2007. E-government services maturity models. In Proceedings of the 2007 Computer Science & Information Technology Education Conference (CSIT Ed 2007), Mauritius, Nov 16-18, 2007.

Ojha, A., Palvia, S., and Gupta, M. P. 2008. A model for impact of E-government on corruption: Exploring theoretical foundations. In J. Bhattacharya (Ed.), *Critical Thinking in E-Governance,* pp. 160–170. New Delhi: Gift Publishing.

Pina, V., Torres, L., and Royo, S. 2010. Is e-government leading to more accountable and transparent local governments? An overall view. *Financial Accountability and Management,* Vol. 26, Issue 1, pp. 3–20.

Reddick, C.G. 2005. Citizen interaction with e-government: From the streets to servers? *Government Information Quarterly,* Vol. 22, pp. 38–57

Sein, M. K. 2011. The "I" between G and C: E-government intermediaries in developing countries. The *Electronic Journal on Information Systems in Developing Countries,* 48 (2), 1–14.

Shahkooh, K. A., Fasanghari, M., and Abdollahi, A. 2008. Clustering the countries according to relation between e-government and transparency. Paper presented on 3rd International Conference on Information and Communication Technologies: From Theory to Applications, 2008. ICTTA 2008. ITRC, Tehran Date: 7-11 April 2008.

Shahkooh, K. A., Saghafi, F. and Abdollahi, A.. 2008. A proposed model for e-government maturity. Paper presented at the 3rd International Conference on Information and Communication Technologies: From Theory to Applications, 2008. ICTTA 2008. ITRC, Tehran Date: 7-11 April 2008

Shim, D. C., and Eom, T. H. 2008. E-government and anti-corruption: Empirical analysis of international data. *International Journal of Public Administration*, 31(3), 298–316.

Singh, H. 2003. Government in the digital era and human factors in e-governance. Paper presented at the Regional Workshop on E-government, Sana'a.Web: unpan1.un.org/intradoc/groups/public/.../ unpan015248.pdf (accessed on May, 2011)

Teicher, J., Hughes, O., and Dow, N. 2002. E-government: A new route to public sector quality. *Managing Service Quality*, 12(6), 384–393.

Tripp, A. M. 1997. Changing the rules: The politics of liberalisation and the urban informal economy in Tanzania. Berkeley: University of California.

UN. 2008. UN e-government survey 2008. New York. unpan1.un.org/ intradoc/groups/public/.../un/unpan028607.pdf (accessed on May, 2011)

UN and ASPA. 2002. Benchmarking e-government: A global perspective. New York: UN Publication. unpan1.un.org/intradoc/groups/public/.../ un/unpan021547.pdf accessed on May, 2011)

West, D. M. 2000. *Assessing e-government: The internet, democracy, and service delivery by state and federal governments*. Providence, Rhode Island: Brown University.

Williamson, O. E. 1985. *The economic institutions of capitalism: Firms, markets, relational contracting*. London: Collier Macmillan.

Yonazi, J., Sol, H., and Boonstra, A. 2010. Exploring issues underlying citizen adoption of eGovernment initiatives in developing countries: The case of Tanzania. *Electronic Journal of e-Government*, 8(2), 176–188.

Yong Hyo, C., and Byung-Dae, C. 2004. E-government to combat corruption: The case of Seoul Metropolitan government. *International Journal of Public Administration*, 27(10), 719–735.

Chapter 9

The Quantity-Quality Balance: Reforms in University Education in Uganda

Roberts Kabeba Muriisa

Abstract

Uganda has reduced state financing of universities and promoted commercialisation and privatisation in response to demand for greater capacity and relevance. The findings show that reforms increased access and equity but compromised quality. This chapter uses scholarly works and university documents to analyse the access, quality and equity trajectory over the past 30 years. It establishes that the impact of commercialisation of higher education has been affected by lack of careful planning and minimal government involvement/ resources. It recommends a combination of commercialisation and government and public investment to ensure access, quality and equity going forward. Education, being a public good, should be supported by both state and private resource to optimise the people's wellbeing.

Introduction

Neo-liberalism — reducing the role of the state while increasing access to services — has been a primary reform strategy around the world. In the neo-liberal framework, consumers pay for services and both quality and quantity are driven by market demand. Likewise, in the higher education sector, commercialisation and privatisation have become the norm (Mamdani 2007) making university education a product that can be bought; students exercise consumer choice (Brown 2005,43). The higher education stakeholder map has also become more complex. It includes parents, students, the business sector, the state, donors, international education service providers, and the academic community – all demanding more relevant programmes of higher quality (Muriisa 2010). Universities have also changed their curricula, introduced brand-name courses, and, as part of a solution to the lack of teaching space caused by increased enrolment, have started parallel programmes such as evening, weekend and summer classes. The above and other related changes have different implications for quality, equity and access. Although the changes have increased enrolment, some argue that the quality of education has deteriorated (NCHE 2007), following the entry of sub-standard providers (World Bank 2008); changes also resulted in increased - but not always healthy - competition between departments and faculties (Mamdani 2007).

Much of the literature on the relationship between privatisation and commercialisation versus equity, quality and access has focussed on the quantitative aspects (see for example Bacwayo 2010; Elhadary 2010; and Kasozi 2009). This chapter investigates the implications of Uganda's public sector reform in the higher education/university sector on quality, equity and access.

This paper critically reviews the existing literature from Muriisa (2010), Bacwayo (2010), Mayanja (2007), Kasozi (2009), Musisi (2003), Musisi and Muwanga (2003), Mamdani (2007), and university archives such as periodic reports and memos. These offer a rich base for discussion. For example, Mamdani (2007), Kasozi (2009) and Muriisa (2010) provide data on how different financing models affect the quality of education, while Bacwayo (2010) and Elhadary (2010) provide data on access. Literature was first arranged according to themes (privatisation and commercialisation, quality, equity, access, quality assurance), then analysed for content and resonance with themes of focus.

Uganda's Higher Education Reform Process at a Glance

Uganda's university education in the 1980s, already in crisis due to the civil strife and war that devastated Uganda's educational system, was further hobbled by the "structural adjustment" fashion of the period which called for limits on public funding of higher education. The viability of investing in higher education for social, economic and political development was questioned. By 1993, the Uganda government had completely stopped financing higher degrees and instead shifted all funding to primary education. The logic was that higher education increased social inequality while primary and basic education were more equitable and more cost effective (World Bank 1995). The World Bank recommended privatisation of higher education as the alternative financing strategy, arguing that cost-sharing (with consumers) and the promotion of private higher education would help free up scarce public resources for improving basic education; that privatisation of higher education would induce countries to adopt reforms that would increase efficiency and reduce public costs (*Ibid*).

In 1992, Uganda's white paper on strategic investment recommended a complete halt to full sponsorship of higher education by government, to be replaced by cost-sharing and private sponsorship (Musisi 2003). This took various forms:

• Introduction of privately funded programmes in public universities;

• Fee-paying students on some or all programmes. There were two phases of this form, one involving entry of private students into university (1991 – 1995), and then a curriculum change to attract more privately-funded students (1995 onwards) (Mamdani 2007,11).

• Private service providers were allowed to set up colleges and universities. The first private university in Uganda — the Islamic University in Uganda (IUIU) — was established in 2001. By the end of 2008, Uganda had 26 private and 5 public universities (Muriisa and Bacwayo 2010).

When privatisation was allowed at Makerere University, there was careful planning but there was no clear agreement between the university and its staff on various issues. The reform began by withdrawing student allowances (for example, personal needs and transport). There was also endless negotiation between academic staff and government for better pay. Formal staff associations created for this purpose included the Makerere University Academic Staff

Association (MUASA) and later the Mbarara University Academic
Staff Association (MBUASA). The heat in the economic issues, often
flaring to strikes, persists to the present day.

The financial squeeze on university facilities and staff
precipitated an educational crisis, which privatisation later sought
to solve (Mamdani 2007; Muriisa 2010). According to Mamdani,
privatisation was a survival strategy, recruiting private students
at Makerere University purely as revenue streams. This trend
expanded in the 1990s and other private universities opened up the
education service for competition.

Driven by privatisation and commercialisation, traditional
curricula were changed to offer more marketable programmes.
Management structures decentralised and faculties sought
autonomy in deciding which programmes to teach and how to
allocate money (Muriisa 2010). Faculties and departments became
power centres, making major decisions on programme development
and financial administration (Muriisa and Bacwayo 2010). At the
Makerere University Business School (MUBS), "saleability" rather
than academic quality became the driving force of programme
expansion. There was duplication of programmes among different
departments, gross mismanagement of funds, and inter-departmental
conflicts over pay differences caused by privately funded salary top-
ups (Mamdani 2007).

At Mbarara University of Science and Technology, student
numbers increased at the rate of 20 per cent per year between 2005
and 2010 (Mbarara University, 2011). By 2006, privately-sponsored
students accounted for the highest percentage of enrolment
and education financing at public universities. At Mbarara and
Makerere, the private proportion was about 80 per cent (Kasozi
2009). World Bank (2010) notes that between 1997 and 2006 the
number of university students in Uganda increased from 14,400 to
34,500.

Moreover, the share of private financing in public university
budgets increased from 30 per cent to 60 per cent, the largest
contribution coming through student fee payments. For example,
Makerere's total budget for 2005/2006 was Uganda shillings 98.5
billion, of which 38.5 billion (39 per cent) came from government,
56.2 billion (57 per cent) came from private students' contributions,

while 3.9 billion (4 per cent) came from donors (Mayanja 2007,2). Almost all students who enrol at private universities pay fees. The 2006–2007 budget for Bugema University was Uganda Shillings 2.765 billion of which 1.536 billion (55.6 per cent) was expected from student fees, with the balance of 44.4 per cent coming from donors and non-fees sources (Katamba 2007). These figures reflect the important contribution of the private sector, and the probability of its influence on programme design and management. In short, by the end of the 1990s, access to university had been greatly increased and the state had been relieved of responsibility for university student support (Kwesiga and Ahikire 2006).

Implications of Privatisation and Commercialisation of Education for Access, Quality and Equity

Government reforms in higher education include privatisation and commercialisation, the quota system, affirmative action programmes, performance management, and programme diversification – aimed at attracting more finances through more marketable programmes. The following section will discuss the resultant issues of access, quality and equity.

Reforms and Access

Access means the extent to which there is provision for everybody in higher education institutions. UNESCO's measure of access demands an equitable chance of tertiary education based on merit, capacity, effort and perseverance. This applies not only to university access, but lifelong educational opportunity. (http://www.unesco. org/education/educprog/wche/declaration_eng.htm. accessed on 11th June, 2011).

In Uganda, pre-1990s higher education was dominated by state provision and there was one state university. The space limit not only restricted access, but also polarised eligibility to an elite — a few rich families were able to pay fees for the best education *before* university entrance. Good secondary school education was available only in urban areas, effectively denying people from rural areas (85 per cent of the population) access to university (Ministry of Finance Planning and Economic Development (MFPED 2011).

Privatisation and commercialisation increased the number of higher education institutions and more than doubled student numbers. As noted above, at present, there are 5 public and 26 private universities. In 2009/2010, Makerere University alone had 33,112 registered students and 31,035 (94 per cent) were on undergraduate programmes (Makerere University, 2010: 16). Kasozi (2003, 2009) notes that overall university student numbers in Uganda rose from fewer than 10,000 in 1990 to about 100,000 in 2009. Despite this increase, access of the poor to tertiary education is still limited. As in the pre-reform period, government continued to sponsor only 2,000 students — chosen from those who deliver outstanding results in the advanced level examination set by Uganda National Examinations Board, plus a few selected for mature entry, and few exceptional performers from other tertiary institutions.

Annual fees for a programme of study at Mbarara University during the 2011/2012 academic year ranged from US$706 to US$1,167 (Mbarara University of Science and Technology 2011). By 2006, most private universities were also charging USD$ 947 per year for a single programme of study (Katamba 2007). Average earnings per month for a person employed in agriculture is slightly above US$ 5 (sic) (Uganda Bureau of Statistics 2010:16). Poor students who obtain the required grades cannot possibly pay for the university place their academic performance has earned. Even some of those who do muster the fees to enter, eventually drop out through fees default (Bacwayo 2010, 108).

Reforms and Equity of Geography and Gender

The reforms have allowed more students living outside of the capital city to enter university.

Previously, the great majority of students at Makerere University came from Gayaza High School, Nabbingo, Namagunga, Namilyango College School, and St. Mary's Kisubi, all of which are in and around Kampala. Some came from schools outside the capital, but schools dominating the wider list - like Ntare and Mbarara High School – were in urban centres, too.

The creation of four other public universities after the reform (Busitema in the eastern region, Gulu in the north, Mbarara in the west and Kyambogo in central), balanced the geographic spread and improved equity (Muriisa and Bacwayo 2010).The new universities are physically more reachable from rural schools. The dispersed locations of the new public universities help compensate for the market-driven decision of most new private universities to locate in and around the central region. Of the 31 universities in Uganda at the end of 2008, 17 were located in central – 9 universities and 2 degree-awarding institutions in Kampala, 2 in Wakiso, 3 in Mukono, 1 in Mpigi and 2 in Luwero – (Muriisa and Bacwayo 2010).

The entry requirements for the new public universities at Mbarara, Gulu, Busitema or Kyambogo are generally lower – sometimes by several exam points — than for Makerere. In the 2008/2009 academic year, the cut-off points for Bachelor of Medicine and Bachelor of Surgery was 49.6 and 48.4 at Makerere and Mbarara universities, respectively; for Gulu the benchmark was 45.5. Similarly, the cut-off points for Bachelor of Science with Education-Biology, were 39.9 and 33.8 for Makerere and Mbarara Universities, respectively and for Gulu it was 33.3 (Public Universities Joint Admissions Board - PUJAB - 2008). This has improved equity of access for rural students.

Table 1: **Undergraduate students registered in selected faculties at Makerere University, 2009/2010**

Faculty/Institute/School	Male	Female
Arts	1,641	2,239
Library and Information Science	143	294
Law	515	657
Social Sciences	1,077	1,536
Agriculture	690	297
Computing and Information Technology	2,178	1,354
Medicine	612	302
Science	752	346
Technology	1,701	465
Veterinary Medicine	355	164

Source: Makerere University Fact Book (2010)

In parallel, the affirmative action policy from 1990 automatically awarded women 1.5 extra points. The policy was directed to females seeking direct entry to undergraduate programmes at Makerere only (in 1990, Makerere was the only public university) but the policy has applied to all other public universities since their establishment. Enrolment of female students increased from 25 per cent in 1990 to 46 per cent in 2008 (Makerere University Gender Mainstreaming

Directorate 2012). In 2009/2010, more females than males were registered on most arts subjects and Library and Information Science at Makerere (see Table 1). Indeed, the system arguably disadvantages males on some programmes, and there now calls for the abandonment of the 1.5 point bonus (Vaughan 2009).

Males retain a significant majority on science programmes. Table 1 illustrates relatively low female enrolment on subjects such as agriculture, medicine and veterinary medicine, suggesting the overall increase in enrolment is skewed towards the arts.

Precise figures vary at other universities, but the trend is similar. Males still dominate enrolment on all study programmes (see Table 2), but female enrolment has the greater increase.

Table 2: **University enrolment by gender 2009/2010**

Field of Study	2009 Male	Female	2010 Male	Female	Change (%) Male	Female
Soc. Sciences	30,903	26,367	32,251	27,937	4.4	5.9
Humanities	6,877	5,959	7,489	6,770	8.9	13.6
Agric. Sciences	1,207	420	1,611	526	33.5	25.5
Med. Sciences	2,059	1,948	2,163	2,067	5.1	6.1
Eng. Sciences	3,215	786	3,685	1,797	14.6	128.7
Nat. Sciences	6,759	3,887	7,465	4,672	10.4	20.2
Total	**51,020**	**39,376**	**54,664**	**43,769**		
Share by Gender (%)	**56.4**	**43.6**	**55.56**	**44.5**	**7.1**	**11.2**

Source: UNCST (2011, 32).

The increased percentage of females accessing university education would not have been possible without privatisation, which increased the overall number of places available — especially in the arts and social sciences subjects. It is a combination of this growth and affirmative action that has achieved these results.

Reforms and Quality of Higher Education

In this chapter, quality is measured by the availability of teaching infrastructure and teaching facilities, availability of teaching staff and the quality of research.

Both private and public universities in Uganda lack necessary educational facilities, although they have increased their student population. Between 2009 and 2010 the total enrolment rose by 8.9 per cent and the greatest growth was in engineering, agriculture and medical sciences (18.3 per cent) while social sciences was 5 percent and humanities stood at 13.2 per cent (UNCST 2011, see Table 3).

The increase in student enrolments has not been accompanied by expansion of facilities such as computers, teaching space and library facilities; which are critical for quality education. Both private and public universities lack facilities for optimum learning (NCHE 2004, 2005, 2006, 2007) and the quality of education suffers. Many universities do not meet the minimum facility requirements set by NCHE (2005; 2006) in terms of space, student-teacher ratio, computers, library resources such as journals, books, e-resources and more. For instance, Mbarara University of Science and Technology library has a seating capacity of 700 for a student population of 3,163 (Mbarara University of Science and Technology 2010). E-resources are also not generally available. Mbarara and other universities still depend on the hardcopy books. Kasozi (2005) notes that private suppliers of higher education have joined government in delivery of the service, but there is a mismatch between resources and facilities versus student numbers, and this will inevitably lead to inferior performance.

Table 3: **University enrolment, 2007 – 2010**

Year/Program	Social Sciences	Humanities	Agric. Sciences	Med. Sciences	Eng. sciences	Nat. Sciences	Total enrolment
2007	62,901	3,344	1,678	3,489	3,447	8,781	83,640
2008	58,834	8,033	1,990	3,971	3,866	8,928	85,622
2009	57,279	12,836	1,627	4,007	4,001	10,646	90,396
2010	60,188	14,259	2,137	4,230	5,482	12,137	98,433

Source: UNCST (2011, 8)

One of the reasons for the lack of facilities is lack of finance that results from lack of government support for the gap between what students can pay and what quality service costs.

Table 4: **Fees charged by Mbarara University for different programmes**

Program of Study	Fees charged 2009/2010	Fees Charged 2010/2011	Fees Charged 2011/2012	Unit Cost (2010)
Human Medicine	1,327,000	2,106,000	3,267,500	8,142,740
Development Studies (Arts)	962,000	1,420,000	1,979,500	3,633,121
Information Technology	1,067,000	1,762,000	2,579,500	3,169,330
Business Administration	1,067,000	1742,000	2,539,500	3,633,121
Science	967,000	1,462,000	1,979,500	7,795,591

Sources: AH Consult (2010); Mbarara University of Science and Technology (2009, 2011)

The Mbarara example in Table 4 shows the disparity between cost and price. University charges are limited by consumer purchasing power; they are simply unable to collect sufficient revenue to provide quality education. At public universities, the same effect is caused by declining government expenditure. For instance, in the fiscal year 1997–98, the government approved 60 billion shillings for Makerere but released only 20 billion by the end of the financial year (Kwesiga and Ahikire 2006). According to an internal memo circulated by the Mbarara University Bursar in January 2011 (Musana 2011) the government released only 173 million Uganda shillings of the expected 736 million budgeted for the third quarter. The communication read in part: "This is a cut by 76 per cent and no explanatory circular has been attached. The allocation on development is nil" (Musana 2011). Four months later, in a communication memo of 18th April, 2011, the University Secretary indicated that the recurrent and non-wage budget for the 4th quarter of 2010/2011 had been cut by 46.1 per cent. The memo read in part that: "the consequence of budget cuts is that certain activities will have to be suspended...meetings, workshops, conferences and newspapers" (Kibirige 2011). According to Mbarara University Annual Report 2010, the government has not released any funds for staff recruitment in the past six years (Mbarara University of Science and Technology 2010, 9). Clearly, defaults on funding cascade to declines in quality.

Research is one of the first victims of funding limits in both private and public universities. In 2006, the national council for higher education reported that private universities were spending 0.4 per cent of their budgets on research and more than 50 per cent on infrastructural development. A NCHE (2005) report on 16 universities, four of which are public (Makerere, Mbarara, Kyambogo and Gulu), shows 1.1 per cent of budget spent on research and 70.2 per cent on staff welfare (cited in Kasozi 2009, 145–146). Even the little that is allocated to research often gets diverted to other uses more crucial to mere survival (NCHE 2005). Mbarara University indicates that government released only 28 per cent (US$25,000 instead of US$89,000) of funds allocated for research in 2010/11 (Mbarara University of Science and Technology 2010a). The result is minimal research activity at any university. Also, research inputs such as books, equipment, subscription to journals and qualified academic staff are very limited (Ajayi, Goma and Johnson 1996).

Lack of finance has negatively affected attraction and retention of qualified staff. Table 6 shows staff required versus staff available in terms of academic position at Mbarara University.

Table 5:   **Approved vis-à-vis available academic staff establishment at Mbarara University, June 2011**

Category/Rank	Required	Available	Shortfall
Professor	69	3	66
Associate Professor	76	8	68
Senior Lecturers	102	25	77
Lecturers	162	99	63

Source: Mbarara University (2010)

In 2006, there were 3,927 lecturers in Uganda. Only 684 (17 per cent) of these had PhDs. The distribution of qualified staff among the universities is lopsided. Kasozi (2009:86) shows that Makerere

University had 363 of the 439 PhD holders employed in all public universities.

While higher education regulations stipulate that in any academic programme 10 per cent of teaching staff should be PhD holders, by June 2010 Mbarara University had 22 PhD holders (including expatriates), and was running more than 40 programmes. Six of the twenty-two (27 per cent) of the PhD holders were employed in the biology department alone, while most departments and faculties did not have any PhD holders (Mbarara University of Science and Technology 2011a). The Faculty of Development Studies with a staff establishment of 38 had only 2 (5.3 per cent) holding PhDs and no professor or associate professor. The faculty was running two undergraduate and two postgraduate programmes. In the Institute of Computer Science, staff ranks started at lecturer level and there was no PhD holder. The Faculty of Medicine relies on expatriates.

Universities face not only a shortage of qualified staff, but also a high turn-over of the inevitably overloaded staff they do have. Research time, a key function of academic staff, is almost non-existent in such overload conditions (Mbarara University of Science and Technology 2011a,18).

In short, privatisation of higher education in Uganda, combined with poor government financing of higher education, has resulted in loss of qualified staff and lack of new knowledge arising from research. There is increasing evidence that in countries with inadequate public financing and resource diversification, an increasing number of students results in deterioration in quality of education (World Bank 2010). The impact of under-funding affects both private and public universities in almost the same way. The bottom line is that while access to university has improved, the quality of education at either public or private universities has deteriorated.

Conclusion

In almost any endeavour known to modern man, there is a trade-off between quantity and quality. With a given resource, more of one invariably means less of the other. If both are to be improved, then more resources will be needed. If such resources are not forthcoming, the only remaining choice lies in the point of balance:

more access means less quality; more quality will mean less access (and almost certainly less equity). This chapter shows that quality of higher education in Uganda is compromised; that privatisation and commercialisation is in effect changing universities into glorified high schools.

Reforms in Uganda have led to minimal investment in higher education. Public universities receive less funding from government; private universities receive none. In both cases, the state's role has been reduced to that of a watch-dog. The question is whether universities (public or private), which work for the public good, warrant public investment. Government should recognise that investment in education is a benefit to the people that the government represents, and should be financially supported in some way — through direct funding and/or other incentive structures such as tax waivers.

References

AH Consult. 2010. Unit cost study of education at public universities in Uganda (draft report). Kampala: Office of the Auditor General.

Ajayi, J.F, Ade, K.H. L. Goma, and G. A. Johnson. 1996. *The African experience with higher education*. Accra: Association of African Universities.

Bacwayo, E. K. 2010. Private higher education in Uganda: Implications for equity, access, knowledge creation and research. In *Reshaping research universities in the Nile Basin countries, Book 2*, edited by B. A. Kassahun, C. M. Mwiandi and T. Halvorsen. Kampala: Fountain Publishers.

Brown, W. 2005. *Edgework: Critical essays on knowledge and politics*. Princeton NJ: Princeton University Press.

Elhadary, A. E. Y. 2010. Equity in and access to higher education in Nile Basin countries. In *Reshaping research universities in the Nile Basin countries Book 2*, edited by B. A. Kassahun, C. M. Mwiandi and T. Halvorsen. Kampala: Fountain Publishers.

Kasozi, A. B. K. 2003. *University education in Uganda: Challenges and opportunities for reform*. Kampala: Fountain Publishers.

———.2005. The development of a strategic plan for higher education in Uganda 2001–2005: The interplay of internal and external forces in higher education policy formation in a southern country. In *NUFFIC- A changing landscape*. The Hague. web: http://www.ruforum.org/sites/default/files/Development of a Strategic Plan for Higher Education in Uganda ABK Kasozi.pdf (accessed on May, 2011)

———.2009. *Financing Uganda's public universities: An obstacle to serving the public good*. Kampala: Fountain Publishers.

Katamba, P. 2007. Government philanthropy towards private universities in Uganda and its implications for access, equity and quality of higher education: The case of Bugema University. *The Uganda Higher Education Review* 4 (2):9 –16.

Kibirige, C. 2011. "Government reduces fourth quarter release." Mbarara: Mbarara University of Science and Technology.

Kwesiga, C. J. and J. Ahikire. 2006. On student access and equity in a reforming university: Makerere in the 1990s and beyond. *Journal of Higher Education in Africa/RESA* 4 (2):1–46.

Makerere University. 2011. *Makerere University fact book 2010*. Kampala: Makerere University.

Makerere University Gender Mainstreaming Directorate. 2012. Gender equality landmarks in Makerere University. http://gender.mak.ac.ug/index.php?option=com_content&view=article&id=168&Itemid=153, (accessed on October, 2012)

Mamdani, M. 2007. *Scholars in the market place: The dilemmas of neo-*

liberal reform at Makerere University, 1989–2005. Kampala: Fountain Publishers.

Mayanja, K. M. 2007. Improving income from internally generated funds without provoking students or staff strikes at Makerere and other universities. *The Uganda Higher Education Review* 4 (2):2–8.

Mbarara University of Science and Technology. 2009. Mbarara University of Science and Technology entry requirements—Fees structure for 2009/2010. Mbarara: Mbarara University of Science and Technology, Office of Academic Registrar.

——.2010. *Mbarara University annual report 2010.* Mbarara: Mbarara University of Science and Technology.

——.2010a. Mbarara University of Science and Technology budget estimates 2010/2011 Financial Year. Mbarara: Mbarara University of Science and Technology.

——.2011. Mbarara University of Science and Technology admissions requirements—Fees structure for 2011/2012). Mbarara: Mbarara University of Science and Technology, Office of Academic Registrar.

——.2011a. Mbarara University of Science and Technology status report sent to The President of Uganda. H.E. Yoweri Kaguta Museveni June 2011. Mbarara: Mbarara, Mbarara University of Science and Technology.

Ministry of Finance Planning and Economic Development (MFPED). 2011. The background to the budget 2011/2012 fiscal year. Kampala: MFPED.

Muriisa, R. 2010. It is not all about money: Financial governance and research in public universities in Uganda. In *Reshaping research universities in the Nile Basin countries, Book 2,* edited by B. A. Kassahun, T. Halvorsen and C. M. Mwiandi. Kampala: Fountain publishers.

Muriisa, R. K. and E. K. Bacwayo. 2010. The state of university education in Uganda: A situational overview. In *Shaping research universities in the Nile Basin countries, Book 1,* edited by T. Halvorsen, C. M. Mwiandi and A. Kassahun. Kampala: Fountain.

Musana, D. 2011. Non-wage recurrent cash limits, January–March 2011. Mbarara: Mbarara University of Science and Technology.

Musisi, B. Nakanyike. 2003. Uganda. In *African higher education: An international reference handbook,* edited by D. Teferra and G. P. Altbach. Bloomington Indiana University Press.

Musisi, B. Nakanyike, and K Nasozi Muwanga. 2003. *Makerere University in transition 1993–2000.* Oxford: James Currey.

National Council for Higher Education (NCHE). 2004. The state of higher education: A report of a survey of Uganda's institutions of higher learning. Kampala: NCHE.

——.2005. *The state of higher education and training in Uganda.* Kampala: NCHE.

——.2006. The state of higher education: A report of a survey of Uganda's institutions of higher learning. Kampala: NCHE.

——.2007. The state of higher education and training in Uganda: A report on higher education delivery and institutions. Kampala: NCHE

Public Universities Joint Admissions Board (PUJAB). 2008. Cut-off points for study programs at public universities, 2008–2009 academic year. Kampala: PUJAB.

Uganda Bureau of Statistics (UBOS). 2010. *Statistical abstracts 2010*. Kampala: UBOS.

UNCST. 2011. *Science, technology and innovation in Uganda: Status report, 2009/2010*. Kampala: UNCST.

Vaughan, J. 2009. 'It is time to get rid of 1.5 at Makerere.' *The Monitor*, 01.08.

World Bank. 2010. *Financing higher education in Africa*. Washington, D.C: World Bank.

——.1995. *Higher education: The lessons of experience*. Washington, D.C: World Bank.

——.2008. *Progress of higher education in developing world*. Washington, D.C: World Bank.

Chapter 10

Making Outcomes Matter: Programme-Based Budgeting for a Better Public Sector in Mauritius

Verena Tandrayen-Ragoobur and Kesseven Padachi

Abstract

Mauritius has implemented Programme-Based Budgeting (PBB) at all ministries and departments, as a key public sector reform. This chapter assesses the adoption and implementation of PBB. Using a survey that covers 22 ministries and departments, this study finds set-backs in the training of staff involved in the new system, with some progress in large ministries where there is now greater public accountability, better monitoring of projects and a rise in efficiency. PBB may not have met all expectations and there is certainly room for improvement, but it constitutes a major step forward in comparison with old-fashioned input budgeting.

Introduction

Globalisation, deregulation, technological improvements and public expectation have triggered radical changes in the performance of the Mauritian public sector. The role of the government has moved from public service provider to private service facilitator. Reforms include performance management across all ministries and departments, improvement in service delivery, introduction of Gemba Kaizen principles, 24/7 response, several online services, application of customer charters by different ministries, creation of a Public Service Quality Association, and the introduction of the Public Service Excellence Award (Ministry of Civil Service and Administrative Reforms 2008).

In 2006/07, the Mauritian government launched an economic reform programme focused on increasing the competitiveness of the economy, attracting foreign direct investment, empowering the poor, and strengthening fiscal management. As part of the fiscal management reform measures, Programme-Based Budgeting (PBB) has been implemented to improve expenditure efficiency and effectiveness by systematically linking funding to results, and making use of performance information to achieve that connection.

Five years after starting PBB implementation, there has been no study analysing its effectiveness and challenges. The system has been adopted as part of public sector reform policy, but there remain unanswered questions on the adoption, implementation and evaluation of this new tool. This study fills that gap, and analyses the opportunities and the challenges encountered in the execution phase.

The study's methodology rests on survey analysis, sampling 17 ministries and 5 departments where PBB has been adopted. A questionnaire was administered to key officials, especially officers in the finance sections (the core implementers)[1]. The questionnaire embraced the timing and scale of adoption; motivating factors; difficulties encountered; training offered; status of implementation; benefits to budgeting structure; and monitoring and reporting.

The next section of this chapter reviews literature which conceptualises PBB. Section 3 discusses the public sector reforms in Mauritius during the past two decades. Section 4 outlines the public sector reforms and PBB in Mauritius. Section 5 discusses findings on the opportunities and challenges of PBB reform. Conclusions are presented in Section 6.

Conceptualising Programme-Based Budgeting

Public sector reforms have increasingly followed a New Public Management (NPM) approach that recommends a results-orientated managerial approach aimed, inter alia, at improving quality of public services; enhancing efficiency of governmental operations; making policy implementation more effective; and obtaining value for money by focusing on performance management and auditing (Aucoin 1990; Pollitt and Bouckaert 2000; Laffin and Painter 1995; Minogue 2001). NPM constitutes various reforms including the PBB system, which links the funding of public sector organisations to the results they deliver, through the systematic use of performance information (Tügen et al. 2009).

PBB is an advanced budgeting process and an annual, integrated programme plan, indicating the relationship between levels of funding and anticipated outcomes. It refers to a single or a set of performance target(s) which must be achieved at a given expenditure level, and involves three major elements:

- the ultimate outcome of a particular performance (Objective);

- the strategies - diverse means of attaining the final result (Strategic Plan); and

- the activities performed in order to achieve the final outcome (Operational Plan).

(Segal and Summers 2002).

PBB informs the public about the amounts expended on various services, the anticipated benefit which the users will derive, the destinations of spending, and the cost (user price) of the expected benefits. It gives policy and decision makers a transparent view of the trade-offs between alternative expenditure plans, so they can make more up-to-date, beneficial and effective allocation of financial resources. By shortening the traditionally lengthy budgeting and reporting procedures, PBB helps public sector institutions focus on objectives on a constant basis, save money and time simultaneously, align data collection and reporting procedures, and improve performance on a continuous basis (Robinson and Duncan, 2009).

Technically, PBB reforms sound promising in improving the public sector financial system. In practice, however, reformers face many difficulties. Recurring problems include the formulation of (sound) objectives, getting useful performance data and linking government performance (the output) to societal impact (the outcome) (Van Nispen and Posseth 2006). The literature also indicates that performance budgeting is difficult to implement for a wide range of countries, including most Low-Income Countries (LICs) (Rose 2009). However, a "scaled-down" model of PBB — which aims to make the budget preparation process more "performance-informed" — can be implemented in some LICs and could be of significant benefit to a country's development. However, this should only be attempted where sound macro-economic fiscal policy has been established; where PBB systems and procedures ensure that budgets are executed as planned; where information systems are able to provide timely and reliable budgetary data; and where enhanced capacities are available to handle the more demanding analysis that PBB requires. Countries with serious governance problems are unlikely to be able to reap the full benefits of PBB (*Ibid*).

The Public Sector in Mauritius

The Mauritian economy is one of the fastest growing in sub-Saharan Africa and is classified by the World Bank as upper-middle income. Mauritius has developed from a low-income, agriculturally-based economy to a middle-income diversified economy with growing industrial, financial, and tourist sectors. In recent years, annual growth has been in the order of 5 to 6 per cent. In 2011, with difficulties on the international scene following the global financial crisis, the euro debt crisis and the oil crisis, economic growth was 4.1 per cent, slightly lower than the 4.2 per cent registered in 2010 (Statistics Mauritius 2011). The main contributors to the 4.1 per cent GDP growth were real estate; renting and business activities; manufacturing; transport storage and communications; and financial intermediation. This achievement has been reflected in an equitable income distribution, increased life expectancy, lower infant mortality, and an improved infrastructure.

In 2006, Mauritius's Gross National Income (GNI) per capita at market prices was around USD 5,723 and today it stands at US$ 7,740 (World Bank 2012), representing a 35.2 per cent rise over a period of 5 years. The objective of the government is to achieve a per capita GNI of US$ 20,000 by the 2020s (Mauritius International Investment Forum 2011). Fiscal deficit was also reduced from 5.3 per cent of GDP in 2005/06 to 4.3 per cent in 2006/07. The overall 2010 budget deficit was estimated at 4.7 per cent of GDP against 6.6 per cent in 2009. It stood at 4.2 per cent in 2011 and was expected to fall to 3.8 per cent in 2012. Government revenue and grants amounted to only 19.8 per cent of GDP in 2010, compared with 24.5 per cent for government expenditure and net lending. In 2011, revenue and grants were expected to rise to 20.5 per cent while expenditure and net lending was projected to rise to 24.9 per cent (see Table 1). The

2008 Public Debt Management Act (PDMA) puts a limit on the debt-to-GDP ratio. In 2010, the ratio was estimated at 59 per cent - close to the legally mandated 60 per cent ceiling.

Table 1: **Public finances as a share of GDP, (2002–2012)**

	2002	2005	2007	2008	2009	2010	2011	2012
Total revenue & grants	18.5	20.0	17.6	19.6	18.8	19.8	20.5	20.6
Tax revenue	15.2	18.1	15.5	16.8	15.6	16.6	17	17
Oil revenue	–	–	–	–	–	–	–	–
Grants	0.2	0.2	0.1	0.2	0.8	0.8	1	1
Other revenues	3	1.7	2	2.6	2.4	2.4	2.5	2.5
Total expenditure and net lending	22.2	25.3	19.7	21.7	25.4	24.5	24.9	24.9
Current expenditure	18.5	21.4	16.9	17.2	17.7	16.5	17	16.9
Excluding interest	16.2	17.7	14.3	14.3	14.9	13.2	15.2	15.2
Wages and salaries	7.3	6.3	6.4	6.5	6.6	6.5	7	6.9
Goods and services	2.5	2.3	2.1	2.1	2.4	1.7	2.3	2.4
Interest	2.4	3.8	2.6	2.9	2.8	3.3	1.8	1.7
Capital expenditure	3.4	3.6	2.6	3.1	6.8	6.5	6.7	6.7
Primary balance	-1.4	-1.4	0.6	0.7	-3.8	-1.3	-2.6	-2.6
Overall balance	-3.7	-5.3	-2.1	-2.1	-6.6	-4.7	-4.4	-4.3

Source: ADBG et al. (2010)

Since 2006, with the adoption of PBB, there has been better monitoring of government funds and expenditure targeted to improve standards of living and achieve sustainable development. Mauritius has also followed prudent macro-economic policies in the recent past. In particular, it has taken measures aimed at fiscal consolidation and has been implementing PBB as well as the Mid-Term Expenditure Framework (MTEF). By doing so, it seeks to restructure public expenditure, strengthen expenditure controls and improve budgetary processes. The gradual implementation of PMS (Performance Management System) and PBB is expected to strengthen governance and the strategic budgeting process across all government agencies (ADBG *et al* 2009).

The Mauritian government has also embarked on a major reform programme targeting both revenue and expenditure to contain the budget deficit. On the revenue side, in the hope of boosting economic growth and entrepreneurship, the government announced in its 2006/07 budget the introduction of a flat-rate personal and corporate income tax of 15 per cent. Revenue collection has been enhanced by consolidating agencies under the single Mauritius Revenue Authority, eliminating overlap, duplication of functions and waste. In an effort to get more individuals and businesses to pay taxes, the government introduced a Voluntary Disclosure Incentive Scheme (VDIS) and a Tax Arrears Payment Incentive Scheme (TAPIS). VDIS allowed individuals and companies to come forward and make voluntary disclosure of undeclared earnings with only 25 per cent of the penalty and interest that would have been imposed under normal provision. Although the government has moved to PBB, some high expenditure items - such as subsidies to bus owners in exchange for providing free transportation to students and old-age pensioners - are still in the budget.

More than 50 per cent of government expenditure (Statistics Mauritius, 2010) is directed towards community and social services with social security and welfare presenting the largest share, followed by education and health. Mauritius has a wide range of social protection schemes. It provides free education from pre-primary to tertiary level, free health services, including costly tertiary health care procedures like heart surgery. It also gives subsidies on basic foodstuffs like rice and flour and cooking gas as well as many free social services and social security schemes.

Public Sector Reforms and PBB in Mauritius

In the wake of independence in 1968, the Mauritian public service structure resembled the British system. It was the only model Mauritian civil service had been extensively exposed to and followed the premise that government should be an important provider of goods and services. During this time, the Ministry for Civil Service Affairs was created and has played a key role ever since in improving the level of service offered by ministries and departments.

In the 1980s, several institutions were set up to modernise the civil service system, especially through information technology. These included the establishment of the National Computer Board for development of national policies in informatics, the Central Informatics Bureau to co-ordinate computerisation in the civil service, and the State Informatics Limited for software development. Several ministries and departments computerised their systems to improve administrative efficiency. Training of staff in different fields has been an ongoing feature.

In the 1990s, a number of new bodies were set up to cope with rising demand for better services. Government launched the Public Sector Management Investment Programme (PSMIP) with three key areas for reform — Financial Management, Human Resource Management and Physical Assets Management. New Financial and Personnel Management Manuals were introduced. Other measures included One-Stop Shops to reduce bureaucratic delays and simplify processing of applications for industrial licences, investment projects and work permits. Strict budgetary measures were adopted; posts in the public services that were left unfilled for a specified period were abolished; voluntary early retirement was used to optimise the size of the public sector workforce in parallel with job inspections and manpower utilisation/needs/performance audits. The setting up of Work Improvement Teams and measures to enhance the quality of service to customers through ISO 9000 Standards have been introduced to promote improvement of service quality in some sectors and to reassure the people that their interests are being catered for. The government also introduced reforms in the judiciary, local government, education, health and other public services. Moreover, the selection of public officers is undertaken by the separate Public Service Commission that is mandated to ensure transparent recruitment and equal opportunities. There is a strategy for civil service training to equip officers with the necessary knowledge, skills and tools to enable them to perform their day-to-day duties in a most efficient and effective manner.

To expand and increase the delivery of public services to citizens, one strategy has been to make public sector managers more customer-aware and focused. Quality of service delivered is a management priority. Hospitals, schools, town halls, district councils, police and prisons, the Accountant-General's Office, the Central Electricity Board, the Central Water Authority, the Telecommunications Service and banks have been encouraged to formulate citizens' charters, in which organisations commit themselves to provide prompt, efficient, courteous, honest and fair service. A Public Service Counter-Service Award Programme has been instituted to motivate and recognise best performers and create healthy competition.

In 2003, pilots were launched on PBB, PMS and MTEF. These have been progressively extended throughout the public administration. Prior to 2003, Mauritius used a traditional budgeting system where expenditures were classified by ministries and departments. The budgets were very detailed and included several thousand line items. These were "input-orientated", with detailed *ex-ante* controls and/or rigid appropriation rules. This system does not deal with key issues of government objectives, their links to the budget, the services to be delivered by the government, and the most efficient combination of inputs to deliver services. PBB within an MTEF was the chosen solution, but the initial attempt to introduce the reform to six pilot ministries in 2003 was unsuccessful.

In 2006, the Ministry of Finance and Economic Empowerment (MoFEE) became the main reform driver of PBB. Enabling legislation included the Finance and Audit (Amendment) Act of 2008, which allows for estimates of expenditure to be submitted to the National Assembly (NA) according to programmes and sub-programmes on a three-year rolling basis, together with outputs to be delivered and outcomes to be achieved. In parallel, government has encouraged ownership by sector ministries, coherence with the reform programme, internal consistency, and programmes which are fully financed and consistent with economic reform (MoFEE 2009). The MoFEE employed a 'big bang' approach, introducing PBB to all ministries simultaneously (see Appendix 1), with related reforms such as revising the chart of accounts (COA) and implementing a new Financial Management Information System (FMIS) (UNDP 2009).

PBB in Mauritius is based on a logical planning framework. It gives the detailed costs of every programme/sub-programme, consisting of activities in a budget that clearly links the funds to outputs (the goods and services produced by government) and outcomes (changes that people perceive in their daily life, like, for example, faster travel on roads). Performance measures are identified so each activity can be accurately costed and monitored. The relationships are shown in Figure 1.

Figure 1: **The relationship between activities and performance measures**

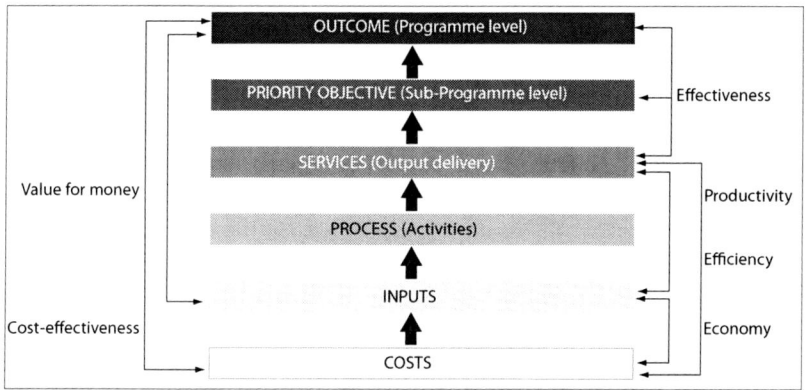

Source: Manual for Programme-Based Budgeting, MoFEE (2009)

By developing and implementing PBB, the Mauritian government aims to achieve seven objectives:

- To reform the framework governing public management to make it more results-orientated and geared towards achieving development outcomes;

- To promote high quality, client-responsive public services and to maximise value for money in service delivery;

- To use performance and evaluation data for policy planning and management purposes, in particular for enhancing operational and technical efficiency, expenditure prioritisation and optimum allocation of resources;

- To provide information to help re-allocate resources within and between programmes and sub-programmes and to help reduce expenditure (efficiency savings);
- To institutionalise gender equity throughout the process and increase the transparency and accountability of the system;
- To improve effectiveness of government ministries/departments when developing and implementing their programmes and sub-programmes of activity; and
- To provide more concrete performance information to the Cabinet for decision-making and setting future targets and priorities (MoFEE 2009).

Mauritius has a straightforward PBB statement. It is a three-fiscal-year rolling agreement between each ministry/department and the Ministry of Finance and Economic Development. It outlines the *outcomes* at the programme level, the *priority objectives* at the sub-programme level, or at the programme level when there are no sub-programmes, and *services* provided by programmes/sub-programmes (output delivery) with related performance indicators/targets (MoFEE 2009). Each ministry/department has to prepare annually a three-year rolling PBB statement, and has to elaborate or regularly update its strategic plan. This defines objectives in line with overall government priorities and includes specific actions and target outcomes as well as the ways in which the actions are to be implemented over the medium term. For example, a strategic plan will not only stipulate construction of clinics (the "what") but also indicate the process by which the results will be achieved (the "how"), including assignment of responsibility for achievement. However, some of the objectives in a strategic plan are not measurable; some of them are not a current strategic priority; and some may not be affordable within the resources currently available to the Ministry/Department (MoFEE 2009).

Analysing the Adoption and Implementation of PBB

The list of surveyed ministries and departments is given in Appendix 1. Respondents assessed PBB's perceived usefulness, benefits, pace of implementation, motivating factors, ease of implementation and difficulties. The following section discusses the survey results.

Perceived Usefulness of the PBB across Agencies

Respondents in the ministries and departments surveyed were asked whether PBB was a useful tool in their respective organisations (see Figure 2 & Figure 3). Large institutions (Ministry of Education and Human Resources, Ministry of Finance and Economic Development or the Public and Disciplined Forces Service Commissions and the Department of Civil Aviation) were more positive than smaller ministries and departments (for example, Ministry of Gender Equality, Child Development and Family Welfare).

Figure 2: **Perceived usefulness of the PBB**

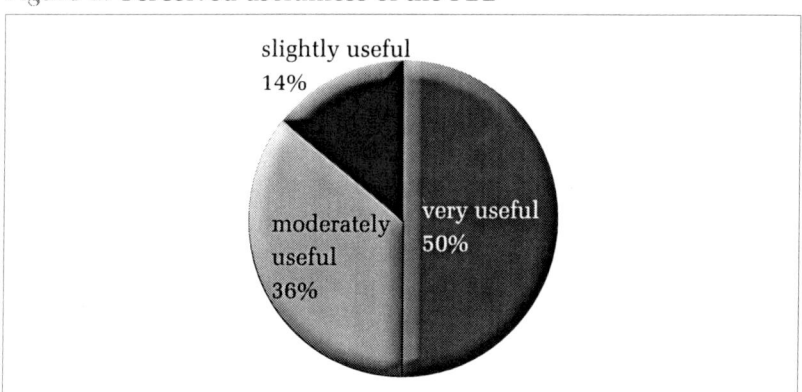

Benefits of PBB for Ministries and Departments

Survey answers ranked public accountability as the foremost benefit, with 64 per cent (14 of 22) ministries and departments stating that PBB had led to better monitoring of budgets and increased public accountability of funds used and projects undertaken. Although PBB has had mixed results in improving budget efficiency (Pressman 2011), in Mauritius it has led to clear accountability improvements, because it indicates what funds accomplish, not merely what they are spent on.

Figure 3: **Ministries' and departments' responses to whether PBB was a useful tool in their respective organisations**

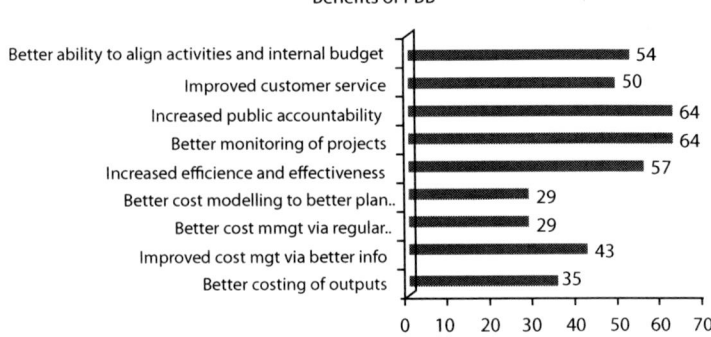

Benefits of PBB

The survey also shows that PBB leads to better monitoring of projects and a better way to align activities to organisational units. It has also led to a more meaningful costing of outputs, improved cost management via improved information, improved efficiency and effectiveness[2] of the unit, and improved customer service.

Fifty seven per cent of respondents maintain that PBB has improved the efficiency and effectiveness of each unit or department, and 54 per cent are now in a better position to align activities of units/departments and ultimately monitor properly the internal budget allocation. This is in line with previous works in different countries which argue that PBB allocates funds to achieve programmatic goals and objectives as well as some measurement of work, efficiency[3], and/or effectiveness (Snell and Hayes 1993; Garsombke and Schrad 1999; Epstein 1984). Effectiveness indices in the Ministry of Health and Quality of Life show that the number of pathological tests carried out has increased from 1.4 million in 2010 to 1.5 million in 2011, but the average access time (weeks) to specialised services has deteriorated.

PBB concentrates on performance measurement as well as customer satisfaction (Young 1998). For 43 per cent of ministries, PBB has led to improved cost management due to regular analysis; 29 per cent claim a better cost management via regular monitoring of activities; and 36 per cent postulate for a better costing of outputs. Another 29 per cent state that there has been improved cost modelling to better plan the activities of the unit/department. Many ministries have a structured and robust system in place to monitor the performance of PBB. Monitoring at quarterly intervals was the general recommendation. Despite the benefits attributed to PBB, the National Audit Report (2010) on the performance of the public sector shows incidents of misuse and wastage of public funds and assets in some ministries and departments. Cases in point were over-payment of pensions, which has been increasing from year to year, as well as misuse of government vehicles and laptops (*Ibid*).

Pace of Implementation

The survey results show 80 per cent of the ministries and departments believe PBB has been implemented in a gradual and well-structured manner, while 20 per cent believe the process was not properly established. The 2010 report from the Collaborative Africa Budget Report Initiative (CABRI) indicated that Mauritius developed a well-sequenced reform strategy and action plan in 2007, which described well the various tasks that needed to be performed, the deadline for each task and the individuals responsible. However, the report observed frequent changes during implementation, suggesting that more time could have been spent on planning the reform process and developing definitions and guidelines before actual implementation (CABRI 2010). Changes during implementation also caused misunderstanding of what was required in terms of defining outcomes, outputs and performance indicators, and undermined confidence in the PBB concept. There is still a lack of clarity regarding definitions, which has resulted in inconsistencies in the way performance information is used in PBB documentation (*Ibid*).

Motivating Factors to Adopt PBB

On the "why" behind adoption of PBB, a point system was used to prioritise the factors - first-ranked scored 10, second scored 8, third 6, fourth 4, and the one ranked last scored 2. Table 2 shows that "better budget monitoring" emerges as the leading motivation. Budget monitoring comprises tracking and registering operations, and their use of appropriations; it covers appropriations, apportionment, any increase or decrease in appropriations, commitments/obligations, expenditure at the verification/delivery stage, and the payments system. Similar studies show the main motivation is to enable policy and decision makers to track progress and demonstrate the impact of a given project, programme or policy (Kusek and Rist 2003; MoFEE 2009). Lack of budget monitoring and recording makes sound analysis of input use, outputs, or outcomes impossible. In order of priority, other motivating factors include: greater level of accountability, better performance assessment, greater transparency, better disclosure of methodologies used, and mutually beneficial relationships across different stakeholders.

Table 2:   **Ranking of motivating factors in adopting PBB**

Characteristics	Score	Percentage
Better monitoring - results and indicators are vital for continuous monitoring across the entire results chain from inputs, outputs, outcomes and impacts	214	17.6
Greater level of accountability	200	16.5
Better performance assessment - broad dissemination and active discussion of performance information (progress made toward the achievement of outcomes)	192	15.8
Greater transparency	184	15.2
Better disclosure of the methodologies used to collect valid and reliable performance indicators	178	14.7
Mutually beneficial relationships based on trust among the different stakeholders involved in a project.	138	11.4
Simple procedure	98	8.1
Others	10	0.8

Source: Authors' compilation

Ease of Adopting and Implementation of PBB and Difficulties Faced

Many respondents (58 per cent) found implementation very complex; only the Public and Disciplined Forces Service Commission found adoption of PBB an easy process.

The survey highlighted six main difficulties, all receiving roughly equal weight – 16–18 per cent – (see Figure 2). Marginally heading the list was lack of staff training, followed by the radical change from the existing system. Further difficulties were additional administrative work, the time-consuming burden of detailed procedures, and difficulty in fully understanding the new system. A critical area was the complicated nature of estimating the actual costs of public sector activities. In the private sector, estimation of costs for activities is relatively easy as data are available at a very detailed level. The design of public sector accounts makes information on all input costs, in particular at a disaggregated level, difficult to obtain. Estache, Gonzalez, and Trujillo (2007) stress that public budgets are not really designed to track down specific sectoral expenditure.

Figure 4: **Ranking of difficulties encountered in adopting PBB**

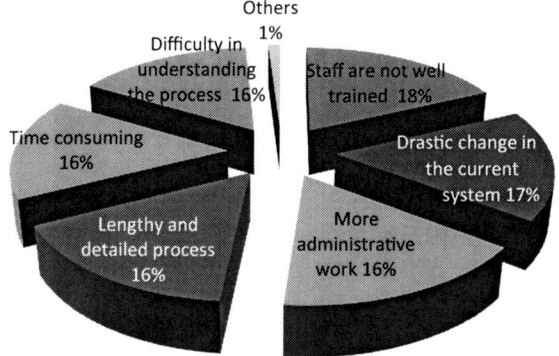

Data from interviews and documents indicate that a tailor-made training programme using 12 modules was provided for Mauritian officials. External consultants trained approximately 65 people from the parent ministry, line ministries and universities; the best 15 were chosen to become trainers, and they then trained 400 officers from a range of line ministries. This first round of training was fairly broad, and was followed by mentoring and support from IMF experts. More specific, specialised training (sometimes taking the form of extensive consultation) was developed at the request of individual ministries. At the time of the training, a PBB manual was developed to assist understanding and implementation in a multi-year framework.

Nevertheless, line-ministry officials felt that too few people were trained. Most of the training was given to persons involved in finance, and not enough to those involved in developing policy and implementing service delivery. In some instances, it was felt that the 15 chosen trainers were inexperienced, having just received training themselves, had not had the opportunity to internalise practical implementation of PBB before training others. Respondents considered the training programmes were too compact, with insufficient time allocated to sessions. In hindsight, many officials would have liked to spend more time on training prior to, as well as during implementation.

Reports from Collaborative Africa Budget Report Initiative (CABRI 2010) echo these problems and note that although the Ministry of Finance and Economic Development made a concerted effort to provide training, most officials from the line-ministries felt that it did not go far enough, and that this shortfall limited their ability to implement PBB successfully (CABRI 2010). Currently, no training is taking place. This especially affects officers who are new to the civil service (*Ibid*).

Conclusion

In just five years, the Mauritian government has made great progress in the implementation of PBB. The Ministry of Finance and Economic Development has managed to instil a sense of performance orientation throughout the government. Recognising that implementation is still in the early stages, there remains much to be done to reap the benefits of aligning resource allocation to policy priorities and improving service delivery.

While PBB may not have met all expectations, it constitutes a major step forward in comparison to old-fashioned input budgeting. There is still room for improvement in some spheres and some key elements for successful implementation, based on other countries' experience, need to be considered. For instance, one of the major shortcomings of the Mauritian PBB was lack of training. Introducing PBB requires intensive training of officials, so ministry personnel have a good understanding of the concepts and the system by the time of implementation. More capacity-building is required to deepen the understanding of officials ranging from operational levels to top management.

Enabling ministries and departments to design their own programme structure fosters a sense of ownership. For some ministries in the study, the adoption of the PBB system was not well established. Thus, a gradual approach may be most appropriate given the magnitude of change that PBB involves. The advantage of a gradual approach is to make sure the new budget system is accepted and well understood and, at the same time, allow time for other ministries to learn more about the new system and its effects. There is also a need to institute systems to monitor and evaluate programme performance. The system should include quality assurance arrangements and the use of IT facilities to support the production of progress reports.

Appendix 1: List of ministries and departments and implementation date of the PBB

Ministries and Departments	Implementation Date
Ministries	
Ministry of Health and Quality of Life (MOH) – Pilot Phase in 2007	2007
Ministry of Tourism and Leisure (MOT)	2008
Prime Minister's Office (PMO)	2008
Ministry of Local Government and Outer Islands (MLG)	2008
Ministry of Gender Equality, Child Development and Family Welfare (MOG)	2009
Ministry of Finance and Economic Development (MOFED)	2008
Ministry of Information and Communication Technology (MICT)	2008
Ministry of Environment and Sustainable Development (MESD)	2008
Ministry of Industry and Commerce (MIC)	2008

Table Continued	
Ministry of Labour, International Relations and Employment (MOL)	2008
Ministry of Education and Human Resources (MEHR)	2008
Ministry of Housing and Lands (MHL)	2008
Ministry of Public Infrastructure (MPI)	2008
Ministry of Arts and Culture (MAC)	2008
Ministry of Social Security, National Solidarity and Reform Institutions (MSSNSRI)	2008
Ministry of Energy and Public Utilities (MEPU)	2009
Ministry of Agro-Industry and Fisheries (MAIF)	2011
Departments	
Public and Disciplines Forced (PDF)	2008
Companies Division (CD)	2008
Department of Civil Aviation (DCA)	2008
Department of Prisons (DP)	2009
National Audit Office (NAO)	2009

Source: Authors' Compilation

Notes

1   In all we obtained 22 responses, the Principal Factor Analysis could not be applied since the minimum sample size for applying this method is 50.

2   **Effectiveness Measures:** These are the indices that assess how well a programme achieved its goals and objectives; for instance, percent of wetlands preserved as a result of permit issuance; percent of inmates convicted of another crime after release, percent of placements successful after 30 days.

3   **Efficiency Measures:** These are indices that assess or compare how much output was achieved per unit of input (costs); for example, cost per complaint processed, cost per license issued, cost per prisoner incarcerated.

References

African Development Bank Group (ADBG), OECD Development Centre, UNDP, and UNECA. 2009. African Economic Outlook, Mauritius 2009. www.africaneconomicoutlook.org. (accessed on February, 2011)

———.2010. African Economic Outlook, Mauritius 2010. www.africaneconomicoutlook.org.(accessed on February, 2011)

Aucoin, P. 1990. Administrative reform in public management: Paradigms, principles, paradoxes and pendulums. *Governance*, 3: 115–137.

Collaborative Africa Budget Reform Initiative (CABRI). 2010. *CABRI joint country case study*. London: CABRI.

Epstein, P. D. 1984. *Using performance measurement in local government: A guide to improving decisions, performance, and accountability*. New York, NY: Van Nostrand Reinhold Company, Inc.

Estache, A., Gonzalez, M., Trujillo, L. 2007. *Government expenditures on education, health and infrastructure: A naïve look at levels, outcomes and efficiency*. City University London, *Department of* Economics, Discussion Paper Series: 07/03.

Garsombke, H. P. and Schrad, J. 1999. Performance measurement systems: Results from a city and state survey. *Government Finance Review:* 4.

Kusek, J. Z. and R. C. Rist. 2003. Readiness assessment: Toward performance monitoring and evaluation in the Kyrgyz Republic. *Japanese Journal of Evaluation Studies*, 3(1): 17–31.

Laffin, M. and M. Painter. 1995. *Reform and reversal*. Melbourne: Macmillan.

Mauritius International Investment Forum. 2011. Celebrating 10 years of progress: Board of Investment. http://www.miif.mu/Mauritius.aspx (accessed on February, 2011)

Ministry of Civil Service and Administrative Reforms. 2008. *Guidelines on providing quality counter/customer services*. Republic of Mauritius.

Ministry of Finance and Economic Empowerment (MoFEE). 2009. Programme-based budgeting manual. Mauritius.

Minogue, M. 2001. The internationalization of new public management. In *The internationalization of public management: Reinventing the Third World state*, McCourt, W. and M. Minogue (Eds.), pp. 1–19. Northampton: Edward Elgar Publishing, MA.

National Audit Office. 2010. *National audit report 2010*. Mauritius: National Audit Office.

Pollitt, C. and Bouckaert G. 2000. Public management reform: A comparative analysis. New York: Oxford University Press.

Pressman. 2011. http://www.brighthub.com/office/entrepreneurs/articles/123697.aspx. (accessed on February, 2011)

Robinson, M. and Last D. 2009. A basic model of performance-based budgeting. International Monetary Fund, Fiscal Affairs Department.

Rose, A. 2003. *Results-oriented budget practice in OECD Countries*. London, UK: Overseas Development Institute.

Segal G. and Summers, A. 2002. Citizens' budget reports: Improving performance and accountability in government. Reason Public Policy Institute, Policy Study, 292: 4. http://heartland.org/sites/all/modules/custom/heartland_migration/files/pdfs/8771.pdf (accessed on February, 2011)

Snell, R. and Hayes K. 1993. Performance budgeting and the states. Presented to the Nebraska Legislative Appropriations Committee. Lincoln, NB.

State Services Commission. 2002. Public service chief executives *http://www.ssc.govt.nz/CEs/CEs.asp?MenuID=4&Content=CEs/CEs.asp.* (accessedon on February 2011)

Statistics Mauritius. 2011. National Accounts Estimates (2008–2011). Mauritius.

Statistics Mauritius. 2010. Digest of Public Finance Statistics (2009) Mauritius.

Tügen K., Akdeniz, H., Aksarayi, M., Egeli, H. and Özen, A. 2009. Critical control points on performance-based budgeting system. *Review of Social, Economic and Business Studies*, 9(10): 161–178.

UNDP. 2009. Strategic budgeting in the government of Mauritius, April 2007–March 2009. UNDP Mauritius.

Van Nispen, Frans K.M. and Johan J.A. Posseth. 2006. Performance budgeting in the Netherlands: Beyond arithmetic. *OECD Journal of Budgeting* 6 (4): 1–26.

World Bank. 2012. *Doing business 2012*. Washington, D.C.: World Bank.

Young, R. D. 1998. A statewide strategic planning process: The need for the state's leadership in South Carolina to plan ahead. Unpublished manuscript. University of South Carolina.

Chapter 11

Good Intentions, Poor Results: Reforming the Academic Organisational Structure and Performance Management System at the University of Botswana

Keene Boikhutso

Abstract

In the wider context of examining public sector reforms in sub-Saharan Africa, this chapter uses the University of Botswana as a case study on two reforms: revision of the academic organisational structure and introduction of a Performance Management System (PMS). It assesses the choice of objectives and methods (the good intentions) and follows both design and implementation (the less positive results) to better understand the processes, to identify key challenges and mistakes, and to draw lessons which might guide remedy and future efforts. Information was collected through interviewing 20 members of academic staff in the faculties of Education and Humanities; and content analysis of official documentation such as the university's Strategic Plan to 2016 and Beyond, a proposal paper for restructuring, and Minutes of the Faculty of Education Board Meetings. This chapter finds that reform failed to bring the desired transformation of performance; indeed, the restructuring programme was suspended during the course of this study, and the PMS project faces widespread internal dissatisfaction and some active resistance.

Introduction

Public sector reforms (PSR) in Botswana straddle performance management systems, human resource management, job evaluation, work improvement teams, public information management, transparency, national integrity and anti-corruption. These are applied to central government, local governments and state-owned enterprises (Hope, 1995). The state-owned enterprises include the University of Botswana (UB), the Botswana Development Corporation, the Botswana Meat Commission, the Botswana Telecommunications Corporation, the Botswana Housing Corporation and the Botswana National Development Bank (Crisculo and Vincent 2008; Simwanza and Samaratunge 2010).

The reforms have been implemented within the broader framework of the New Public Management (NPM) movement taking place in many countries (Simwanza and Samaratunge 2010). The NPM is part of the neo-liberal ideology that sees PSR, among other things, as an avenue for attracting foreign investment and creating employment (Marobela 2008). To consolidate these initiatives, the Botswana government has set up a specialised training body, the Botswana National Productivity Centre (BNPC), to facilitate productivity and quality improvement programmes (Andrews, 2006). The BNPC is similar in origin and mandate to the Ghana Institute of Management and Public Administration (*Ibid*). Botswana also established the Botswana Institute for Development Policy Analysis (BIDPA) to act as an external policy advisor to the government (*Ibid*).

The UB is one of the few publicly-funded organisations that have dominated Botswana's higher education landscape since independence. Government has constantly called on the UB to restructure its programmes in line with development objectives and national policies, especially to tackle human resource shortages which have bedevilled the country since independence in 1966. The UB is working to transform itself from a predominantly teaching institution to a research-intensive organisation, more tuned to the trend of a knowledge-based world economy.

The UB wants to be at the cutting edge of innovation and knowledge creation driven by neo-liberal reforms and globalisation. In 2006, the university initiated a strategic planning exercise to facilitate effective teaching and learning, advance excellence in research, improve economic and social development, provide high-quality programmes, promote a research strategy and culture, strengthen international collaboration and local community involvement, and build a graduate employability strategy (University of Botswana 2008 a & b). It has developed an organisational structure accordingly, and has introduced a Performance Management System (PMS), which aims to deliver 360-degree evaluation of teaching based on standardised competency rating scales by students, peers and supervisors.

This chapter analyses the process involved in initiating, designing and implementing academic restructuring and PMS; examines the intended and unintended outcomes; and discusses the differences and similarities of the reforms in terms of design, implementation and outcomes. While these two sets of reforms are intricately tied together, they are tackled as separate for the purpose of systematic analysis.

This study used interviews and document analysis as complementary tools. The respondents were 20 academic staff drawn mainly from the Faculty of Education and the Faculty of Humanities, who are actively involved in the teaching and learning process and are members of faculty leadership. Face-to-face interviews were conducted in the first two weeks of February 2011 and e-mail interviews during the last two weeks of July 2011. The study also relied on content analysis of the following documents:

- A strategy for Excellence: University of Botswana Strategic Plan to 2016 and Beyond;
- Proposal Paper: Revision of the Academic Organisational Structure; and
- Minutes of Faculty of Education Board Meetings.

Section 1 provides the introduction. Section 2 highlights the concepts of restructuring higher education and performance-based measurement systems. Section 3 analyses the reforms, and Section 4 looks at the results and draws lessons.

Defining Restructuring and Performance Management in Higher Education Systems

Higher education institutions in Africa have been beleaguered by the twin challenges of rapid enrolment increase and declining educational quality (World Bank 2008; King 2005; Swayerr 2004; World Bank 1997). Enrolment at African universities more than trebled from 181,000 to 600,000 between 1975 and 1980 and nearly trebled again to 1,750,000 by 1995 (Swayerr 2004). Public subventions – the main source of higher education funding in Africa – were not adequately provided to enable the hugely expanded universities to provide a quality learning environment (*Ibid*). This was mainly due to the collapse of national economies across Africa, especially in the 1980s and 1990s, that resulted in sharp reductions in governments' capacity to support universities, especially amid heightened competition for resources from other social and economic sectors (World Bank 2008; Swayerr 2004). The consequent fall in quality had a disastrous effect on the learning environment. Facilities built for a small student population became so overcrowded that some students had to take lessons while standing and others had to listen from outside the lecture rooms (Swayerr 2004).

Higher education institutions in Africa have since undertaken major reforms and strategic planning to address the quality and relevance of their academic programmes (Sawyerr 2004). The overriding concern has been to raise the standard of higher education through the use of quality assurance audits of institutional teaching and learning processes (Chalmers 2008; Sawyerr 2004; Burke, Minassians and Yang 2002).

Academic restructuring essentially focuses on the 'value' added to students in terms of satisfaction with the quality of their experience and the quality of skills they develop (Chalmers 2008; Romainville 1999). It ensures that learning outcomes are aligned with the student's needs as the customer (*Ibid*). It is also expected to address the key problem of rapid enrolment that is causing decline in educational quality which then undermines the contribution of higher education to economic growth. It also involves the design of new curricula, courses and academic programmes tailored to the needs of the labour market (University of Botswana 2010; World Bank 2008). Such restructuring can, however, have unexpected and possibly negative consequences as it can lead to a gap between how executive managers and their subordinates perceive the quality of educational programmes, student satisfaction, learning and teaching policies (Chalmers 2008; Borden and Bottrill 1994).

PMS is a continuous process of systematically and effectively evaluating performance, providing feedback and assessing the present and potential capabilities of human resources (Nyaoga *et al.* 2010). According to Davis (1995), it is a process in which both the supervisor and supervised identify common goals which correlate with the university's strategic plans. The joint effort itself improves efficiency, productivity and morale.

PMS can be traced to the use of management control, budget control systems, setting targets, and techniques of performance assessment which were designed as steering mechanisms in business organisations and intended to help organisations achieve specific objectives (Nyaoga *et al.* 2010). At higher education institutions, PMS and other forms of performance appraisal are designed to provide documented, constructive feedback regarding performance expectations and an equitable means to determine rewards for contributions to the university (Rogers 1995; Nyaoga *et al.* 2010). Among strategies to measure teaching effectiveness are student evaluation of teaching, which includes student ratings; peer ratings; self-evaluation; administrator ratings; and teaching portfolios using multiple sources of evidences (Berk 2005; Artley and Stroh 2001).

Higher Education Reforms in Botswana

Since the early 1990s, Botswana's long-standing international reputation as a nation with sound development management was tarnished (Hope 1995). Principles of honesty and integrity appeared to be giving way to creeping corruption, and public service standards declined (Hope 1995; Moleboge 2003). This concern was translated into a series of reform measures designed to bring about rapid remedy (*Ibid*). Botswana's commitment to reform was also partly the result of a continuous quest to increase efficiency (Simwanza and Samaratunge 2010).

An underlying problem Botswana has faced since independence is lack of high-level and skilled human resource. The country has relied on expatriates to fill the gap. To build local capacity through higher education, the government introduced the Organisation and Methods (O&M) review strategy. This covers all ministries, departments, local governments and parastatals (including the UB). O&M is designed to improve the institutional capacity of the public sector; to enable it to implement development policy and meet national objectives by improving organisational arrangements, accountability and operational work procedures (Hope 1995). In this regard, higher education organisations, like the UB, the Botswana Institute of Administration and Commerce (BIAC) and the Institute of Development Management (IDM) have constantly restructured their programmes to conform to the country's development objectives and national policies. For example, in the early 1990s the IDM and the UB introduced a certificate programme in local government administration and a Master's Degree in public administration as part of capacity-building (*Ibid*).

Academic Organisational Restructure at the UB

The University of Botswana (UB) was established in 1982 by an Act of Parliament. Previously it was called the University of Botswana, Lesotho and Swaziland (UBLS). The main campus was based in Lesotho with two small satellite campuses in Botswana and Swaziland. However, in 1975 the Lesotho government nationalised the main campus to form its own national university. The remaining University of Botswana and Swaziland (UBS) operated for seven years before formal inauguration of a stand-alone University of Botswana (University of Botswana 2010/2011)

The UB's first-year intake was 1,200 students, projected to increase to 2,400 over the following two decades. But after one decade, the growth was revised first to 6,000 and then to 10,000 (Republic of Botswana 1993). All three forecasts did not work and according to the Institutional Research Unit (2009), in 2003/04, the UB had a total student enrolment of 15,425. Of this number, 13,104 were full time, 2,080 part time, and 241 were distance learners. However, enrolment figures fluctuated significantly and, in 2008/09, total enrolment was down to 14,420. The decline was wholly in the full time student cadre (13 per cent down) while part time enrolments increased by about 36 per cent in the same period. The disaggregated figures for 2008, according to academic programmes, were as follows: Certificate 13, Diploma 2,450, Bachelors Degree 10,541, Postgraduate Diploma 239, Master's Degree 1,089, and MPhil/PhD 88 (University of Botswana, 2011a). In 2011, total enrolment was up again, and the entire increase was in the full time cadre, with part time and distance learning enrolments holding steady. The number of staff (academic, support and industrial) in 2011 was 2, 805, of which the academic staff was 813 or 29 per cent (*Ibid*).

A cursory look at the organogram of the UB shows that at the apex of the structure is the Chancellor of the University, whose role is largely ceremonial. The UB Council is the top decision-making body that approves policies on academic affairs, finance and administration, student affairs and institutional planning. The Executive Management is headed by the Vice Chancellor who is the Chief Executive Officer of the UB, assisted by three Deputy Vice Chancellors (Academic Affairs, Finance and Administration, and Student Affairs). In particular, the Deputy Vice Chancellor (Academic Affairs) oversees the Deans and faculties, academic development, library services and research and development (University of Botswana, 2009/10). Then, there are the faculties and their respective non-executive Deans, who oversee academic programming and course development in their faculties under the supervision of the Deputy Vice Chancellor (Academic Affairs).

Currently there are seven faculties - Business, Education, Engineering and Technology, Health Sciences, Humanities, Science, and Social Sciences. There are also two schools – the School of Graduate Studies and the Medical School – and their Deans. In addition, there are academic centres and their Directors — the Office of Research and Development (ORD), the Centre for Continuing Education (CCE) and the Okavango Research Institute (OR) based in Maun, and the Centre for Academic Development (CAD). Attached to the UB are affiliates, like nursing institutions and colleges of education, and the Botswana College of Agriculture (University of Botswana 2011a).

At inception, the UB offered limited courses and programmes at diploma, first degree and Master's levels in education, humanities, social sciences and sciences (Republic of Botswana 1993). However, in the 2010/11 academic year students were enrolled in 16 academic programmes at the certificate and diploma levels. During this year there were 52 Bachelors Degree programmes, two postgraduate Diploma programmes, 40 Master's Degree programmes and 26 MPhil/PhD programmes (University of Botswana 2011a).

The first of several phases of restructuring was initiated in the late 1980s, involving largely administrative and management reforms, giving the executive more powers on day-to-day governance. A second phase of restructuring in 2002 was the replacement of the year-long academic programme with a "semesterised" system (Daka 2008; Tanna and Kumar 2002). Under the latter system, students are examined twice per year to allow those who failed one or two courses to proceed to the next level while re-sitting the failed courses, instead of wasting their own and university resources by repeating the entire year (Gabathuse 2004). The system also allowed more flexible tailoring of programmes. However, the semester set up was beset by challenges, often arising from inconsistent interpretation and application of regulations, and the use of a manual system. This was ameliorated in 2007 through revision of the academic regulations and computerised implementation (Daka 2008).

The latest phase of restructuring, which started in 2008, was a major university overhaul to address the rise of the knowledge-based economy; high growth in student numbers putting extra strain on quality; reluctance of government to fund a rapidly expanding sector, leading to a new dimension of private enrolments and institutions; and the need for the UB to fit in the international academic discourse. In its battle to survive and become a centre of excellence, the UB used an all-stakeholder strategic planning exercise and SWOT anaysis (University of Botswana 2010). These consultative processes unanimously called for a change to the university's academic structure, to transform it from a predominantly teaching function into a research-intensive institution (*Ibid*).

In 2008, an independent consultancy report concluded that re-organisation was imperative for the UB to survive competition from within and outside Botswana. In the same year, the UB Council approved its Strategic Plan for 2009-2016 and Beyond. This strategy envisioned coherent, inter-disciplinary and more efficient and effective academic operations and management (*Ibid*). In the second half of 2009, the Academic Affairs Divisional Management Team visited other higher education institutions in the region on a fact-finding and benchmarking mission.

At the beginning of 2010, a proposal paper called "Revision of Academic Organisational Structure" was presented to the various faculties for adoption. At this juncture, the UB was grappling with two main issues:

- competition from other providers, both public and private, both locally and internationally; and

- the new mode of funding that was phasing out treatment of the UB as a department of government (including salary levels and increases) and developing new forms of financing such as 'third stream' approaches (University of Botswana 2010).

The concept of 'third stream' funding is modelled on the blueprint of the United Kingdom's Higher Education Innovation Fund. It is a collaborative effort between businesses and community to support higher education's contribution to economic development through engagement in 'knowledge exchange' or 'knowledge transfer'. Universities that engage with business receive a significant increase in state funding (HEFCE 2011; Hatakenaka 2005).

The UB's academic re-organisation follows six over-arching principles:

- institutional expansion, including enrolment growth and new fields of study;

- international status and visibility;

- intellectual focus which requires inter-disciplinarity and avoidance of duplication;

- institutional coherence;

- institutional effectiveness where bureaucracy does more to enable and ensure than to obstruct academic goals; and

- decentralisation, giving Deans of faculty greater administrative and financial autonomy.

The prevailing structure comprised seven faculties housing 43 departments and two schools. The proposed structure called for the disestablishment of departments and the introduction of inter-disciplinary programmes, defined as a "plan of study lasting for a specified period that leads to a qualification and which has a related set of research activities" (University of Botswana 2010,11). The school was defined as an "academic unit that links cognate and related subject disciplines to facilitate the generation, application and teaching of inter-disciplinary knowledge" (*Ibid*). The Faculty was conceptualised as a "strategic unit that brings together a group of cognate and related schools to facilitate strategic planning, effective management, optimal resource usage, and the quality of education, research and engagement activities" (*Ibid*). So, the new faculties would be sub-divided into schools rather than departments, and some existing faculties would be merged.

Decentralisation was a key driver, in the interests of "more efficient and effective academic operations and management" (University of Botswana 2010,17). Accordingly, the Vice Chancellor and the three Deputy Vice Chancellors (Academic Affairs, Finance and Administration, and Student Welfare) would retain their positions but with reduced responsibilities and duties. A fourth Deputy Vice Chancellor would be appointed with responsibility for graduate studies and research. Academic Deans would be replaced by a new Executive Deans cadre, whose management responsibilities would include finance and entrepreneurship to diversify funding sources; human resources; information technology; oversight on teaching, research engagement; and facilitation of academic services. The Executive Dean was to report to the Deputy Vice Chancellor Academic Affairs, but also oversee the mainly administrative Heads of School, who in turn would supervise Programme Co-ordinators who were to look after curriculum development, implementation, review, programme quality, teaching and research, and management of student experience (University of Botswana 2010).

Perceptions of Members of Academic Staff Towards Restructuring at the UB

As one of the objectives of restructuring higher education is to enhance academic performance and value, academic staff are key stakeholders and their perceptions and opinions matter. In this study, a number of academic staff members were asked to give their personal assessment regarding their degree of involvement, the amount of consultation, the pace of implementation of reform, and any gaps in the design and implementation of restructuring.

The perception of the respondents on degree of involvement of the staff is given in Table 1.

Table 1: **Level and nature of staff involvement in restructuring**

Nature of Involvement	Number of Responses
High involvement	0
Moderate involvement: at committee level; commented on documents discussed at departmental and faculty board meetings	6
Minimal involvement: mere attendance at departmental and faculty board meetings	10
Not involved at all	4

Accompanying comments from the less-involved (majority) included: "I am only being told what will happen and where I will fit in the restructuring. Individuals with their own agenda are attempting to realise them." Another respondent observed that "... it seems decisions have been made elsewhere and just sent to us for formality's sake." At the extreme: "The authorities will do what they want to do." In sum, it would appear that the consultation processes was generally weak.

An in-depth interview with one key informant who participated in activities tasked to spear-head the formation of a Centre for Enhancement of Learning and Teaching (CELT) revealed that restructuring was not only sensitive but was also "bound to fail." This informant indicated that some groups in the university were key drivers of the reform while others were by-standers. The formation of CELT was a case in point. It was to be created by merging the existing Centre for Academic Development (CAD) and part of the Centre for Continuing Education (CCE). In the process, the CAD staff were active in the restructuring but the CCE staff did not know specifically what restructuring had in store for them. The respondent noted there had been rumours that people involved in working committees already had posts waiting for them. Some of the rumours had been propelled by lack of information and lack of buy-in into the reform effort.

The second survey question was on the amount of consultation involved and the pace of implementation of the restructuring process. Four (20 per cent) of the respondents thought that the fast pace of restructuring did not allow adequate time for consultations with all the stakeholders. Five (25 per cent) thought implementation lacked coordination and adequate consultation with all crucial stakeholders. 8 (40 per cent) thought the pace of implementation was very fast while the other 3 (15 per cent) said it was too early to evaluate the exercise. One respondent stated that "...it looks like the university has a well laid out roadmap — crucial dates have been set and the restructuring is unfolding. The momentum is high but most people are like passengers on the way to an uncertain destination." Another respondent said "...there is a serious cause for concern in every aspect. The pace is just too high and stakeholders are not able to digest and feedback meaningfully. It is already predetermined from above."

The third survey question explored issues on design and planning gaps. Some respondents were worried about retrenchment and exit packages, contract obstacles, as well as permanent and pensionable appointments. Others revealed concerns regarding staff promotion opportunities, confusing supervisory roles in "lumped-together" and "huge" and "bureaucratic" structures. One respondent observed that the merging of the Faculty of Education and the Faculty of Humanities into the new Faculty of Arts and Education "...will be like another university inside the UB."

The level of staff involvement and consultation was not impressive. It would appear that the UB top management tended to focus on the hardware of reforms – strategic plans, income generation and cost-cutting — but ignored the core business of universities, which is the promotion of effective learning and teaching and research output that is dependent on the all-important software aspect of the reform: human beings.

PMS at the University of Botswana

The University of Botswana introduced the PMS in 2005 (University of Botswana 2005). The university had hitherto used the academic staff annual appraisal system, with staff completing annual forms and meeting with heads of department to discuss issues. Such meetings produced a brief report which was subsequently used for status review in terms of confirmation, crossing the proficiency bar in the pay structure, renewal of contract, or promotion (Dzimbiri 2009). A weakness was that "...whatever one did was what was appraised, irrespective of whether it had a bearing on the objectives and goals of the department, faculty or the university" (*Ibid*:4). Under the 2005 PMS, however, performance measures are aligned to the organisation's mission, vision, values and strategic goals (University of Botswana 2005; Artley and Stroh 2001).

The planning and design of the PMS project was driven by an Internal Project Team (IPT) advised by external consultants (University of Botswana 2005). Working groups had representatives from each key structure - services, academic disciplines, human resources and the Centre for Academic Development, but in practice the general process was a top-down approach dominated by the senior management team (Dzimbiri 2009). In designing the PSM, the UB did not conduct a thorough environmental scan to identify factors that could affect the successful implementation of the PMS (*Ibid*). The steering committee, chaired by the Vice Chancellor, ultimately approved the PMS manual and other policy documents (University of Botswana 2005).

An integral part of the PSM is student evaluation of courses and teaching (SECAT). So, the SECAT was revised to align with the dictates of the PMS (University of Botswana 2005). In the SECAT, students complete a three-section questionnaire. The first two sections contain closed (convergent) questions, on teaching and courses, respectively. Evaluation is based on a five-point scale offering: poor, satisfactory, good, very good and excellent. A third section asks open-ended (divergent) questions based on the appraisal.

In the first section on teaching, items to be ranked include the extent to which the lecturer: helps students learn and understand course material; explains concepts; organises content; encourages students to express their own view; has an effective management style; gives marking and feedback; engenders interest in the subject matter; and is available to take personal interest in the progress of students.

The second section on course evaluation focuses on: clarity and coverage of learning objectives; course organisation; contribution of course materials like readings, written assignments, handouts, small group discussion, tutorials and tests.

Examples of open-ended questions in the third section are: *what did you like most about the lecturer? What did you like most about the course?* Students are also asked to reflect on and explain some of their ratings.

In order to study the process of implementation of the PMS at the UB, 20 academic staff were interviewed using semi-structured questionnaires. The survey was intended to assess the degree of acceptance of the PSM. As shown in Table 2, there was a lot of resistance from academic staff.

Table 2: **Resistance to implementation of the PMS**

Nature of resistance	Number of Responses
There is a lot of resistance to the PMS	15
There is a fair amount of resistance to the PMS	3
Not sure	2
There is no resistance to the PMS	0

Through in-depth interview, it emerged that some members of academic staff refused to sign PMS contracts. Some interviewees also stressed that strike action by the UB staff was partly related to the PMS. One of the respondents observed that "...people seem not to understand what the intentions really are; even those who run the PMS seem to be confused - nobody really understands it."

Interview results show a large measure of scepticism and dissatisfaction. Here is a litany of comments:

- "I have a feeling that no one likes the PMS"; "...a lot of resistance and animosity..emanates from the fact that when it comes to remuneration the management seems not to have clear system of rewards. It frustrates folk most of the time";

- "PMS demands and involves a lot of paperwork in addition to the lecturers' core business of research and teaching... very few people are certain about what the PMS wants from them."

- "The idea of 'forced distribution' based on the PMS scores is seen as 'a deliberate strategy by senior management to deal with what they perceive to be unduly high ratings - perhaps most disturbingly, the Head of Department can apparently deduct points on a case-by-case basis, unilaterally."

Generally, the PMS was perceived to lack adequate consultation in its design and implementation. Some respondents, however, noted that the PMS provides at least some framework and roadmap. It is seen as helpful (in principle more than in practice) in target-setting; planning; evaluation; accountability; audit of performance and efficiency; enhancement of productivity; creation of teaching portfolios; and monetary rewards. Respondent statements endorsing this include: "Since the PMS is evidence-based, it encourages research and publication."

These interview results are consistent with the experience of Malaysia, where almost identical reforms have been implemented. Lack of ownership, absence of consistent performance standards, lack of standardised criteria and methods for performance evaluation are cited as issues plaguing the Malaysian system (Shafie 1996). Perceptions at the UB are the same.

Conclusion

The key findings of this study are that the UB's reforms were implemented too quickly and without adequate consultation among all stakeholders. This is a well established recipe for resistance and failure. In April 2011, restructuring was suspended pending further consultation of all stakeholders both within and outside the university. In a memorandum addressed to the university community two weeks after his appointment, the new Vice Chancellor noted:

It has come to my attention that as a result of... implementation of the revision of the academic organisational structure, there is confusion regarding the official status of the envisaged and existing organisational structure, functioning, roles, and responsibilities... As a new Vice Chancellor, I need an opportunity to carefully study the ideas that are contained in the proposed revision... and satisfy all stakeholders and myself that adequate provisions are in place to address the practical issues that may arise at the stage of implementing a major organisational change (University of Botswana, Office of the Vice Chancellor 2011b, 1–2).

Although "new" to his current post, the Vice Chancellor is one of the longest serving members of the UB community.

Similarly, the design and implementation of the PMS at the UB adopted a top-down approach, which equates to lack of consultation. Some sections of the academic staff are advocating that the exercise be suspended pending further review.

The revision of the academic organisational structure and the implementation of the PMS at the UB offer valuable insight for higher education policy makers in Africa.

Firstly, higher education is a complex and 'high stakes game' with the possibility of producing potential 'winners' and 'losers.' Top managers and their subordinates tend to perceive organisational and institutional reforms differently. For example, generally, top managers experience restructuring as bringing about organisational and institutional efficiency and accountability. In contrast, subordinates perceive restructuring as bringing uncertainty to their daily operations.

Secondly, well articulated reforms at the planning and formulation phase do not guarantee a successful implementation phase. It is evident that the planning cycles for both restructuring and the PMS at the UB were well thought out (with the exception of heavy reliance on the 'top-down' approach to planning) and guided by good intentions. However, implementation of reforms was somewhat 'hijacked' by well positioned individuals with entrenched perceptions and vested interests. Failure to implement restructuring also stemmed from lack of 'buy-in' by subordinates who had limited awareness about the positive and negative impacts.

Thirdly, the PMS project is still being implemented despite widespread resistance.

The question arises: is the implementation of the PMS at the UB achieving the desired goals? The results of this study highlight the danger of going ahead with reforms without drawing lessons from past mistakes and challenges which might guide remedy and future efforts. The puzzling thing is that the PMS office is now undertaking some initiatives to revamp the PMS although still following the 'top-down' planning model. In fact, this is a recipe for failure because the success of any organisational reform is contingent upon 'ownership' by the end-users: that is, subordinates.

Lastly, in coming up with public sector reforms, policy makers need to take into account both the expected outcomes and unexpected outcomes with a view of putting mitigating strategies in place.

References

Andrews, M. 2006. Beyond 'best practice' and 'basics first' in adopting performance budgeting reforms. *Public Administration and Development* 26: 147–161.

Artley, W. and Stroh, S. 2001. *The performance-based management handbook:* A six-volume compilation of tools and techniques for implementing the Government Performance and Results Act of 1993. Performance-Based Management Special Interest Group. Retrieved on 20th March, 2011 from http://www.orau.gov/pbm .

Berk, A. R. 2005. Survey of 12 strategies to measure teaching effectiveness. *International Journal of Teaching and Learning in Higher Education*, 17, no. : 48–62.

Borden, V. and Bottrill, K. 1994. Performance indicators: Histories, definitions and methods. *New Directions for Institutional Research* 82: 5–21.

Burke, J.C., Minassians, H. and Yang, P. 2002. State performance reporting indicators: What do they indicate? *Planning for Higher Education,* vol 31, no.1: 15–29.

Chalmers, D. 2008. *Teaching and learning quality indicators in Australian Universities.* Paris: Organization for Economic Co-operation and Development.

Crisculo, A. and Vinicent, P. 2008. Reform teams: How the most successful reformers organized them-selves. *Public Policy for Private Sector, From World Bank Findings, Number 318.* Washington, D.C.: World Bank.

Daka, J. S, J. 2008. Information system based implementation of semester progression at University of Botswana. *International Journal of Education and Development Using ICT,* 4 no. 3.

Davis, R. 1995. Choosing performance management. *A Holistic Approach Journal.,* New Dehli: CUPA publication.

Dzimbiri, B. Lewis. 2009. Challenges in managing change: The case of performance management system at the University of Botswana. *Review of Higher Education in Africa,* 1 no. 1: 1–10.

Gabathuse, R. 2004. Discussions underway on UB expansion. *Mmegi,* 26 March.

Hatakenaka, S. 2005. Development of third stream activity. Lessons from international experience. Higher Education Policy Institute. Retrieved on 6th December, 2011 from http://www.hepi.ac.uk .

HEFCE. 2011. Business and community. Retrieved on 6th December, 2011 from http://www.hefce.ac/uk .

Hope, R. Kempe. 1995. Managing development policy in Botswana: Implementing reforms for rapid change. *Public Administration and Development,* 15 no. 1: 41–52.

King, K. 2005. The commission for Africa: A changing landscape for higher education and capacity development in Africa. Nuffic Conference on 'A Changing Landscape'. the Hague, 23rd – 25th May, 2005.

Marobela, M. 2008. The political economy of Botswana's public sector management reforms: Imperialism, diamond dependence and vulnerability. Retrieved on 10th June, 2011 from http://globalization. icaap.org/content/v7.1/Marobela.html.

Moleboge, S. Norman. 2003. Public sector reforms challenges and opportunities: The case of Botswana Police Service. Paper presented at the Commonwealth Advanced Seminar, Wellington, 24th February – 8th March, 2003.

Nyaoga, B. Richard., Simeon, K. and Magutu, O. P. 2010. The effectiveness of performance appraisal systems in private universities in Kenya. An assessment of Kabarak university performance appraisal systems. *African Journal of Business & Management,* 1: 123–134.

Republic of Botswana. 1993. *Report of the National Commission on Education 1993.* Gaborone: Government Printer.

Romainville, M. 1999. Quality evaluation of teaching in higher education. *Higher Education in Europe,* 24 no. 3: 414–424.

Sawyerr, Akilagpa. 2004. Challenges facing African universities: Selected issues. *African Studies Review,* 47 no. 1: 1–59.

Shafie, B. Halim. 1996. Malaysia's experience in implementing the new performance appraisal system. *Public Administration and Development,* 16: 341–352.

Simwanza, J. and Samaratunge, R. 2010. Public sector reforms in Africa: A comparison of Zambia and Botswana. Paper presented at International Research Society for Public Management (IRSPM XIII), Berne, Switzerland, 6th – 8th April.

Tanna, N. J. and Kumar, K. L. 2002. Curriculum innovations in design and technology at the University of Botswana, Southern Africa. *The Journal of Design and Technology Education,* 7 no. 1: 54–63.

University of Botswana. 2011a. *Fact Book 2010/11.* Gaborone: Department of Institutional Planning.

——.2011."Suspension of the implementation of the proposed revision of the academic organizational structure." Office of the Vice Chancellor. Memorandum addressed to all staff and students, 12th April, 2011.

——.2010/2011. Undergraduate academic calendar 2010/2011. Gaborone: Public Affairs.

——.2010. Proposal paper: Revision of the academic organizational structure (Final version, 24th January, 2010).

——.2009/10. *Annual Report 2009/10.* Gaborone: Public Affairs Publications Section.

——.2009. *Graduate employability strategy.* Gaborone: Institutional Research Unit (Version 4).

——.2008a. University research strategy. Approved by Senate, 20th February, 2008.

——.2008b. *A strategy for excellence: University of Botswana strategic plan to 2016 and beyond.* Gaborone: Department of Institutional Planning.

——.2005. *Performance management manual.* Gaborone: PMS Internal Project Team.

World Bank. 1997. *World development report 1997: The state in a changing world.* New York: Oxford University Press.

——.2008. *Accelerating catch-up: Tertiary education growth in sub-Saharan Africa.* Washington D.C.: World Bank.

Chapter 12

Big Growth and Big Mistakes: Telecoms in South Africa

Maxwell Chanakira

Abstract

This chapter explores fundamental features of the public sector reform process in South Africa's telecommunication sector. Using case study methodology, it asks whether the public sector reform has resulted in higher quality of service and better governance of state enterprise. It argues that while the reform contributed to the accelerated growth of mobile telephony and foreign capital inflows, the reform was deeply flawed; tender procedures were chaotic and hostage to vested interests; there were significant job losses; and the quality of service and corporate governance did not improve. Deduced remedies include safeguarding the independence of the regulator by making it accountable to parliament, making quality of service and corporate governance the key deliverables.

Introduction

Key approaches to public sector reform have been liberalisation, commercialisation, privatization, and out-sourcing. The trend is motivated by widespread perception that the public sector is inherently inefficient; pursues investment projects that benefit politicians rather than consumers; and implements skewed pricing policies (Shleifer and Vishny 1994). Chanakira (2003) points especially to the potential causes of inefficiency in State Owned Enterprises (SOEs) – government interference to serve political interests, pervasive corruption and inadequate motivation or monitoring of management. In many cases, SOEs are a source of unsustainable fiscal haemorrhage. Accepted wisdom is that SOEs need to shift from a bureaucratic mindset to a more open, accountable and consumer-focused approach, so they make a positive economic contribution to their countries (OSSREA 2010).

Since the 1990s, many African governments have been restructuring their state-owned and monopolistic telecommunications sectors. Independent regulatory bodies have been established to oversee the entry of competitive private providers, to resolve disputes, to set up inter-connection rates, support fair competition and encourage growth. The industry landscape has changed significantly: the number of mobile phone systems in Africa has increased more than four-fold in little more than a decade - from 35 (1995) to 160 (at the end of 2009). The rise in subscribers has been meteoric. Research by Frontier Economics on behalf of the Global System for Mobile Association (GSMA) found that the mobile industry in sub-Saharan Africa directly or indirectly employed more than 3.5 million people in 2006; contributed an average of 4 per cent to African countries' Gross Domestic Product (GDP); and accounted for 7 per cent of total government revenues in the region (Frontier-GSMA 2008). Recognition among African policy makers of the role telecoms can play in development is now emphatic (Gillward and Stork 2007).

This chapter focuses on South Africa - a middle-income emerging market which, according to the World Bank (2011), had a population of 49.2 million people, a GDP of US$285.37 billion and a GDP per capita of US$5,786 at the end of 2009. South Africa has four mobile communications network operators (Vodacom, MTN, Cell C and 8.ta) and two fixed line network operators (Telkom SA Ltd. and Neotel). It is the third largest (by numbers) telephone market in Africa, after Nigeria and Egypt. The telecoms sector contributed 2.9 per cent of the country's GDP in 2008 (Esselaar *et al.* 2010). At the end of 2010, the country had 52.2 million mobile subscribers and 4.3 million fixed-line connections (see Table 1), accounting for almost 15 per cent of the total telephones on the continent.

Table 1: **South African telecommunications indicators**

Indicator	2008	2009	2010
Fixed line networks			
Number of fixed-line operators	2	2	2
Lines connected	4,450,000	4,300,000	4,300,000
Teledensity	9.14	8.83	8.83
Digitalisation switching (%)	99.9%	99.9%	100%
Mobile networks			
Number of mobile operators	3	3	4
Total mobile subscribers	49,320,000	49,640,000	52,210,000
Teledensity	99.62	104.54	107.24
Number of internet subscribers	1,380,000	2,363,000	14,000,000

Source: BMI-T (2011)

This chapter examines South Africa's public sector reform of the telecoms. It covers initiatives from 1991 to 2009; focuses on the Telkom SA parastatal, and examines the off-shoots of Vodacom and MTN. Specifically, the chapter:

- explores the fundamental features of the SA public sector reform process encompassing the various telecommunication policies enacted, strategies employed and the rationale behind those actions; and

- analyses the outcomes and implications and, in particular, assesses whether the process resulted in improved quality of service to consumers and better governance of the reformed enterprise.

Telkom SA was chosen as the SOE being reformed. A case-study strategy was used as it is an established and well understood research approach in public sector reform (Shirley et al. 2002; Shirley and Walsh 2001; Ramamurti 1997; La Porta and Lopez-de-

Silanes 1997). Information was gathered through a comprehensive review of archival documents, policy documents on legislation, speeches and reports, government gazettes, applications for licences, newspaper articles, company annual reports, media releases, analysts' reports on the industry, and previous research studies on the subject.

This chapter is organised into four sections. The first provides an introduction and brief outline of the methodology. The second provides an overview of the telecommunication sector, and key theoretical issues on the regulatory system, quality of service and corporate governance in the sector. The third looks at key features of the reform process in South Africa, with analyses of outcomes. The fourth offers a conclusion and recommendations.

An Overview of the Telecommunication Sector

The International Telecoms Union (ITU) acknowledged in 2002 that the sector had become a major economic engine as well as an enabler of social, educational, technological and medical progress worldwide. Since then, the telecoms industry has become an even higher revenue industry that makes a substantial and growing contribution to the world economy. The Telecommunications Industry Association (TIA) estimates that the industry's worldwide revenue was US$3.85 trillion in 2009, with global telecoms spending expected to grow at a compound annual rate of 6.3 per cent to US$4.9 trillion in 2013 (TIA 2010). This growth has been spurred by global market reforms since the early 1990s, which show increasing privatisation of the industry and dominant take-over by transnational companies in the market structure (Ojo 2004).

The World Trade Organisation (WTO) has insisted that member countries commercialise and privatise certain aspects of their telecoms markets. Hence, member countries are legally bound to liberalise (WTO 2002). The IMF and World Bank have stipulated public sector reform (telecoms included) as part of Economic Structural Adjustment Programmes (ESAPs) and as a condition for financial assistance (ALRN 2002). Their central argument has been that restructuring allows competition, which in turn leads to efficiency and innovation.

Ayogu and Hodge (2001) argue that the way competition evolves in liberalised telecoms will depend on the nature of regulation. Melody (2002) asserts there is increasing recognition that the success of reform and the ability of telecoms markets to improve efficiency and achieve public policy objectives depend largely on the establishment of a credible, competent and effective regulatory system. Frempong and Aturba (2001) weigh in with similar arguments, calling for a strong and independent regulator to provide constant monitoring, arbitration, legal guidelines and a level playing field. It is important that the regulator be independent from powerful and influential operators and from undue government influence (Habeenzu 2003). Regulatory authorities are crucial to ensure that operators stick to their licence terms, increase network rollout and treat consumers and competitors fairly.

The regulatory model can focus either on *infrastructure bias* (where infrastructure requirements are stipulated as conditions for issuing licences) and/or on competitive *cost-driven pricing* (Borrmann 2001). In the early years of fixed-line development, many countries focused on infrastructure bias and introduced competition at a later stage. In mobile telephony, the approach has been to apply both strategies immediately and simultaneously.

Quality of Service (QoS) – an essential function in telecoms supply and maintenance - is the measurement of the performance of a network and the degree to which it conforms to stipulated parameters (NTRC 2007). Yao (undated) lists QoS criteria as billing errors, waiting lists for provision of service, wrong number, time to repair, poor transmission, fault incidence, failure of call completion, and dial tone/post-dialling delay. Indicators are the number of customer fault reports, the time taken for fault repair, and the time taken to provide exchange lines (Sibanda and Akinboade 2004).

Corporate governance refers to the way in which companies govern themselves. The objective could be to maximise the wealth of shareholders, in a way that observes certain standards, laws, regulations and desired practices (Coyle, 2005). In South Africa, the key parameters for governance include remuneration practices, corporate integrity and ethics, risk management practices, broad-based black economic empowerment (BBBEE), and transformation. The first three points tally with the World Bank's (and this study's) parameters of a structure to incentivise performance, internal checks and balances, and active control by visible top managers wielding discretionary power (Girishankar 2001).

Public Sector Reform in the South African Telecommunications Market

The fundamental features of the South African process, encompassing policies, strategies and actions from 1981 to 2009, are briefly discussed in this section - to show conditions prior to reform, how the reform process evolved and the outcomes. At crucial junctures of the narrative, an analysis of the implications of the various policies, actions (and inactions) is provided.

Pre-public Sector Reform Era (1981–1991)

The South African Posts and Telecommunications (SAPT) or the "Post Office," as it was popularly known then, was a government department administered by the Minister of Transport and Communications with the Post Master General (PMG) as head. The Post Office was sole provider of postal and telecoms services. It was subject to close financial oversight and, as a rule, experienced little outright corruption or gross over-spending (Horwitz 1992).

Horwitz (1992) describes the SAPT's network at the time as sophisticated, with a high degree of digitalisation. The company had 3.32 million lines in 1991; equivalent to roughly 40 per cent of all the telephone lines in Africa and hence the highest telephone density on the continent. SAPT's speed of fault clearance was 77 per cent within 24 hours, comparable to the performance of some industrialised countries (Coopers and Lybrand 1992). However, SAPT was heavily in debt following rapid change-over from the electro-mechanical switching system to digital technology in the 1980s (De Villiers 1986). The company had to compete with other government departments for capital to finance projects, and was sometimes short of funds. Political considerations kept tariffs below cost (Taylor 1992). Comparative productivity indices provided in the Coopers and Lybrand (1992) showed SAPT was over-staffed and inefficient.

Corporate users were intensely lobbying government for improved quality of telecoms service to run their enterprises efficiently and sought the freedom to choose their own service provider rather than deal only with SAPT (De Villiers, 1986). Pressure also came from public perception that SAPT was top-heavy, bureaucratic and inefficient. Furthermore, the bulk of SAPT services were in the white and mixed-race areas (13.5 per cent and 8.8 per cent of the population, respectively) while the blacks (74.8 per cent) were largely neglected (see Table 2).

Table 2: **Distribution of residential telephones in the metropolitan areas by race, 1987**

Race	Number of telephones (millions)	Percentage of lines	Percentage of population
White	1.63	72	13.5
Coloured	0.27	12	8.8
Indian	0.16	7	2.9
Black	0.20	9	74.8
Total	**2.26**	**100.0**	**100.0**

Source: Adapted from Kaplan (1990)

These complaints, South Africa's deteriorating economic conditions in the 1980s - in part due to sanctions imposed as a result of the apartheid system but worsened by the plummeting value of the Rand - finally convinced government that reforming SAPT was a better option than carrying the debt-ridden company in its existing state.

The Public Sector Reform Process (1991–2009)

The following section covers the major reforms considered during the period. It discusses the various telecommunication acts, the establishment of regulatory organisations, the privatisation measures and the introduction of various telecom services.

- **Commercialisation of Telkom SA Ltd**: Reform began through the Post Office Amendment Act of 1991, releasing ministerial control so the company could pursue commercial goals and embrace private sector management practices; to separate telecoms from postal operations and create two distinct companies — Telkom SA Ltd and SA Post Office Ltd — and to split the roles of regulator and operator from Telkom SA per international best practice

(Teer-Tomaselli 2002). Telkom SA was formally registered under the South African Companies Act, as a commercialised entity, but with the government as the sole shareholder. The residual Department of Posts and Telecommunications acted as interim regulator, although neither its legal standing nor the scope of its authority was clearly delineated. In line with the new regulations, Telkom SA could now generate profits, pay taxes, receive no state subsidies, and be responsible for obtaining its own financing, subject to ministerial approval. The company was subject to a system of price caps for services in which it had a monopoly.

• **Introduction of Mobile Telephony Service:** Consistent with the recommendations of the Coopers and Lybrand (1992) and in response to market demand, the South African cabinet decided in early 1993 to precede with the introduction of cellular mobile telephone systems. Licences were put out to tender and the Minister of Transport and Communications appointed Ters Oosthuizen, an individual consultant, to oversee telecoms in general and the cellular tender process in particular (Horwitz 1992). Telkom SA was awarded half of the first mobile licence, in consortium with UK-based Vodafone and the Rembrandt Group of South Africa, to form a subsidiary named Vodacom. There were three bidders for the second licence. The first was from Mobile Telephone Networks (MTN), a consortium of South African pay-television providers M-Net (30 per cent), UK-based Cable and Wireless (30 per cent), the NAFTEL association of black businessmen (30 per cent), and state-owned Transtel (10 per cent) (*Ibid*). The other bids were from Cellstar Cellular Networks and the Reunert Group.

MTN won the bid in 1993. Vodacom and MTN would provide cellular service on the GSM communications standard. With 50 per cent shareholding held by Telkom SA, and ultimately controlled by the government, Vodacom's operations could be burdened by indirect state control. MTN, with only 10 per cent share and indirect government control through Transtel, would be able to operate relatively freely.

The introduction of competition was commendable but there were significant flaws. The government introduced mobile telephony without first establishing a legal framework for the sector and its regulation, so there was an uneven playing field between Telkom SA and its mobile competitors. In the absence of a credible and independent regulator and handicapped by price controls, the indirect competition unleashed by mobile operators would prove damaging in the long run. Consumers could suffer from high prices in a market without a regulator.

- **Enactment of the Telecommunications Act 103 of 1996**: Lack of regulation was remedied by the Telecommunications Act 103 of 1996, which was designed to develop telecoms infrastructure; promote universal and affordable provision of telecoms services; reposition Telkom SA for local and global competition; and create an independent regulator (Republic of South Africa 1996). The Act created a framework for the establishment of an independent regulator and required government to sell 30 per cent of Telkom SA.

- **Establishment of an Independent Regulator:** South Africa Telecommunication Regulatory Activity (SATRA) was established as an independent organisation in 1997 to approve licences, monitor networks' compliance with licence conditions, create and supervise pricing policy, regulate the industry and support the development and sustainability of free competition in the market. SATRA battled a heavy workload with limited resources from the outset (Bidoli 1999).

- **Phase 1 of Telkom SA Privatisation – 1997:** Phased privatisation of Telkom SA began with the sale of 30 per cent to a strategic equity partner (SEP) called Thintana Communications LLC. Thintana — comprising Telkom Malaysia Berhad (which bought 12 per cent) and US-based SBC Communications Inc (18 per cent) — paid US$1.26 billion for the stake and was tasked with turning Telkom SA into an efficient telecoms operator, ready for competition by 2002. The award to Telkom SA of a 5-year exclusivity period in which to operate fixed-line services without competition was conditional on a roll-out of 2.8 million lines, of which 1.7 million were earmarked for historically under-serviced areas and priority customers such as clinics, hospitals, schools and 120 thousand public pay phones (MyBroadband, 2010). Telkom SA would retain the exclusive right to supply long-distance and international voice telephony. The exclusivity period was scheduled to expire in May 2002 (Parliamentary Monitoring Group, 2000).

- **Creation of a New Regulatory Body — ICASA-2000:** In July 2000, SATRA was merged with the Independent Broadcasting Authority (IBA) to form the Independent Communications Regulatory Authority of South Africa (ICASA), mandated by an act of parliament to facilitate the effective and seamless regulation and technical convergence of telecoms and broadcasting. The statutory functions of ICASA were to make regulations and policies that governed broadcasting and telecommunications; issued licences to broadcasters and providers of telecommunication services; monitored the market; and enforced compliance with rules and regulations.

- **Phase 2 of Telkom Privatisation:** In April 2001, a further 3 per cent of government shares in Telkom SA were sold to Ucingo, a BEE grouping. Ucingo Investments, a special-purpose vehicle created to secure an empowerment stake in Telkom SA, was the "preferred and exclusive" applicant for the allocation of 3 per cent of Telkom SA stock, valued at more than R600 million (Fin24 2001). The group estimated that its shareholders represented about 2 million people - 5 per cent of the national population.

- **The Award of a Third Cellular Licence – 2001:** Three developments gave impetus to a third licence. These were: a) the success of Vodacom and MTN suggested that the market was ready and viable for a third operator; b) Vodacom and MTN were suspected of colluding and operating a duopolistic cartel (Bidoli 1999); and c) by introducing a third cellular operator, the government would have the opportunity to economically empower the majority black population at both the equity and operational levels. After a chaotic tender process, ICASA recommended the Cell C consortium led by Saudi Oger as the winning bidder (Gardner 2003). Losing bidder NextCom filed a court injunction, and the regulator issued an affidavit that alleged government interference in the licensing process. Despite these dents in public confidence, the Minister of Communications formally announced Cell C as the winner of the third cellular licence in 2001.

- **Phase 3 of Telkom SA Privatisation**: In March 2003, the government sold a further 20 per cent of Telkom SA through a primary listing on the Johannesburg Stock Exchange (JSE) and a secondary listing on the New York Stock Exchange (NYSE). The Initial Public Offering (IPO) valued each share at R28, earning the government R3.9 billion (Giddy 2003) - less than half the R10 billion the government had planned to raise a year earlier, reflecting the relatively weak state of the global telecoms market at the time.

- **The Introduction of Fixed-Line Competition – 2005**: At the end of Telkom SA's five-year grace period in May 2002, licensing of a rival fixed-line operator was delayed (Gardner 2003) through a combination of government actions and squabbling between bidders. After another chaotic tender process, Neotel was awarded South Africa's second network operator (SNO) licence in 2005, with a mandate to tackle the monopoly of Telkom SA. Neotel launched its wholesale, corporate and residential retail services in 2007, by which time Telkom SA had been allowed 10 years to develop a stranglehold on the fixed-line network.

- **The Electronic Communications Act (ECA) – 2005**: To recognise the convergence between telecoms and broadcasting, the Electronic Communications Act (ECA) of 2005 was gazetted in June 2006 (BMI-T 2011), repealing the Telecommunications Act 103 1996 and the Independent Broadcasting Authority Act 1993. The new act regulated and facilitated the convergence of telecoms, broadcasting and IT services, and ushered in services-based and horizontal competition.

- **Sale of 15 per cent Telkom SA Stake to Vodafone PLC – 2007**: In 2008, Vodafone PLC bought a portion of Telkom SA's stake in Vodacom for R22.5 billion, equivalent to US$3 billion (IT News Africa 2009). The transaction raised Vodafone's shareholding in Vodacom from 50 per cent to 65 per cent. Vodacom listed on the Johannesburg Stock Exchange in early 2009, while the remaining 35 per cent shareholding of Vodacom was demerged by Telkom SA to its shareholders.

Key Outcomes of the SA Reform Process

- **Rapid Growth of Mobile Telephony**: GSM mobile services have experienced rapid growth (see Figure 1) since MTN and Vodacom were licensed in 1993. In the following 17 years, the number of mobile subscribers rose from 12,510 to 52.2 million, with Vodacom capturing 48.5 per cent market share (BMI-T, 2011), MTN 36 per cent and the balance of 15.5 per cent shared between Cell C and 8*ta. This prodigious growth speaks above all to enormous and irresistible demand, but also endorses the supply-side assertion of Megginson and Netter (2001) that the privatisation of SOEs and the introduction of competitors (whether fixed-line or mobile) is likely to accelerate telecommunications network development and improve penetration rates.

Figure 1: **Fixed and mobile growth, 1991–2010**

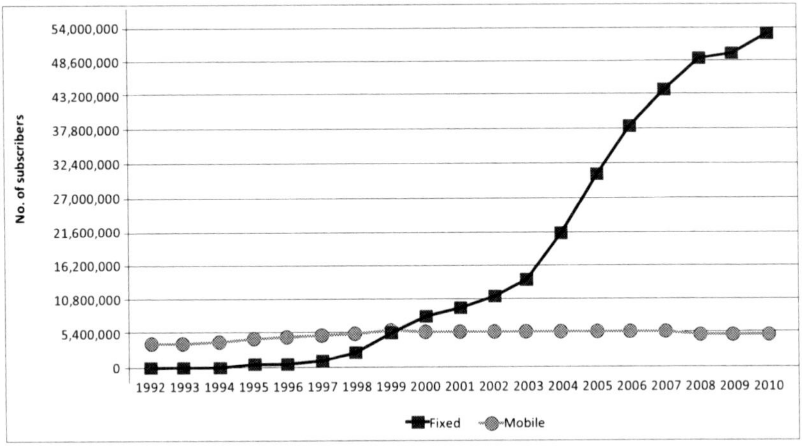

Source: BMI-T (2011)

- **Job Losses:** In 1991, Telkom SA had 67,000 employees (Horwitz 1992). It was over-staffed and inefficient (De Villiers 1986) because, like many SOEs, it was forced to pursue political goals (Boycko, Shleifer and Vishny 1996). Inevitably, Telkom SA's commercialisation in 1991, the introduction of mobile competition in 1993, the subsequent phased privatisation of the company in 1997, 2000 and 2003, adoption of commercial goals and private sector management orientation, have led to deep job cuts. Between

1991 and the end of 2009, Telkom SA's establishment was reduced by 65 per cent, to 23,785 employees (Telkom SA 2010). The trend in direct employment levels is evident across the entire telecoms industry, where formal employment has dropped from a high of 108,215 in 1985, to 63,503 in 2008 (Esselaar *et al.* 2010) - a fall of 41 per cent - driven by competitive pressures for efficiency and protection of margins.

• **Injection of Foreign Capital:** South Africa attracted US$8.5 billion, mainly foreign capital in ICT products consumption and infrastructure between 2004 and 2008 (see Table 3). The introduction of mobile telephony in 1993 was the really powerful driver.

Table 3: **South Africa's strong growth in ICT products, consumption and infrastructure (US$ in millions)**

Country	2004	2005	2006	2007	2008	Growth ('04 – '08) %
South Africa	1,314	1,647	1,836	1,999	1,700	29

Source: UN Comtrade (2009)

Apart from investments in licences and shares, the new operators have made major investments in network development. In January 2010, for example, Cell C signed a deal with China's ZTE worth US $378 million to supply 3G HSPA and network equipment - one of several instances of financial injection (Esselaar et al. 2010). Neotel, which is majority-owned by India's Tata Communications, approved an investment of up to US$300 million in South Africa over a four-year period from 2009. Stock market listings also have attracted foreign investment.

• **Struggle with Handling Tender Processes:** The licensing process of the third cellular operator (Cell C) and the SNO (Neotel) highlighted how the South African government struggled to effectively and transparently manage a tender process because of alleged government interference. Insufficient checks and balances were evident. The protracted and controversial nature of the process generated negative perceptions for international investors (Gillward and Esselaar, 2004). South Africa's poor performance in this respect shows the lack of transparent and trouble-free processes.

- **Quality-of-Service Challenges**: Telkom SA was bound by Regulation 4.9, which stipulated improvements to be achieved in the five-year (which became 10-year) period before effective competition, in respect of the number of customer fault reports, the time taken for fault repairs, serviceability of public pay-phones, the time taken to provide exchange lines and the number of customers waiting for service. Telkom SA scores 75.85 per cent instead of the stipulated 90 per cent on fault clearance within three days (ICASA 2011), and fails to clear the remaining faults within six days (scoring 90.13 instead of 100 per cent on that criterion). According to the same report, Neotel, Vodacom and Cell C also do not comply with these two regulations; the report is silent on MTN's compliance. These figures demonstrate that across the entire telecommunications sector, quality of service has not met the minimum thresholds set by ICASA. This points to the unsettling fact that privatisation does not necessarily deliver quality of service.

  Telkom SA Group's CEO concedes that the company has lost credibility with some of its customers, especially residential ones, in terms of quality of service and customer communication. The CEO said the company's culture is characterised by lack of innovation and accountability; has a bloated cost structure and, consequently, faces fierce competitive pressures resulting in shrinking revenues and profits (Telkom SA 2010).

- **Regulation Challenges**: Yan (2001) argues that privatised operators often retain strong links with governments, making the application of regulations difficult and undermining the independence of the regulator. In the case of Telkom SA, there are more than strong links with government as government is still the company's largest shareholder.

  Regulators in recently liberalised markets often require considerable time to acquire a full complement of staff with relevant experience, which will then allow them to establish their credibility with operators and consumers. From its inception, SATRA was confronted with a heavy workload and limited resources and battled to fulfil its mandate (Bidoli 1999). Ideally, the regulator should have been introduced in 1991, at the time Telkom was commercialised. Coming almost five years later, the regulator inherited embedded damage.

- **Governance**: According to the Executive and Specialised Skills' report on total emoluments of executives and directors at JSE-listed companies in 2009, telecoms executives took home the most money, with MTN's CEO, Phuthuma Nhleko, earning R15,694,000 in 2009, while former Telkom SA CEO, Reuben September, had a total salary of R12,828,000 (MoneyWeb 2010). Any executive under-achievement is clearly not attributable to under-payment.

The King III corporate governance framework requires that boards of listed companies have a minimum number of independent directors. At a February 2011 shareholder meeting, Telkom SA did not comply. Element Investment Managers commissioned an independent survey of Telkom SA's corporate governance, which was undertaken by Avior Research, and found the company's corporate governance poor (Fin24 2010). Telkom SA made massive losses (at US$1.4 billion, this was approximately half the company's total value) when it bought Multi Links in Nigeria. The Group CEO called it the worst investment in South Africa's investment history, while employees called it corporate fraud (Nigeria Communications Week 2011). The New Public Management (NPM) approach encourages active control by visible top managers wielding discretionary power in former SOEs (Girishankar 2001). Telkom SA's recently appointed Group CEO, Ms. Nombulelo Moholi, is the fourth CEO to take the helm in the past five-and-a-half years, since Sizwe Nxasana left the group in September 2005 after seven years as CEO. Government interference is cited as one of the obstacles that top managers at Telkom SA face in wielding the discretionary power necessary to steer the company forward.

A key objective of the commercialisation of Telkom SA in 1991 was to free SAPT from the burdens of ministerial control, which made decisions on the basis of political rather business considerations. Two decades later, government is still the major shareholder with 39.7 per cent.

Conclusion

In a sector over-brimming with potential for growth, business viability, consumer benefit and national development, South Africa's reform of the telecoms sector has made significant gains but also failed to maximise the opportunities.

Firstly, the lack of a strong and independent regulator, above any other single factor, has led to the under-achievement of key reform objectives. Hence, there is a need to re-look Africa's objectives in the public sector reform process and to ensure strong and independent regulators are a fundamental part of the process.

Secondly, Telkom SA remains under the control of the government as the majority shareholder with 39.7 per cent. This has created instability, with CEOs installed in an acting capacity at times for close to a year and a weak governance structure.

Thirdly, the reform has failed to deliver quality of service and good corporate governance in Telkom SA. Part of the problem lies in the prioritisation of objectives of the reform process. More often than not, key objectives are financial receipts to ease the government's financial burden, expanding service to the entire population, and reducing job losses. As companies pursue these objectives, other ideals, like quality of service and sound corporate governance, which rank very low in priority, tend to suffer.

References

ALRN. 2002. *Privatisation - African experience*. African Labour Research Network.Windhoek, Namibia

Ayogu, M. and Hodge, J. 2001. *Understanding the nature of reforms in the telecom sector in South Africa: A political economy perspective*. Cape Town: School of Economics, University of Cape Town.

Bidoli, M. 1999. SATRA: Bulldog needs more teeth. *Financial Mail*, 6th August.

BMI-T. 2011. *Communication technologies handbook*. Fourways. South Africa: BMI-TechKnowledge.

Borrmann, C. 2001. Corporate strategies in the telecommunications sector in an environment of continuing liberalisation. HWWA Discussion Paper, Hamburg.

Boycko, M., Shleifer, A. and Vishny, R. 1996. A theory of privatisation. *Economic Journal*, Vol. 106:435.

Chanakira, M. 2003. A critique of the privatisation strategy of Lesotho telecommunications corporation. An unpublished Master's thesis in Business Administration (MBA), Mancosa.

Coopers and Lybrand. 1992. *Telecommunications sector strategy study for the department of posts and telecommunications*. Pretoria: Government Printer.

Coyle, B. 2005. *Corporate governance*. London: ICSA Publishers Ltd.

De Villiers, J.W. 1986. *Condensed report of the study by Dr. WJ de Villiers regarding the strategic planning, management practices and systems of the South African transport services*. Pretoria: Government Printer.

Esselaar, S., Gillwald, A., Moyo, M. and Naidoo, K. 2010. *South African ICT sector performance review 2009/2010: Towards evidence-based ICT policy and regulation, Volume two*. Policy Paper 6. www.npconline.co.za/MediaLib/Downloads/Home/Tabs/Diagnostic/MaterialConditions2/South African ICT sector performance review 2009-2010.pdf (accessed on March, 2011)

Fin24 2010. *Feathers fly at Telkom AGM*. Available from: http://www.fin24.com/Companies/Feathers-fly-at-Telkom-AGM-20100824 (accessed on 20th July, 2011).

Fin24 2001. *Ucingo seals stake in Telkom*. Available from: http://www.fin24.com/Economy/Ucingo-seals-stake-in-Telkom-20010403 (accessed on 15th July, 2011).

Frempong, G.K. and Aturba, W.H. 2001. Liberalisation of telecoms: The Ghanaian experience. *Telecommunications Policy*, 25(2): 197–210.

Frontier-GSMA Report 2008. *Taxation of Mobile Services in Sub Saharan Africa*. Available from: http://s3.amazonaws.com/zanran_storage/www.gsmworld.com/ContentPages/21047163.pdf (accessed on 16th May, 2012).

Gardner, S.P.N. 2003. The effect of commercialisation, privatisation and liberalisation on universal access in South Africa. An unpublished Master's Degree dissertation, Rhodes University, South Africa.

Giddy, I. 2003. *Case study: The IPO of Telkom South Africa*. New York: New York University.

Gillward, A. and Esselaar, S. 2004. South African 2004 ICT sector performance review. *LINK Centre Public Policy Research Paper* No 7, December 2004. http://link.wits.ac.za/papers/tspr2004.pdf (accessed on December, 2011)

Gillward, A. and Stork, C. 2007. Towards an African ICT e-index: Towards evidence-based ICT policy in Africa. Research ICT Africa, LINK Centre, Johannesburg: Witwatersrand University.

Girishankar, N. 2001. *Evaluating public sector reform: Guidelines for assessing country-level impact of structural reform and capacity building in the public sector*. Washington, D.C.: World Bank.

Habeenzu, S. 2003. Telecommunications sector reform. Zambia Trade and Investment Enhancement Project (ZAMTIE). pdf.usaid.gov/pdf_docs/ PNACX613.pdf (accessed on December, 20011)

Horwitz, R.B. 1992. The politics of telecommunications reform in South Africa. *Telecommunications Policy*, 16(4): 291–306.

ICASA. 2011. ICASA compliance reports on Telkom SA, Cell C, Vodacom and MTN. ICASA, August. ICASA: Johanesberg

——.2010. Overview/Mandate http://www.icasa.org.za/AboutUs/ OverviewMandate/tabid/56/Default.aspx (accessed on 15th July, 2011).

IT News Africa. 2009. "Vodacom, Vodafone deal gets green light from high court." IT News Africa, May 19. http://www.itnewsafrica.com/2009/05/ vodacom-listing-gets-green-light-from-high-court (accessed on 20th July, 2011).

Kaplan, D. 1990. *The crossed line: South African telecommunications industry in transition*. Johannesburg: Witwatersrand University Press.

La Porta, R. and Lopez-De-Silanes, F. 1997. Benefits of privatisation: Evidence from Mexico. NBER working paper # 6215. NBER: Cambridge MA, USA

Megginson, W.L. and Netter, J.M. 2001. From state to market: A survey of empirical studies on privatisation. *Journal of Economic Literature*, 39: 321–389.

Melody, W. H. 2002. *Telecomm reform: Principles, policies and regulatory practices*. Johannesburg: LINK Centre, University of Witwatersrand.

MoneyWeb. 2010. South African ICT executives' salaries revealed. 19 October.

MyBroadband. 2010. Telkom's fixed line numbers: A brief history since 1993. http://mybroadband.co.za/news/telecoms/17131-telkom-s-fixed-line-numbers-a-brief-history-since-1993.html (accessed on July, 2011).

Nigeria Communications Week. 2011. Multilinks: Aggrieved staff cry foul, allege fraud. Available from: http://www.nigeriacommunicationsweek. com.ng/details.php?category=topnews&id=429 (accessed on July, 2011).

NTRC. 2007. *St. Lucia telecommunications quality of service regulations 2007*. Statutory Instrument No. 148, NTRC, St. Lucia, August.

Ojo, T. 2004. Old paradigm and information and communication technologies for development agenda in Africa: Modernisation as context. *Journal of Information Technology Impact*, 4(3): 139–150.

OSSREA. 2010. "Call for papers: Three decades of public sector reform in Sub-Saharan Africa". OSSREA: Addis Ababa.

Parliamentary Monitoring Group. 2000. 'Labour and public enterprises select committee on telecom's monopoly', 20 June.

Ramamurti, R. 1997. Testing the limits of privatisation: Argentine railroads. *World Development*, Vol. 25:12.

Republic of South Africa. 1996. *The telecommunications Act No. 103 of 1996*. Government Printers.

Shirley, M.M., Tusubira, F.F., Gebreab, F. and Haggarty, L. 2002. Telecommunications reforms in Uganda. *World Bank Policy Research Working Paper 2864*, June 2002.

Shirley, M. and Walsh, P. 2001. Public vs. private ownership: The current state of the debate. *World Bank Policy Research Working Paper* No. 2420. Washington, D.C.: World Bank. http://jpkc.ecnu.edu.cn/ggzcgl/shoukejiaoan/minyinghuazhengce/public%20and%20private%20ownership-the%20curent%20state%20of%20debate.pdf (accessed on July 2011)

Shleifer, A. and Vishny, R. 1994. Politicians and firms. *Quarterly Journal of Economics*, Vol 109:4.

Sibanda, F. and Akinboade, O. 2004. Regulating for competition: The case for Telkom SA. UK: Centre for Regulation and Competition, University of Manchester. https://www.wbginvestmentclimate.org/uploads/15. Regulatingdev.pdf (accessed on Sepetember, 2010)

Taylor, W.J. 1992. Former Deputy Postmaster General for Telecommunications: Interview with Horwitz, R., July 7. In in Communication and Democratic Reform in South Africa (2001) By Robert B. Horwitz Cambridge University Press: Cambridge, UK

Teer-Tomaselli, R. 2002. Transforming state-owned enterprises in the global age: Lessons from broadcasting and telecommunications in South Africa. Paper presented at "Convergence: Technology, Culture and Social Impacts", International Research Seminar, 6–10 May, University of Natal, Durban.

Telkom SA. 2010. *Telkom SA 2010 Annual Report*. Pretoria, South Africa: Telkom SA.

TIA. 2010. ICT is key driver for global economy: TIA's 2010 ICT market review and forecast. Trends, analysis and projections from 2002 to 2013. Research and Markets: Dublin, Ireland

UN Comtrade. 2008. International trade statistics. http://comtrade.un.org (accessed on 16th March, 2011).

World Bank. 2011. Development indicators. http://data.worldbank.org/data-catalogue (accessed on 23rd September, 2010).

WTO. 2002. Telecommunications services: Uruguay round decision on negotiations on basic telecommunications. http://www.wto.org/english/tratop_e/serv_e/telecom_e/tel22_e.htm. (accessed on 20th March, 2011).

Yan, X. 2001. The impact of the regulatory framework on fixed-mobile interconnection settlements: The case of China and Hong Kong. *Telecommunications Policy*, 25(7): 515–532.

Yao, W. [Undated]. Brunel University EE5302 Network Design and Management. people.brunel.ac.uk/.../14-Access%20Network%20Design. pdf (accessed on May, 2011).

Chapter 13

The Performance of Decentralisation and Public Sector Accountability Reforms in Uganda

William Muhumuza

Abstract

Good governance reforms have had paradoxical outcomes in Uganda. Some have been relatively successful, even if not yet with long-term stability. Others have made no effective progress. The stark difference in results is not explained by any distinctive shortfalls in the 'usual suspects' of design, resources or implementation process. Yet the differences in outcome are certainly dramatic. This chapter investigates why, using juxtaposed case studies, decentralisation and public sector accountability reforms have had paradoxical outcomes in Uganda. It establishes that the outcomes of reforms depend neither primarily on donor objectives, or on the stated commitment of aid-recipient states, nor on the potential of the reform to build good governance or give better service and value to people. The outcome will depend, above any other factor, on whether the reform consolidates or obstructs the government's political power base, and whether it is likely to assure or threaten the government's tenure. This chapter identifies, pursues and evidences that fact, and how incumbent neo-patrimonial states ensure the process works exactly as they want it to.

Background

Uganda's early years of independence held great promise. There was a competitive democratic political system, devolution of central

267

power to sub-national governments, and an effective civil service. However, the "golden" phase was short-lived. By the mid-1960s, democratic good governance was replaced by authoritarian rule; in 1971 there was a military coup that ushered in nearly a decade of economic collapse and institutional decay. Even when the Idi Amin era came to an end, there was political instability as the traditional parties - Uganda People's Congress (UPC), Democratic Party (DP) and Conservative Party (CP) - wrangled over the ruins (Apter 1995; Museveni 1997) for several more years.

Some normality was restored when President Museveni's National Resistance Movement (NRM) took over in 1986. Political party activities were suspended to unify and stabilise the country which had for long been devastated by strife (Museveni 1997). A monolithic system of government, popularly known as the "Movement system", was created where both local and national leaders were elected on the basis of individual merit rather than party affiliation (Mugaju and Oloka-Onyango 2000). Ugandans would have to wait until 2005 for a national referendum to open the way for a multi-party system.

Meanwhile, reconstruction of the economic debris had to begin with virtual "emergency" state-control of barter trade, foreign exchange, key enterprises and more (Ochieng 1991). But sustained international support to rebuild a broken country – economically, structurally and socially – was essential, and it was conditional on good governance. Uganda soon adopted the World Bank/IMF's neo-liberal strategy (Mugyenyi 1991; Botchwey *et al.* 1998), and the NRM government embarked on a broad agenda of public sector policy reforms. These began with reconstruction of a market-led economy, later supplemented by decentralisation of power, civil service overhauls, and focus on public sector accountability (Therkildsen 2001). Clearly, these are closely linked and complementary in the quest for efficiency and effectiveness in government, albeit the fundamental ingredients of the reforms were not well achieved (Kuteesa *et al.* 2010).

The main thrust of this chapter is to critically analyse the varied outcomes of decentralisation and public sector accountability reforms — examine their nature, the process of implementation, and the reasons for the relative success of decentralisation and the subversion of the public sector accountability reforms.

Decentralisation is chosen because of its relative success, although even here, there has been recent stagnation and attempt to reverse some earlier gains (Tripp 2010). This "successful" reform is contrasted with conspicuously less progress in public sector accountability. Although a semblance of institutional structure and law has been put in place, accompanied by much political rhetoric, real accountability has not moved forward.

This study relies on secondary sources of data and the lived experience of the author who resides in the country and is an informed observer who has actively participated in research closely related to the subject matter. This section gives background. Based on the extant literature, the next section briefly touches on the motives and challenges of public sector reforms. This is followed by a critical analysis of the performance of the decentralisation and public accountability reforms in Uganda, with explanation for the diverse outcomes.

Motives and Challenges of Public Sector Reforms: Introductory Remarks

The pressure for public sector policy reform in sub-Saharan Africa gained international popularity in the 1980s, coinciding with the end of the Cold War, the ascendancy of conservative political regimes in the rich Western donor states, and the economic crises in sub-Saharan Africa. The advocates of market-based neo-liberal policy reforms championed by the World Bank blamed crisis in governance for sub-Sahara's woes, as captured in the famous World Bank report of 1989. The state-led model of economic development was particularly castigated for creating a poor policy environment, mismanagement, inefficiency and rent-seeking behaviour, all of which contributed to the economic crisis that was rampant in the 1980s.

The conditions set for good governance (Grindle 2004, 533–4) include: decentralising government, reducing corruption, improving accountability, restructuring the civil service, and better management of public resources. In sum, the stated objectives of public sector reforms are to bring about efficiency and effectiveness in government, to improve service delivery and consequently reduce poverty.

For both donors and aid-dependent states, those goals were common and real. But the donors' motives were, of course, not pure altruism (Harrison 2005, 240). Directly or indirectly, they were to serve vested political, ideological and economic interests. The motives of recipient governments were not so selfless, either. Countries like Uganda wanted to access much-needed foreign resources to revive their collapsed economies, service the political patronage machine, and re-invent their legitimacy (Chabal and Daloz 1999).

The crucial issue here is that the underlying motives of donors and receivers differed. And those differences help explain why the outcomes of reforms have been so variable. Universalising neo-liberal policy measures mainly informed by Western value systems and historical experiences, while disregarding peculiarities of non-Western contexts, explains public sector reform paradoxes (De Maria 2008).

The so-called "predatory state" is perceived to be the main obstacle to achieving development in Africa. The nature of contemporary politics in Africa is best understood as the exercise of the neo-patrimonial power (Chabal 2002,450) — a situation where state control and political legitimacy are attained through informal political ties with an elaborate network of patrons and clients whose loyalty is rewarded through the appropriation of public resources (Medard 2002). Although the trappings of formal state institutions and processes remain visible, they are either circumvented in preference for informal channels or manipulated to serve the vested political interests of the power holders (Cammack 2007). Watching events and reforms unfold, the neo-patrimonial paradigm seems to fit very well.

So, the view that the dismal performance of public sector reforms is attributable primarily to poor design or lack of national ownership (Kjaer 2004; Wohlgemuth 2008) or inadequate institutional capacity is incorrect or, at least, incomplete where it does not recognise the over-riding impact of political factors (Crook and Manor 1998). This assertion is corroborated by Van de Walle (2001,54) who argues that some reforms will not be resisted as long as they do not hurt the interests of important clienteles. The socio-economic and political interests in the recipient countries and not the Western donors' preferences primarily shape the agenda (Grindle 2004, 274; Chabal 2002, 459). African politicians have adapted to the new political framework without allowing it to undermine their neo-patrimonial systems. It is against this background that the relative success of some reforms and the subversion of others, or what Van de Walle (2001) has termed the "partial reform syndrome", need to be understood.

The literature on public sector reforms in Africa shows cases of failure and success. In particular, decentralisation has been found to be relatively successful in sub-Saharan Africa because of its capacity to renew regime legitimacy and distribute patronage. As pointed out by Crook and Manor (1998), decentralisation reforms in many sub-Saharan Africa countries were embraced because they helped discredited regimes to spread patronage politics to the grassroots. Decentralisation also advances symbolic participation while real accountability has been undermined. Other public sector reforms, which either lack or even obstruct the regimes' political survival strategies, have fared less well. A case in point is the public sector accountability reforms, which pose a big threat to patronage and state-orchestrated corruption on which neo-patrimonial rule thrives (Mwenda and Tangri 2005). Based on such, some argue that the relative success and failure of reforms show that the general and over-riding motive of most African states in accepting public sector reform has been political self-preservation, in terms of accessing foreign aid and re-inventing legitimacy (Haruna 2001). While there surely are some factors other than neo-patrimonialism that explain outcomes of public sector reforms, the Ugandan context is analysed here using the neo-patrimonial paradigm.

Uganda's Decentralisation Reforms

The incumbent ruling party's – National Resistance Movement (NRM) – early commitment to decentralise power is contained in the Ten-Point Programme of the party's first manifesto. Under Point No.1, a two-tier (or two-dimensional) system was provided by representative democracy (parliament) and popular democracy (NRM 1985, 6–7; Watson 1994) through decentralisation. Populist grassroots assemblies (people's committees) had been implemented in liberated zones as the National Resistance Army/Movement increasingly worked towards national power, and these had made a tremendous contribution to the guerrilla war effort by mobilising new recruits, food, mediating in local disputes, and gathering intelligence.

Building on this, the NRM government set up a five-level hierarchy of Resistance Councils and Committees (RCs) which were later re-named Local Councils (LCs). The RCs were participant grassroots political structures that started from the village level (LC1) and federated to the parish (LC2), sub-county (LC3), county (LC4), and to the district (LC5). The RCs were constituted by all adults aged 18 years and above who collectively deliberated on local issues that affected them, including functioning as local courts to dispense civil justice. Only at the village level (LC1) did all eligible people democratically elect their leaders (executive committees). Leaders of each other level (LC2 – LC5) were elected by the executive committee of the level immediately below them. Plainly, fully-fledged democratic participation progressively deteriorated, and the more senior the power base became, the more disconnected it was from the people's suffrage.

The RC grassroots system of governance was later formalised and translated into policy by the Local Governments (Resistance Councils) Statute of 1992. Under the decentralisation policy reforms, Uganda adopted a devolved form of local government where political, administrative and financial powers were given to districts (LC5). This arrangement meant that district local governments had become corporate bodies with powers to periodically elect their own leaders, recruit personnel, make policies, plan, make annual budgets and raise local revenue with less interference from the central government (Villadsen and Lubanga 1996).

The decentralisation policy reforms were implemented from 1993, beginning with 13 pilot districts after which it was rolled over to 13 more districts in 1994 and finally to the remaining 13 districts so as to cover the entire 39 districts. This policy was embedded in the 1995 constitution and subsequently operationalised by the Local Governments Act of 1997. Decentralisation was effectively institutionalised.

Uganda had an elaborate decentralisation system at independence in 1962, but this was reversed in 1966 by the then President Obote, who abrogated the independence constitution and re-centralised power under the 1967 Republican Constitution (Karugire 1980). This marked the beginning of authoritarianism which climaxed in the 1971 military take-over and the subsequent political dictatorship and state-orchestrated abuse of people's rights. After such a traumatic and prolonged experience, the decentralisation reforms implemented by the NRM government were hailed both domestically and internationally as a landmark in Uganda's democratisation process (Ndegwa 2002). They restored (and hopefully entrenched) people's participation at the grassroots, with the power to make decisions relevant to their circumstances and to hold their leaders accountable. They empowered and brought aboard marginalised groups such as women, the youth and people with disabilities. Women were constitutionally guaranteed one-third of the composition of the local council committees (Muhumuza 2004; Saito 2002).

One of the stated objectives of the NRM government was to enhance accountability. The 26 years of centralisation without accountability had allowed rampant corruption which led to the collapse of service delivery and people's withdrawal from the state to the informal sector (Brett 1993). Decentralisation was presented as a strategy to enforce accountability and, hence, improve service delivery and thereby re-invent state legitimacy.

The NRM's Motive for Decentralising Power

Reasons for decentralisation frequently given by government officials and cited in policy documents created the impression that the drive was to foster democracy and, by empowering the people's initiative, to unlock their potential to undertake development on their own (Villadsen and Lubanga 1996; Nsibambi 1997). While this may be true, so many other measures with similar objectives became so stagnated that these reasons do not explain why decentralisation was implemented with such enthusiasm and speed. What was the driving force?

First of all, the NRM understood that governments which come to power through unconstitutional means are not sustainable. The NRM government needed to build a longer-term power base from which to garner popular support. The experimentation with the people's committees (RCs) during the guerrilla period had helped to mobilise the popular support that propelled the National Resistance Army (NRA) to power as the NRM (Kisakye 1996,36–46). The NRM government had to move with speed to formalise and entrench the RC system. The outcome of returning political power to the grassroots people not only endeared the NRM government to the rural people but also made it difficult to separate LC structures from those of the NRM (especially important when it transformed into a party in 2005). So, decentralisation provided a golden opportunity. The decentralisation carrot worked. In the presidential and local council elections, President Museveni won with 75 per cent of the vote, and more than 80 per cent of councillors winning the district chairs were NRM well-wishers (Uganda Election Commission 1996; Makara, Tukahebwa and Byarugaba 2003).

The NRM has consistently manipulated the LC system and used it to marshal rural support. This partly explains why the support base of the NRM is predominantly in rural areas (Ottemoeller 1998). In fact, when the NRM embraced multi-party politics in 2005, it tried without success to block the introduction of multi-party politics in lower local council levels — village (LC1) and parish (LC2). NRM advocated in parliament that parties should be restricted to the national level, because they were going to divide the people and undermine the unity and stability that had been ushered in by the NRM government (Muriaas 2009).

Uganda's political history had been haunted by sectarian politics fuelled by religious and ethnic cleavages (Apter 1995). Uganda gained independence on the platform of multi-party political competition. However, the major undoing of the three independence parties — UPC, DP and KY (Kabaka Yekka, literally rendered as *Only the Kabaka* – the traditional ruler of Buganda Kingdom) — was that their support was built around ethnicity and religion (Leys 1967). The KY had a strong support base among the Kabaka royalists in the central region of Buganda; DP drew predominantly from the Catholics, while UPC's support was Protestants. There is no doubt that the earlier experience with multi-partism was divisive. This largely explains the popular support given to LCs which were participatory, non-partisan and accommodating people from all walks of life, irrespective of their gender, creed or ethnic affiliation. The NRM's concerns that parties could undermine unity if introduced at the local level were not unfounded, even though the hidden motive could have been to prevent other parties from building a political base at the grassroots, where the ruling NRM party had enjoyed a monopoly for the previous two decades.

Although the NRM's position was rejected and multi-partism was formally mandated at all levels, once elected back to power, the NRM government only allowed other parties to operate at the district and sub-county levels. It defied the new political dispensation and invoked the Local Governments Act 1997 (election on individual merit, not affiliation) for village and parish elections in 2006. Of course, this was in conflict with the new multi-party provisions, but the intended amendment to the act had not been processed.

The main opposition party then, the Forum for Democratic Change (FDC), petitioned the constitutional court which sat on 3rd April, 2007 and ruled in its favour. Facing an unequivocal ruling by the highest legal authority, the NRM government responded by not holding any lower level elections at all! It delayed tabling of necessary laws and cited inadequate funds to conduct the election process with such obduracy that, even today, five years later, lower local council elections (LC1 and LC2) have still not been held. This has had debilitating effects on Uganda's local governance, ranging from increased corruption to poor service delivery (Republic of Uganda 2008; CBR 2005). Although corruption is a nation-wide problem estimated by African Peer Review Mechanism Report to cost Uganda about Shs 569 billion (US$260 million) annually (Republic of Uganda 2007), its impact has been felt most at the local government level.

Local governments were identified as central to implementation of the Millenium Development Goals (MDGs). In Uganda, the national priority programmes to be delivered by local governments include: modernisation of agriculture, water and sanitation, primary education, primary health, and community roads (Republic of Uganda PRSP 2001). The central government channels conditional grants to the local governments to implement these priority programmes. According to the Ombudsman's report of 2010, most of the complaints received were against district administrations and were corruption-related (Republic of Uganda 2010 (a): 7 and 30). Increasing corruption and deterioration of service delivery in local governments translated into citizen apathy – reflected in the Electoral Commission's very low turn-out figures for the 2011 district, municipality and sub-county polls (http://www.ec.or.ug/ Elec-results/2011-District-Chairperson.pdf). The simple explanation is that the local electorate is disenchanted with political candidates who serve their own selfish interests. This was confirmed by a study sanctioned by Konrad Adenauer Stiftung (2010) on Uganda's state of political pluralism and democracy at the local level. One of its major findings on citizens' perception was the lack of trust of local leaders because they were perceived to pursue individual interests.

The early years of decentralisation were promising because popular participation was emphasised in local policy-making, local council courts and election of local leaders. This led to relative stability and development, conditions which legitimised the NRM government, evidenced by its landslide victory in the 1996 elections with 75 per cent of the total votes (Makara, Tukahebwa and Byarugaba 2003). Also, the enthusiasm with which decentralisation reforms were being implemented encouraged significant international donor assistance. Many donors channelled their aid - even for MDGs - through local governments. The percentage of national budget transferred to local governments has grown from UGX. 40 billion in 1992 when decentralisation was initiated to the current UGX 2,234 billion, which was 37 per cent of total government expenditure in the fiscal year 2009/2010 (Mutabwire 2010).

It should, however, be noted that local governments were denied buoyant sources of locally generated resources. They were only allowed to generate revenue from insignificant sources, such as market dues, graduated tax, rates and licences, among others, that together constitute less than 20 per cent of total national revenues while the centre retained the lucrative and elastic sources such as the VAT, income tax, pay-as-you-earn and corporate tax and more (Kiwanuka-Musisi 1999). The financial constriction (and or dependency) of local governments was not accidental. It gave central government carrot-and-stick leverage to prevent "alternative" power centres that could eventually pose a political challenge.

The progressive withdrawal of local government autonomy and increased control by the central government seem to confirm this argument. Graduated tax, which used to generate 80 per cent of local government revenue (Bitarabeho 2008) was suspended indefinitely in 2005. That did more than clip local government's financial wings; it also dive-bombed an opposition strategy to win votes by promising to abolish the tax, which, although lucrative to LCs, was unpopular with the electorate.

Local governments no longer have the resources to implement local priority programmes that differ from the national priority programmes (determined by NRM) that are funded via stringently conditional grants. The central government currently funds more than 90 per cent of the local governments budgets (Mutabwire 2010). These conditional grants reduce innovation at the local level, and increase manipulation at the central level.

While decentralisation was robust, local governments were empowered to establish District Service Commissions (DSCs) and appoint relevant commissioners. In return, the DSCs appointed, promoted and disciplined local government employees, including Chief Administrative Officers (CAOs) for the rural districts and the town clerks (TCs) for the urban authorities with no interference from the centre. The allowances for local governments' elected leaders were internally-decided, provided only they did not exceed 20 per cent of locally-generated resources.

All these democratic gains have been gradually reversed since 2006. The NRM government scrapped the District Tender Boards whose members were controlled by and accountable to elected councils and replaced them with Contract Committees. The argument of the NRM government was that District Tender Boards were abused by elected leaders who controlled them; they were accused of awarding themselves tenders for goods and services, without accountability. Contract Committee members are now appointed by the CAO from among the senior civil servants at the district level. These members are neither controlled by nor accountable to the political leaders of local government. It must be stressed that the key responsibility for controlling the Contract Committees (responsible for procurement) was removed from the elected leaders and given to the accounting officers.

Equally important, the payment of salaries of elected leaders has been taken over by the central government. The district chairpersons, executive committee members, speaker, the sub-county chairperson, deputy chairperson and sub-county speaker are now directly paid by the central government from the national consolidated fund. The implied threat to any local leader who seeks higher political status or challenges the actions of government is evident. Also, the chairpersons of parish and village councils are paid by the central government an annual ex-gratia allowance of UGX 150,000/= (approximately US$65) "to help them perform their duties". This is a not a small amount considering the fact that a primary teacher diploma holder earns a monthly salary of UGX 270,000= (approximately US$108) while a police constable and a private in the army earn about UGX 200,000= (approximately US$80). This is yet another lever in the hands of central government (Muhumuza 2008; Kjaer 2005).

In such ways has central control of local authorities intensified since murmurings of multipartism in 2002 and particularly since multi-party elections (2006 - to date) — the very period that has posed the greatest political challenge to the NRM's grip on power. Indeed, Barkan *et al.* (2005) and Kjaer (2005) assert that local councils have been used to serve the partisan organs of the NRM government. Where independent candidates have won the district chairmanship in local government, they have been put under pressure to sign memoranda of understanding with the NRM party to support the ruling party position. NRM has tooled-up to ensure that anyone who chooses to be defiant and confrontational will find themselves operating under difficult conditions. Defiance is anyway minimised in advance. In Bukomansimbi District, for example, the LC5 chairperson belongs to the JEEMA party but the majority of elected councillors are from the ruling NRM party. Reportedly, the "independent" chairperson had to enter a memorandum of compliance with the NRM Secretary General as a condition of any support by his councillors. A similar incident was reported from Pallisa District in 2007 (Amama-Mbabazi 2007).

Another indicator is the escalating number of districts. Since the introduction of a competitive political climate, the NRM government has opportunistically created many unviable districts contrary to constitutional provisions (Green 2008), especially during the presidential election period. Eleven new districts were created in 1996 and another 11 in 2001 to bring the total to 56 (Jesper 2006). With multi-partism came even more. By 2006, Uganda had

79 districts and by 2010 these increased to 112. Another 21 were promised during the 2011 presidential campaigns. Every one of these is dependent on central government funding. Article 179(4) of the constitution clearly stipulates the principles for the creation of a new local authority — particularly population density and economic viability (Republic of Uganda 1995). Proliferation under NRM government (the number of districts has risen from 33 to 112 on their watch) has ignored those requirements, and instead cited the necessity for effective administration, the need to bring services closer to the people, and responsiveness to the wishes of the people concerned. Political opportunism may be nearer the truth (Jesper 2006). The NRM leadership has increasingly used the creation of new local authorities as a political strategy to renew its grassroots support base and consolidate power (Green 2008).

Bear in mind that Uganda's decentralisation reforms won political commitment from the NRM government on the grounds of defusing political strife and ethnic sub-nationalism. Earlier, concentrated power created stiff competition for limited civil service jobs and political positions which were available only at the centre (Barongo 1989). This was partly because Uganda's private sector had largely been destroyed by the reckless policies of nationalisation in 1969 (Obote 1969), and by Idi Amin's declaration of economic war in 1971 (Schultheis 1975; Kuteesa *et al.* 2010). This competition needs to be put into context, given that Uganda is a multi-ethnic country where factional groups compete for a fair share of the national resources and influential jobs (Kabumba 1989). Furthermore, the Buganda region, which is populous and centrally located around the capital city, has always had a precarious relationship with all central governments since the colonial era. It has always agitated for a federal system of government which it had from 1955 to 1966 before the radical reforms that re-centralised power in 1967 (Kanyeihamba 1975; Mulindwa 2003). The potential for strife is not short of fuel.

The NRM leadership realised that it needed less political competition at the centre while buying time to consolidate its fragile tenure. Decentralisation was not only to appease Buganda's aspirations but also generally diffused ethnic nationalism and competition for power and resources at the centre (Ehtisham, Brosio and Gonzalez 2006,7). According to the Uganda Bureau of Statistics (2009), local governments employ 70.3 per cent of Uganda's total civil service establishment. By distributing resources at local levels, the "fair share" tension is addressed.

Like in many parts of the world, the Ugandan decentralisation reform was introduced to achieve the objectives of bringing government closer to the citizens and giving the people a voice to hold government accountable. The foregoing discussion, however, revealed Uganda's decentralisation reform was embraced as it was instrumental for the ruling party to mobilise the popular support that propelled the NRM to power. For a long time, local governments were identified as central to implementation of the many national development programmes including the Millennium Development Goals (MDGs). Later on, however, this situation has been reversed and the autonomy of local governments was abandoned and they became controlled by the central government. The Ugandan case shows that, as Manor (1999:38) pointed out, 'In neo-patrimonial systems, decentralisation has been diverted from conventional objectives and is used as an instrument to pursue narrow political objectives and entrench regime interests'.

The Nature of Public Sector Accountability Reforms Implemented

The NRM government established the first government Ombudsman in 1988 (Statute No.2 of 1988), empowering the Inspector General of Government (IGG) to fight public sector corruption and abuse of public office – with powers to investigate and prosecute. Other initiatives included activating the Public Accounts Committee (PAC), an oversight committee of parliament; the Office of the Auditor General (OAG), and the enactment of the Leadership Code of Conduct in 1992. To guard against illegal accumulation of wealth through fraudulent channels and to ensure integrity, the Leadership Code of Conduct required both politicians and public servants to declare their wealth every two years.

These measures had legal backing. The institution of Ombudsman, or the IGG, as it is known in Uganda, and the Leadership Code of Conduct were provided for by the Inspectorate of Government Act of 2002 and the Leadership Code of Conduct of 2002, respectively. Other reinforcing legislation has followed in a steady stream: the Audit Act, the Disposal of Assets Act and the Financial and Accountability Act, all in 2003; the Local Government Procurement (Amendment) Act in 2006; the Financial and Accounting Regulations in 2007; the Anti-Corruption Act in 2009 and the Whistleblowers Act in 2010.

Uganda's policy and legal measures to fight corruption have been rated highly at 99.6 per cent (Global Integrity Organisation 2008). The NRM government has also signed international conventions against corruption, including the African Union Convention on Preventing and Combating Corruption (AUCPC) and the United Nations Convention against Corruption (UNCAC) – both ratified in 2003.

But these much lauded demonstrations of intent have not been matched by results. Uganda's anti-corruption efforts are judged to have regressed since 1996 (World Bank 1998:34). This situation is well documented in the CSAR of APRM (2009:94) which describes corruption in Uganda as endemic and widespread – an extraordinary paradox.

The NRM's Ambivalence in Fighting Corruption

This paper's posit – that vested political interests run the show – becomes clarion. The NRM government has not distanced itself from ostracised cabinet ministers implicated in corruption scandals; rather, it has protected them (Tangri and Mwenda 2006:116; Furley 2000:88; Flanary and Watt 1999). Fighting corruption and consolidating power are not naturally harmonic when patronage secures the power base; less still in the glare of opposition pressure. The NRM government has had to manage a trade-off between these two "irreconcilable" issues.

Consolidating power has taken ever-higher priority as opposition has mobilised. Paul Ssemogerere, former President of the Democratic Party, resigned from cabinet to challenge President Museveni's monopoly of power, maintained since 1986 under the guise of "No-Party democracy" (Mugaju and Oloka-Onyango 2000). And even more serious threat was posed by Dr Kiiza Besigye, who broke away from the ruling NRM party and stood on the Reform Agenda platform in 2001, and later formed the Forum for Democratic Change (FDC) party when multi-party politics was revived. The FDC's challenge saw NRM's electoral popularity reduced from 75 per cent in 1996 to 59 per cent in 2006 (EC 2006).

The NRM leadership had all along nurtured the desire to cling to power as evidenced by the removal of presidential term limits in 2005. In these circumstances, corruption is not just more likely; it must be guaranteed. NRM has effectively abandoned the concept of a broad-based government of national unity with commitment to integrity (Muhumuza 2009; Barkan *et al* 2005; Mwenda and Tangri 2005; Tripp 2010). It has needed to pursue patronage politics with more vigour than ever, rewarding political support with benefits from the state, protecting corrupt but loyal officials, flouting public procurement rules, and – if necessary – election bribery and rigging are menu options (Mwenda and Tangri 2005; Agaba and Shipman 2007:383; Flanary and Watt 1999). True accountability is simply not compatible with these strategies.

Mindful of the implications of failure to observe good governance practices, the NRM government has conducted a balancing act to gradually put in place the relevant accountability institutions and laws (to satisfy both international conditions and the expectations of the people) while ensuring they did not have the autonomy, facilitation and political clout to be effective (note many foregoing examples). Where anti-corruption efforts might become inconveniently successful, remedial steps were taken: for example, there was an attempt to strip the IGG of its prosecution powers and reduce it to a department within the President's Office in 2003, as evidenced by proposals submitted to the Constitutional Review Commission by the NRM government (Republic of Uganda 2003). In sum, a semblance of good laws and institutions were put in place but without the necessary autonomy, mandate, capacity, and facilitation to enforce accountability and fight corruption (APRM-CSAR 2009: 95–96).

This balancing act has worked, politically, for a quarter of a century. Uganda has taken a spectacular number of measures to fight corruption, yet it is rated by Transparency International (TI) (2010) as the second most corrupt country in East Africa, with a prevalence of 33 per cent.

According to the findings of the Commission of Inquiry in 2002, which was chaired by Justice Ssebutinde to investigate irregularities in the Uganda Revenue Authority (URA), the driving force behind rampant corruption was politicians (Republic of Uganda 2004). The East African Bribery Index of 2010 report ranked the URA 4th out of 44 as the most corrupt agency in the East African community. Much of the corruption in the National Social Security Fund (NSSF), the custodian of people's pensions, has involved senior NRM politicians. The recent Temangalo land procurement scandal involved the then Minister of Finance and the Secretary General of NRM party (Republic of Uganda 2010(b); Ssemujju 2008, *The Weekly Observer* 6–12, 2008). Although tendencies to bureaucratic corruption characterised the early years of the NRM government, the phenomenon of politically-inspired corruption intensified and became politicised in 2006 — the moment a threat to the NRM's rule emerged through competitive politics. The general elections of 2006 and 2011 witnessed bribery of voters by the NRM on a huge scale (Makara, Rakner and Svasand 2009:197; Oloka Onyango 2011). Thereafter, NRM supporters have been appointed to government positions (Tripp 2010:39-58).

Any remaining semblance of NRM commitment to fight public sector corruption has been severely compromised by corruption cases involving NRM loyalists. The Sixth Parliament censured two NRM cabinet members — Sam Kutesa in March 1999 and Jim Muhwezi in May 1998 — for being corrupt. Two other corrupt ministers, Kirunda Kivejinja and Mathew Rukikaire, resigned before they were censured.

The government's reaction? Kutesa and Muhwezi were promoted to full cabinet ministers in 2001 (Tangri and Mwenda 2006:116). They were later involved in bigger corruption scandals. Muhwezi was later implicated in a corruption scandal involving the misuse of US$ 1.6 million from the Global Fund for AIDS and Malaria (*Daily Monitor* 2007: 1–2), while Kutesa was implicated in the Commonwealth Heads of Government (CHOGM) corruption scandal (see later). This strategic deception delivered one of its most poignant ironies when Dr Nsaba Buturo, who had been implicated by PAC in a corruption scandal that involved the irregular soliciting of UGX 20 million from MEGA FM radio, was appointed to head the key Department of Ethics and Integrity (Olupot and Mary 2006:1; Nanduto 2006:3) – a move viewed as a mockery of the institution and contemptuous of policy integrity.

The Auditor General (AG) and the IGG were not allocated adequate resources and lacked the necessary power to enforce their decisions. Until 2002, the IGG could investigate cases of public sector corruption, but had to report to the Directorate of Public Prosecutions (DPP) to prosecute the culprits. The DPP often interminably delayed or dropped cases.

The NRM's tactics were not shy. When persistent pressure earned the IGG powers of prosecution, the NRM government openly lobbied to restructure the IGG, turn it into a department within the President's Office, and strip it of the powers to prosecute (Republic of Uganda 2003). The proposal raised such a public outcry and donor outrage that the NRM government was forced to withdraw its recommendations.

The AG and Public Procurement and Disposal of Assets (PPDA) were also denied the power to enforce, and could only make recommendations. The AG, which is the government's Chief Auditor, makes recommendations to the Public Accounts Committee (PAC) — an oversight committee of parliament. The PAC is also powerless, since its role stops at conducting investigations and compiling reports which are debated by parliament. If the recommendations are endorsed by parliament, they are then forwarded to the Ministry of Finance (on the lap of government) to pass them on to the appointing authorities and disciplinary commissions for appropriate action. Even the PPDA lacks enforcement powers. Its sole recourse of recommendations to the appointing authorities is rarely acted on. The strategy of breeding tigers but removing their teeth is blatant, chronic and all pervasive. Evidence to corroborate this assertion is provided by Agaba and Shipman (2007:383) who noted that the main obstacles to the success of procurement reforms in Uganda have been identified as vested interests and lack of political will despite the government's declaration of a zero-tolerance policy towards corruption.

The tactics used to achieve this objective varied. One was to delay enactment of relevant legislation — a comprehensive anti-corruption bill tabled in 2003 did not become an act until 2009. That does not happen accidentally. Besides, legal loopholes were often deliberately built-in to laws and institutions as a contingency. The Leadership Code of Conduct was passed to please donors and Uganda's electorate. The law was enacted in 1992, but was not enforced until 1997. It did indeed demand that senior government officials and politicians declare their wealth but made no mention of their spouses and children.

The IGG caught up Mr Kakooza Mutale, a senior political assistant to the President, for failure to declare his wealth. The IGG made a direct and formal recommendation to the President to sack Mutale for failure to abide by the Leadership Code of Conduct. The power of the IGG to do this was challenged through a petition to the Constitutional Court filed by the President's Principal Legal Secretary, Mr. Fox Odoi, while the President agreed to swear an affidavit in court to support the appeal by Kakooza Mutale (Tangri and Mwenda 2006:109–110). Among other things, this removes the possibility that loopholes arise from poor legal drafting or insufficient grasp of crucial litigious detail. Government is the master, not the victim, of these nuances.

As long as anti-corruption laws and institutions do not threaten the NRM regime, they are allowed to work. The key phrase is "selective" authority and enforcement. Take the case of another member of parliament, without patronage, who failed to declare his wealth. On the recommendation of the IGG, he lost his seat. Contrast that with the corruption scandal involving a Minister of Security who doubled as a Secretary General of the ruling NRM party. He was accused of selling his land (exorbitantly) to the National Social Security Fund (NSSF), in contravention of government procurement rules. The PAC was required to investigate and assemble evidence. The President personally chaired the NRM party caucus meeting (which enjoyed an overwhelming majority of 221 - 72 per cent - out of the total 332 MPs) to drum up support for the embattled minister, but also compromised the chairperson of PAC by including him on a delegation that accompanied the President on a state visit to Iceland (Ssemujju 2008:18–19). The minister was subsequently exonerated by the PAC. Through all this, the IGG was silent. When challenged to explain, the IGG attributed inaction to a legal detail: the law bars the IGG from investigating an incident of corruption unless a complaint has been registered in writing.

Another case that exposed the NRM government's complicity was Uganda's hosting of the CHOGM in 2007. Government officials in the organising team were accused of malfeasance and the PAC was mandated to investigate. It unearthed high incidences of corruption that cost government billions of shillings. These scandals involved top government officials, including the Vice President, the Minister of Foreign Affairs, the Minister of Works and Agriculture, and other key officials of the NRM government who had flouted procurement procedures. The President again galvanised NRM party members through a parliamentary caucus meeting. Attempts to have the culprits censured in Parliament were defeated by the majority NRM party members (*Daily Monitor*, November 18, 2010).

The message is clear: irrespective of any rhetoric, legislation or institutional mechanism, accountability reforms have successfully scaled down the levels of corruption only where the political leadership has been committed to making that happen, as exemplified by Malaysia, Hong Kong, Singapore and Botswana (Marican 1979; Skidmore 1996; Quah 2001).

Conclusion

The NRM government has implemented a number of administrative reforms since it came to power in 1986. Some of these reforms, especially those relating to good governance, were pursued under pressure from donors (as a condition for accessing aid). The assumption of donors was that the adoption of Western-inspired "best practices" such as good governance would enhance efficiency and effectiveness in government, promote accountability, reduce the opportunities for rent-seeking behaviour (LeVine 1993,7) and consequently improve service delivery. The outcomes of administrative reforms have been disappointing. This poor performance is reflexively blamed on institutional incapacity and poor design (ECA 2003); less attention has been paid to the influence of the political context. Where there is neo-patrimonial rule, the objectives of administrative reforms are likely to be subverted. The nature of politics and character of leadership play primary roles in the success or failure of reforms. Where such reforms threaten the leader's hold on power, they tend to have limited chances of success; especially where patronage-driven politics go hand-in-hand with the use of public resources to sustain patron-client networks (Bayart 1993; Szeftel 2000; Medard 2002). Foreign pressure is usually eroded by local political manipulations. The fact that donors must weigh their own national motives vis-

´a-vis pressing for reforms in dependent states, may allow the aid-recipient country latitude to escape donor sanctions (Hauser 1999). Uganda's administrative reforms have been influenced by, more than any other factor, the neo-patrimonial nature of the NRM government. Reforms which helped NRM consolidate its power base and prolong its life were implemented with speed and relative success; those that threatened patronage politics were manipulated and/or undermined. This pattern was worsened by Uganda's transition to competitive electoral politics in 2006.

Public Sector Reform – no matter how well designed, resourced and implemented – will have almost no chance of sustained success if it does not, first and foremost, allow for the real political motives of the government it seeks to improve. Donors cannot be oblivious to the manipulations of aid-recipient governments. They are therefore, at least by default, complicit in the less-than-good governance they seek to reform. In balancing rhetoric with reality, change with control, compliant action with vested interest, neo-patrimonial regimes demonstrate an uncanny understanding of donor motives and tolerance levels; where to draw the line and when and how to safely cross it. Equating poor governance with incompetence or negligence would be a grave mistake. The result of any public sector reform is not a matter of skill or effort or chance. It is the deliberate choice of the regime in power.

References

Agaba, E. and N. Shipman. 2007. Public procurement in developing countries: The Uganda experience. In G. Piga and K. V. Thai (Eds.), *Advancing public procurement: Practices, innovation and knowledge-sharing*, pp. 373–391. Boca Raton, FL: PrAcademics Press.

Amama-Mbabazi. 2007. *Political situation in Pallisa district after the By-election for LC5 chairperson*. Kampala: Office of the Secretary General. National Resistance Movement.

Apter, D. E. 1995. Democracy for Uganda: A case for comparison. *Daedalus* 124 (3): 155–91.

Barkan, J., S. Kayunga, J. D. S. Ngethe and N. Titsworth. 2005. The political economy of Uganda: *Managing a donor-financed neo-patrimonial state*. Kampala: World Bank Commissioned Report.

Barongo, Y. 1989. Ethnic pluralism and political centralization: The basis of political conflict. In K. Rupesinghe (Ed.), *Conflict resolution in Uganda*. London: James Currey. pp. 65–90.

Bayart, J. 1993. *The state in Africa: The politics of the belly*. London: Longman.

Bitarabeho, J. 2008. The experience of Uganda – Local government's role as a partner in the decentralization process to strengthen local development. A Paper Presented at a Conference on: Access to Development Funding for Local Governments in Africa, Johannesburg, September 15–17, 2008.

Botchwey, K., P. Collier, J. W. Gunning and K. Hamada. 1998. *External evaluation of the ESAF. Report by a group of independent experts*. Washington, D.C.: IMF.

Brett, E. A. 1993. *Providing for the rural poor: Institutional decay and transformation in Uganda*. Kampala: Fountain Publishers.

Cammack, D. 2007. The logic of African neopatrimonialism: What role for donors? *Development Policy Review*, 25 (5): 599–614.

Centre for Basic Research (CBR). 2005. The impact of political corruption on resource allocation and service delivery in local governments in Uganda. A report submitted to Transparency International Uganda.

Chabal, P. 2002. The quest for good government and development in Africa: Is NEPAD the answer? *International Affairs*, 78: 447–462.

Chabal, P. and J.P. Daloz. 1999. *Africa works, disorder as political instrument*. Bloomington: Indiana University Press.

Crook, R. and J. Manor. 1998. *Democracy and decentralization in South Asia and West Africa*. New York: Cambridge University Press.*Daily Monitor*, May 28, 2007.

288

De Maria, W. 2008. Cross-cultural tresspass: Assessing African anti-corruption capacity. *International Journal of Cross-Cultural Management* 8 (3): 317–341.

Economic Commission for Africa (ECA). 2003. *Public sector management reforms in Africa*. Addis Ababa: ECA.

Ehtisham, A., G. Brosio and M. Gonzalez. 2006. Uganda: Managing more effective decentralization. *IMF Working Paper, No WP/06/279*. Fiscal Affairs Department.

Electoral Commission (EC) 2011. *Election results report 2011*. Kampala: Uganda. http://www.ec.or.ug/Elec-results/2011-District-chairperson.pdf (accessed on December, 2011).

———.2006. *Uganda election results 2006*. Kampala: Election Commission.

Flanary, R. and D. Watt. 1999. The state of corruption: A case of Uganda. *Third World Quarterly* 20 (3): 515–36.

Furley, O. 2000. Democratization in Uganda. *Commonwealth and Comparative Politics*, 38 (3): 79–102.

Global Integrity Organization. 2008. http://report.globalintegrity.org/images/08index_uganda.git (accessed on December, 2011)

Green, E. 2008. District creation and decentralization in Uganda. *CSRC Working Paper No. 24*. Development Studies Institute. London School of Economics (LSE).

Grindle, M. S. 2004. Good enough governance: Poverty reduction and reform in developing countries. *Governance: An International Journal of Policy, Administration and Institutions*, 17 (4): 525–548.

Harrison, G. 2005. The World Bank governance and theories of political action in Africa. *British Journal of Politics and International Relations*, 7 (2): 240–260.

Haruna, P. F. 2001. Reflective public administration reform: Building relationships, bridging gaps in Ghana. *African Studies Review*, 44 (1): 37–57.

Hauser, E. 1999. Ugandan relations with Western donors in the 1990s: What impact on democratization? *Journal of Modern African Studies*, 37: 621–41.

Jesper, S. 2006. Local government organization and finance: Uganda. In Anwar, S. (Ed.), *Local governance in developing countries*. Washington, D.C.: World Bank. pp. 93–136.

Kabumba, I. 1989. Ethnic conflict within the public service. In K. Rupesinghe (Ed.), *Conflict resolution in Uganda*, pp. 158–177. London: James Currey.

Kanyeihamba, G. W. 1975. *Constitutional law and government in Uganda*. Nairobi: East African Literature Bureau.

Karugire, R. S. 1980. *A political history of Uganda*. London: Heinmann.

Kisakye, J. 1996. Political background to decentralization. In Villadsen, S. and F. Lubanga (Eds.), *Democratic decentralization in Uganda*, pp.36–46. Kampala: Fountain Publishers.

Kiwanuka-Musisi, G. G. 1999. Emerging issues in the implementation of decentralization. A paper presented at the National Forum on the Implementation of Decentralization in Uganda, November 15–19 by the President of Uganda Local Authorities Association. The International Conference Centre, Kampala.

Kjaer, A. M. 2005. Central government intervention as obstacle to local participatory governance: The case of Uganda. Paper prepared for ILO Conference on Governance, Geneva.

Kjaer, A. M. 2004. Old brooms can sweep too!' An overview of rulers and public sector reforms in Uganda, Tanzania and Kenya. *The Journal of Modern African Studies*, 42(3): 389–413.

Kuteesa, F., E. Tumusiime-Mutebile, A. Whitworth and T. Williamson (Eds.) 2010. *Uganda's economic reforms: Insider accounts*. Oxford: Oxford University Press.

LeVine, V. 1993. Administrative corruption and democratization in Africa: Aspects of the theoretical agenda. *Corruption and Reform* 7 (3): 271–278.

Leys, C. 1967. *Politicians and policies: An essay on politics in Acholi, Uganda 1962–1965*. Nairobi: East Africa Publishing House.

Makara, S., L. Rakner and L. Svasand. 2009. Turnaround: The National Resistance Movement and the reintroduction of a multiparty system in Uganda. *International Political Science Review* 30 (2): 185–204.

Makara S., G. Tukahebwa and F. Byarugaba. 2003. *Voting for democracy in Uganda*. Kampala: LDC Publishers.

Manor, J. 1999. *The political economy of democratic decentralization*. Washington, D.C.: World Bank.

Marican, Y. M. 1979. Combating corruption: The Malaysian experience. *Asian Survey* 19(6): 597– 610.

Medard, J. 2002. Corruption in the neopatrimonial states of Sub-Saharan Africa. In Arnold J. H. and M. Johnston (Eds.), *Political corruption: Concepts and contexts*, pp. 379–402. New Bruniswick, NJ.: Transaction Publishers.

Mugaju, J. and J. Oloka-Onyango (Eds.) 2000. *No-party democracy in Uganda: Myths and realities*. Kampala: Fountain Publishers.

Mugyenyi, B. J. 1991. IMF conditionality and structural adjustment under the National Resistance Movement. In H. B. Hansen and M. Twaddle (Eds.), *Changing Uganda: The dilemmas of structural adjustment and revolutionary change*, pp. 61–77. Kampala: Fountain Publishers.

Muhumuza, W. 1997. Money and power in Uganda's 1996 elections. *African Journal of Political Science (AJPS)* 2 (1): 168–179.

——.2004. The empowerment of women in Museveni's Uganda: Who benefits? *The Australasian Review of African Studies* 26 (2): 25–40.

——.2008. Between rhetoric and political conviction: The high cost of ignoring the dynamics of decentralization in Uganda and Africa. The *Journal of Social, Political and Economic Studies* 33 (4): 426–457.

———.2009. From fundamental change to no change: The NRM and democratization in Uganda. *Les Cahiers d'Afrique de L'Est* No. 41, pp. 19–38. May–August 2009.

Muriaas, R. L. 2009. Reintroducing local level multiparty system in Uganda: Why be in the opposition? *Government and Opposition* 44 (1): 91–112.

Mulindwa, E. 2003. Buganda's Report to the Constitutional Review Commission. Saturday, 15th February. http.www.mail-archive.com/ugandanet@kym.net/msg03172.html. (accessed on December, 2011)

Museveni, K. Y. 1997. *Sowing the Mustard Seed*. London: Macmillan.

Mutabwire, K. P. 2010. Resource mobilization for implementing decentralization and wealth creation at local level: Ugandan experience. A paper presented at the Joint Meeting of All African Ministerial Conference on Decentralization and Local Development (AMCOD), September, 28–29, 2010, Yaounde, Cameroon.

Mwenda, A. M. and R. Tangri. 2005. Patronage politics, donor reforms, and regime consolidation in Uganda. *African Affairs*, 104 (416): 449–469.

Nanduto A. 2006. MPs order Buturo to pay Shs 20m. *Daily Monitor*, October 31, 2006.

National Resistance Movement (NRM). 1985. *Ten-point programme*. Kampala: NRM Secretariat.

Ndegwa, S. N. 2002. Decentralization in Africa: A stock-taking survey. *Africa Regional Working Paper Series*, No. 40. Washington, D.C.: World Bank.

Nsibambi, A. 1997. *The quest for good governance: Decentralization and civil society in Uganda*. Kampala: Fountain Publishers.

Obote, A. M. 1969. *The common man's charter*. Entebbe: Government Printer.

Ochieng, E. O. 1991. Economic adjustment programmes in Uganda 1985–98. In H. B. Hansen and M. Twaddle (Eds.), *Changing Uganda*, pp. 43–60. Kampala: Fountain Publishers.

Odongotho, C. 2010. MPs clear Mbabazi of CHOGM financial scandal. *Daily Monitor*, 18th November, 2010.

Oloka-Onyango, J. 2011. Uganda elections: An exercise in shame-faced endorsement. *Pambazuka News*, Issue 511. 2nd March.

Olupot, M. and K. Mary. 2006. Buturo ordered to refund MEGA FM Shs 20M. *The New Vision*, October 31, 2006.

Ottemoeller, D. 1998. Popular perceptions of democracy: Elections and attitudes in Uganda. *Comparative Political Studies*, 31 (1): 98–124.

Quah, J. S. T. 2001. Combating corruption in Singapore: What can be learned? *Journal of Contingencies and Crisis Management* 9(1): 29 – 35.

Republic of Uganda. 2007. African Peer Review Mechanism (APRM) country review report. Kampala, Uganda.

———.2009. African Peer Review Mechanism (APRM) country review report No. 7. Kampala, Uganda.

——.2004. Commission of Inquiry into the Corruption in Uganda Revenue Authority. Chaired by Justice Julie Ssebutinde. Kampala, Uganda.

——.2010 (a). IGG Report to parliament. January-December 2010. Kampala.

——.2001. Poverty reduction strategy paper. Progress report 2001: Uganda poverty status report 2001 summary. Kampala: Ministry of Finance, Planning and Economic Development.

——.2003. Proposals for the amendment of the constitution. Kampala: UPPC.

——.2010(b). Public Accounts Committee report 2010. Kampala: Parliament of Uganda.

——.2010. *The background to the budget 2010/11 fiscal year.* Kampala: Ministry of Finance, Planning and Economic Development.

——.1995. *The constitution of the Republic of Uganda 1995.* Kampala: UPPC.

——.2010(d). *The fourth annual review meeting report on public service reform programme (PRSP).* Kampala: Ministry of Public Service.

——.2008. *Third national integrity systems survey (NIS III).* Kampala: Inspectorate of Government.

Saito, F. 2002. Decentralization measures and gender inequalities: Experiences in Uganda. *Ryukoku Journal of Economic Studies* 41 (5). March 2002.

Schultheis, J. M. 1975. The Ugandan economy and general Amin, 1971–1974. *Studies in Comparative International Development,* 10 (3): 3–35.

Skidmore, M. J. 1996. Promise and peril in combating corruption: Hong Kong's ICAC. *ANNALS, AAPSS.* 547:118 – 125.

Ssemujju, I. N. 2008. Bit by bit account of how Museveni saved Mbabazi. *The Weekly Observer,* November 6–12, 2008.

Szeftel, M. 2000. Eat with us: Managing corruption and patronage under Zambia's three republics, 1964–1999. *Journal of Contemporary African Studies,* 18 (2): 207–224.

Stiftung, K. A. 2010. *The state of political pluralism and democracy at local government level in Uganda.* Kampala.

Tangri, R. and A. M. Mwenda. 2006. Politics, donors and the ineffectiveness of anti-corruption institutions in Uganda. *Journal of Modern African Studies,* 44(1): 101–24.

Therkildsen, O. 2001. Efficiency, accountability and implementation of public sector reform in East and Southern Africa. *Democracy, Governance and Human Rights Programme Paper. No. 3.* UNRISD. Geneva.

Transparency International (TI). 2010. *Corruption perception index (CPI) 2010.* Kampala, Uganda.

Tripp, A. M. 2010. *Museveni's Uganda: Paradoxes of power in a hybrid regime.* Boulder, Co.: Lynne Rienner.

Uganda Bureau of Statistics. 2009. *Statistical abstract.* Kampala, Uganda.

Uganda Electoral Commission. 1996. National election results 1996. (www. ec.or.ug/Elec_results/Nat_Res_1996.pdf).

Van de Walle, N. 2001. *African economies and the politics of permanent crisis, 1979–99.* Cambridge: Cambridge University Press.

Villadsen, S. and F. Lubanga. 1996. *Democratic decentralization in Uganda.* Kampala: Fountain Publishers.

Watson, C. 1994. No to multi-party. *Africa Report* 39 (3): 24 (3). May–June.

Wohlgemuth, L. 2008. Can Africa make use of the new aid architecture? *Africa Development* 33 (4): 31–41.

World Bank. 1989. *Sub-Saharan Africa: From crisis to sustainable growth.* Washington, D.C.: World Bank.

——.1998. Report of the World Bank mission to support the programme of the Republic of Uganda to improve economic governance and combat corruption. Kampala: WB Office.

Chapter 14

Contracting Out Public Services to Private Agents: Lessons from the Management of Local Government Contracts in Ghana

Nicholas Awortwi

Abstract

Ghana was among the first countries in sub-Saharan Africa to adopt market-driven public sector reform policies. These included the New Public Management approach in the mid-1990s, with the aim of 'reviving' the public sector and its services. The prescription from the World Bank and other donor agencies pressed specifically for "contracting out" public services to private suppliers. The rationale was that out-sourcing would free the public sector of peripheral duties and enable it to focus on its core roles, harness the power of market competition, raise standards and reduce costs: a win-win for government and its citizens. This chapter investigates how effectively Ghana translated that concept into practical action — the selection of services for out-sourcing, contract designs, management of relationships with private suppliers and, the bottom line is: Did the process work? Did it improve standards and reduce costs, while freeing public sector resources for more weighty tasks? These questions are addressed through case study of local government out-sourcing of solid waste collection services.

295

Introduction

Contracting out is part of the New Public Management (NPM) approach that encourages governments to be more efficient and responsive by applying market strategies to public service provision (Eggers and O'Leary 1995; Hood 2002; Kettl 1997; Osborne and Gaebler 1992). The notion is that out-sourced jobs can be done more efficiently by the private sector because they are specialists in their fields and work in a commercially competitive context. The result should be better services, to the benefit of citizens, at lower cost (Donahue 1989; Savas 1987; Sclar 2000; Kettl 1993; Savas 2000). In contrast, provision of public services by the public sector tends to be monopolistic; lacks competition which drives either cost or quality efficiency; is more subject to political patronage, union influence, and red tape; swamps the public administration system with trivia; and because the same organisations are both providers and monitors of the services objective assessment of service provision will be unlikely (Kelman 2002; Romzek and Johnston 2002; Smith and Smyth 1996; Van Slyke 2003, Smith and Lipsky, 1993).

Since the NPM's advocacy on outsourcing, there has been considerable research on its relative efficiency (Hodge 1999, Averch 1990; Dilger, Moffett, and Struyk 1997; Ferris 1986; Hodge 2000), the implications to public sector contracting (Moe 1987; Romzek and Johnston 2005), and public sector capacity to manage contracts (Brown and Potoski 2003; Cooper 2003; Dehoog 1984; Fernandez 2007). In Africa, key studies include Awortwi (2004); Bartley (1996); Batley and Larbi (2004); World Bank (2004); Devas *et al.* (2001); Bennett and Mills, (1998); Broomberg *et al.* (1997); McPake and Hongoro (1995); Palmer and Mills (2003); Obirih-Opareh and Post (2002).

In Ghana, solid waste collection (SWC) was the first public service to be decentralised to local governments (LGs). In the 1980s, LGs set up production units; defined production technologies; and offered SWC services to residents free of direct charge. The cost of delivery was paid through general LG revenue, usually a central government (CG) grant. As economic conditions worsened in the early 1980s, insufficient capital and operating funds led to regular breakdown of vehicles, plant and equipment; de-motivated management personnel; inappropriate organisation and planning; failure to enforce waste and sanitation by-laws, and negative consumer attitudes. The ability of the LGs to deliver SWC deteriorated sharply. The situation reached a crisis level in 1985 (Benneh *et al.* 1993,38; AMA/Colan Consult 1995) when 82 per cent of the population in cities depended on a few communal container disposal sites from which rubbish was not collected for weeks, while only 10 per cent of the households had front-gate collection. The rest of the population had no access to waste collection service at all, and simply dumped their rubbish anywhere.

In the capital, Accra, by early 1990, more than half the total refuse generated was not collected (AMA/Colan Consult 1995; Awortwi 2003,7). The public viewed LG waste management departments (WDs) as inefficient and ineffective (Agbemabiawo 1996). Following the introduction of the World Bank's structural adjustment and public sector reform programmes in the 1990s, the entire service delivery role of LGs was questioned, and the alternative of private contractors gained momentum (Awortwi 2003; Obiri-Opareh 2002; Crook and Ayee 2006). During the early stages, LGs would continue to provide about 60 per cent of the service, with 40 per cent being in the hands of the private sector, but by 1999 the Ministry of LG planned for 80 per cent of SWC services to be provided by the private sector on a competitive basis. LGs were to maintain a capacity to manage only 20 per cent and make emergency interventions in the event of failures by the private sector (Zanu 1999). By 2000, contracting out to profit and non-profit private organisations had become predominant in all major Ghanaian cities.

This shift required LGs to specialise in the management of standard contracts and to implement strong and effective monitoring, supervision and performance measurement systems. But what effect did the quality of contract have on the quality of SWC service? Did the LGs save money? To what extent did contract management practices tally with the tenets of agency theory? (Note: in this study, LG bureaucrats and politicians are *principals* while profit and non-profit organisations that deliver SWC services are *agents*.)

To answer these questions, empirical data was collected in three Ghanaian cities (Accra, Kumasi and Tema) which have had at least five years of experience in the use of contract documents. Content analyses of 14 contract documents were complemented by analyses of government reports, news sources, and organisational materials. A total of 15 public officers working in the three LG waste departments and 14 private sector managers, two of whom were from community-based organisations (CBOs), were given questionnaire interviews. To maintain the confidentiality of sources of information, fictitious names have been used for the companies involved. A total of 780 households, covering 43 residential communities in the three cities, were asked to assess the quality of SWC services they received. This survey used a report card method.

Theoretical Framework for Contracting out Government Services to Private Agents

LGs have to become smart service buyers in order to define what they want, how to get it, and judge what they have bought (Kettl 1993). Yet they face information asymmetry, adverse selection and opportunism, while *agents* have cost recovery and non-payment problems. The literature shows that these problems are addressed through a web of contractual arrangements. In this research, the *principal-agent* theory is reviewed to provide lessons on contract design and management. While many political scientists and social anthropologists have analysed African public service and management issues using neo-patrimonial literature (Dia 1996; Bratton and van der Walle 1992; Chabal and Daloz 1999) very little has been done using agency theory in economics.

Principal-Agent Theory

The principal-agent theory has been applied extensively to a range of contractual relations (Bogart 1995; Brody 1996; Dharwadkar, George, and Brandes 2000; Lee and O'Neill 2003; Sappington 1991; Bertelli and Smith 2009). It provides a framework for structuring and managing contract relationships in order to explain the behaviours of two actors in an agreement. The principal chooses to contract the agent for reasons of lower cost and higher expertise than it can achieve in-house. Translating this into a contract sounds simple enough: the contract must specify what the agent will do for the principal, and what the principal will pay the agent. However, there is a goal conflict between the principal (public service) and the agent (commercial profit). The agent has more information about the nature and mechanics of the service than the principal. So, the uninformed principal runs the risk of purchasing a service of inappropriate quality (adverse selection); the agent uses their information and expertise advantages to act opportunistically, in their own self-interest, to the detriment of the principal's goals (post-contractual opportunism).

The principal employs a mix of incentives (for instance, adequate fees for services rendered and opportunity for renewal/expansion of contract) and sanctions that will result if the agent does not meet the principal's objectives. Therefore, principals that provide clear and adequate incentives such as vigilant monitoring and credible threat of sanctions might be expected to suffer less than an opportunistic agent and contract goal divergence. Following this proposition, Kettl suggests that, in contractual exchange, a series of questions must be answered that flow from conflict-of-interest and monitoring problems. These questions relate to defining the job, choosing the contractor, selecting incentives and sanctions, and monitoring performance (1993, 24-9). A good contract document will, therefore, have the following clauses specified: contract specification, performance targets, monitoring indicators, conditions for renewal, sanctions and enforcement mechanisms, conflict reduction mechanisms, and the like. (Domberger and Hensher 1993; Domberger *et al.* 1986; Finbar and Allen 2001). According to Crampes and Estache (1998), a quality contract would, therefore, ensure that an efficient private agent is efficient, and an inefficient one is inefficient.

Under conditions of information asymmetry, the agent can inaccurately report high performance to the principal. While more pre-contract preparation and post-contract oversight can reduce many problems, these safeguards increase transaction costs. According to Brown and Potoski (2003), in competitive markets the initial and subsequent bidding processes provide principals with information about trade-offs between quality, quantity, and price. In later bidding rounds, a credible replacement threat disciplines agents to adhere to contract terms. In the absence of a competitive marketplace, a contracting organisation may find it difficult to determine whether the prices and service quality offered by the agent are reasonable because it cannot weigh one bid against the other, and in the event of failure its options are limited.

Critics argue that the principal - agent theory model is one-sided because it negatively characterises an agent's behaviour as self-seeking, and ignores agent loyalty, pride, and identification with the principal's goals (Davis, Donaldson and Schoorman 1997). They argue that some agents are not overwhelmingly motivated by self-interests, and may well place value on collective goals. The agent does not have to be altruistic – merely recognise that mutual benefit ultimately delivers greater personal benefit. Another criticism of the agency theory is that it omits opportunistic behaviour by principals (Waterman and Meier 1998; and Donaldson 1990). This is especially so in public services where politicians and bureaucrats stand to gain personally from colluding with private agents. Literature on episodes of collusion and corruption of government contracts both in developed and developing countries are abundant (Kettl 1993; Schneider 1992).

On these bases, this study postulates that:

- the quality of SWC service would depend largely on the quality of the contract design;

- the effectiveness of contracting out of SWC would depend on contract management provided by LG managers;

- cost savings from contracting out of SWC will arise only if LG managers operate as autonomous principals, able to structure agreements with agents based on their own terms;

- LG contract management with non-profit organisations may be preferred over for-profit making firms, because they are perceived to have less incentive to act opportunistically and thereby enable lower transaction costs for government contract administrators (Commons, McGuire, and Riordan 1997; DeHoog 1984; Kramer 1994; Saidel 1991).

Local Government SWC Service Contracts in Ghana

To enable LGs in Ghana to effectively manage contracts, the Ministry of Local Government and Rural Development (MLGRD), in collaboration with Urban Environmental Sanitation Programme (UESP) of the World Bank, developed project-wide capacity building and training programmes for LG officers (MLGRD 1998a). The outcome was a model of what the contract document for out-sourced SWC services should look like. The model (MLGRD 1998b) covers sets of issues the MLGRD considers crucial in defining the exchange relationship with agents, including preparation of contract bids, evaluation, and award of contracts. The contract preamble requires agents to demonstrate to LGs that they have the required expertise, personnel and technical resources to provide SWC service on the terms and conditions set forth. The following clauses are clearly defined: scope and specification of services, obligations of the contractor, performance monitoring and measurement indicators, payment terms and adjustment in prices, sanctions for poor performance, settlement of disputes, duration of contract, opportunity for renewal and termination, and so on. Each LG was given copies as a guide to writing sound contracts.

Before this model was issued, many LGs had been using a two-page form of agreement. On the basis of the model contract, many LGs have developed their own documents. As previously mentioned, 14 of the LG contracts with SWC enterprises in the three major cities were analysed. They include Accra Metropolitan Assembly (AMA) service contract with Town and Village Waste Limited (Townvil); AMA agreements with 5 small enterprises; Kumasi Metropolitan Assembly (KMA) service contract with Kumasi Litter Management Ltd. (Litterman); and Tema Metropolitan Assembly (TMA) service contracts and agreements with Pitygreen Co. Ltd., Abitod and Keltured Co. Ltd., and so on. The analysis also included two CBOs — the Micro-enterprise Refuse Collection (Microcol) scheme in Kumasi and Ashiedu Keteke Community Participation Project (Comproj) scheme in Accra — and one LG 'in-house' delivery in Tema.

Comparative Analysis of LGs Contracts

Processes of Awarding Contracts

The environmental sanitation policy (MLGRD 1999) and the model contract document (MLGRD 1998b) require contracts to be transparent, through open and competitive bidding. Among other things, this allows LGs to compare agents' proposals, information on their capacity to deliver and, very importantly, reduces risk of non-compliance by unreliable agents. Competitive bidding makes LG procedures strategic - obtaining prior information about agents, comparing rates and selecting the best. However, analyses of the 14 contracts under study show that four other processes were also used, namely:

- agents' connections with people in higher authority, thus usurping LG control over terms;

- constant renewal of existing contracts with no fresh bidding at all;

- gentlemanly agreements based on mutual planning and negotiation, documented as a memorandum of understanding (MoU); and

- LG 'in-house' delivery by WD (contracting-in) which did not pass through any of the other processes.

With the exception of the Pitygreen in Tema, none of the contracts passed through a competitive bidding process. In Accra, the Townvil was registered as a profit-making organisation on 2nd December, 1997, and two days later, it succeeded in signing a contract worth about US$10million - the biggest SWC contract AMA had ever signed with a single private agent. The monopoly contract awarded to Townvil to collect all solid waste in Accra appears to have been influenced by the ruling political party. In Tema, the LG (TMA) gave Abitod and Keltured Companies the first chance to "take" the contract, given that the two companies were already doing the job before the model contract came into effect. The TMA did not open the services to competitive bidding from other contractors.

In principle, the model contract was supposed to regulate exchanges between LGs and all agents in SWC service. In practice, the research reveals that the LG contractual relationship with CBOs did not follow the model in any instance; a MoU with no legally binding terms was used instead. LG 'in-house' provision by the WD had no written agreement and did not go through any competitive bidding process.

Definition of Contract Terms and Scope of Work

The agency theory suggests that it is important to have a contract that defines clearly the relationship and division of responsibility between the principal and the agent. Comparatively, the Pitygreen, Litterman and Townvil contracts were the most comprehensively written. The terms used in the agreement, the scope of work and obligations of each partner were properly defined.

Table 1: **Contract process, definition of contract terms and scope of work**

Name of contract	Open tendering	Proper definition of scope of work
AMA-Townvil Service Contract	No	Yes
AMA-contract with 5 small enterprises	No	Yes
KMA-Litterman Service Contract	No	Partially
TMA-Abitod Agreement	No	Yes
TMA-Keltured Agreement	No	Yes
TMA-Pitygreen Service Contract	Yes	Yes
KMA-ALPHABETS agreement	No	No
KMA-Abbens Service Contract	No	Yes
AMA-Comproj MoU	No	Yes
KMA-Microcol MoU	No	Yes

Notes:'

'Yes' means the contract was competitively tendered. It has clearly defined terms, and specifies the targets to be achieved. 'No' means the indicators were not specified in the contract document. 'Partially' means either one or two indicators were specified.

Financial Incentives to Agents to Deliver Services

Comparatively, the Pitygreen service contract in Tema gives the highest returns per tonne of SWC (collected and disposed of) to agents, followed by the Townvil and Litterman contracts. Contractors in Kumasi and Accra were paid US$10.48 and US$22.17 per tonne, respectively, for collection and disposal distances similar to those in Tema. However, Pitygreen was paid US$51.66 per tonne. The contract appears to provide substantial financial benefit to Pitygreen.

Table 2: **Contract fee per tonne of SWC and haulage within a 15 km radius**

Contract/Company	City	Cost equivalent (US$)
Townvil Service Contract	Accra	22.17
Pitygreen Service Contract	Tema	51.66
5 Small Enterprises Sub-contracts	Accra	5.20
Litterman Service Contract	Kumasi	10.48
Abbens Service Contract	Tema	10.10
WD 'in-house' cost	Tema	7.66
Keltured contract	Tema	10.20
Abitod Contract	Tema	10.20
Comproj MoU	Accra	3.00
Microcol MoU	Kumasi	5.00

Sources: Compiled from various contract documents and organisations' annual reports

Many of the contract documents of the profit-making enterprises state that in the event that payment is delayed beyond three calendar months, the agents shall be entitled to interest. However, it takes a long time before LGs agree to adjust prices to reflect inflation. LGs are aware that once agents buy refuse trucks, they cannot use them for anything else except collecting waste. Given the instability of the Ghanaian currency and delays in adjusting fees, the Townvil and Pitygreen contracts were pegged to the U.S. dollar meaning that as the Ghanaian currency lost value, the Townvil and Pitygreen were paid the dollar equivalent in Ghanaian currency (*cedis*). LGs bear this foreign exchange risk and, therefore, guarantee the two agents stable value of their investment. The other contracts did not have this provision.

In Kumasi, the unit cost of US$10.48 per tonne of SWC that was set in the Litterman contract indicated the principal as the CG through the MLGRD. The amount was arrived at without due consideration of the KMA's budget. Using the LG's own estimates of a minimum waste generation of 800 tonnes a day, the KMA had to pay the agent (Litterman) US$248,497 every month. Considering that the annual revenue generation of the KMA for the same year was US$1.79million, the unit price was far too much for the KMA to afford. Logically, it was impossible for the LG in Kumasi to fulfil its part of the contract, so the MLGRD agreed to pay the full cost of private delivery for six months. The financial inducement that AMA gave to small enterprises sub-contracting in Accra was far less than any of the more formal commercial enterprises.

Monitoring and Supervision

To ensure that agents deliver a level of service that conforms to LGs' prescriptions, contracts specify monitoring indicators and means of verification (Hansen *et al.* 2002). With the exception of the Pitygreen contract and small sub-contracts, where clear performance indicators were set, provision for monitoring just stated that 'the contractor shall allow the LG unimpeded access to its offices, records, and also allow inspection of vehicles and equipment'. They did not make reference to the SWC requirements, thereby leaving the contractor with very loose targets. Items listed for monitoring were only input indicators, rather than outputs. Input indicators are good as far as pre-qualification criteria are concerned, but after a contract is awarded, emphasis on performance ought to shift to outputs. Table 3 shows assessments of monitoring indicators and supervision.

Table 3: **Monitoring and supervision of contract implementation**

Name of contract	Clearly specified monitoring indicators	Supervision
AMA-Townvil Service Contract	Poor	Poor
AMA-small enterprises sub-contracts	Good	Good
KMA-Litterman Service Contract	Poor	Poor
TMA-Abitod Agreement	Poor	Fair
TMA-Keltured Agreement	Poor	Fair
TMA-Pitygreen Service Contract	Good	Fair
KMA-Alphabets Contract	Poor	Poor
KMA-Abbens Service Contract	Poor	Fair
AMA-Comproj MoU	Poor	Poor
KMA-Microcol MoU	Poor	Poor

Notes:

'Good' monitoring means indicators for assessing performance (output, not input, indicators are clearly specified in the contract). 'Good' supervision means the contract clearly states the role of the LG as the supervisor and there are incentives for proper supervision. The opposite, 'poor', means that the indicator is either fuzzily worded or not specified at all. 'Fair' means partial fulfilment of the indicator.

Furthermore, responsibility for monitoring and supervision should, under no circumstances, be blurred between the principal and agents. However, this breach not only occurred, but appears to have been premeditated. For instance, in the Accra-Townvil contract, the agent doubled as the supervisor and sometimes principal at the same time. Townvil was given responsibility to supervise small enterprise sub-contracting with AMA. In Kumasi, a clear differentiation between the principal and the agent was difficult. The LG and the agent (Litterman) shared common facilities (office building, staff, equipment, vehicles and computers). Almost all LG waste management staff were involved in the agent's SWC activities so there was no clear delineation between LG officers' responsibilities and those of the contractor. As the metro engineer explained:

> In many cases, KMA bulldozers at the landfill site were broken down, and we had to fall on Litterman's equipment to clear the site. In cases like that, it becomes difficult for the LG to strictly enforce the rules set out in the contract document. If you are too strict on them who knows when you are going to have problems and you may need the company's help (Interview with the author).

Sanctions

A contract is expected to contain an explicit list of penalties that will be incurred if the rules are not respected. All the SWC contracts, except that of small sub-contracts and CBOs, have clearly specified sanctions. However, deterrence lies not only in the existence of sanctions, but also in how severe they are. In the case of the Townvil's service contract with the AMA, the company had to pay twice the service cost for each premise missed on any collection day.

Table 4: **Severity of sanctions in the contracts**

Name of contract	Stated sanctions	Severity of sanctions
AMA-Townvil Service Contract	Yes	High
AMA-Sub-contracts with 5 small enterprises	No	Non-existent
KMA-Litterman Service Contract	Yes	High
TMA-Abitod Franchise Agreement	Yes	Moderate
TMA-Keltured Franchise Agreement	Yes	Moderate
TMA-Pitygreen Service Contract	Yes	Low
KMA-Alphabets Agreement	No	Non-existent
KMA-Abbens Service Contract	Yes	High
AMA-Comproj MoU	No	No
KMA-Microcol MoU	No	No

Notes:

'Yes' means sanctions are clearly specified in the contract, while 'No' means that sanctions are not specified. 'High' means the cost of default (sanctions) is higher than that of compliance. 'Low' means sanctions are not severe enough to deter willful default.

In contrast, the sanctions to be imposed on Pitygreen are not severe enough to deter the company from non-compliance and non-performance. For example, the agreement states: 'the contractor shall pay the sum of US$126 as liquidated damages to the LG for each and every day that the contractor shall fail or refuse to perform its duties.' Considering that Pitygreen is paid a fixed monthly sum of US$8,140 irrespective of the quantities of waste collected, this means that for each day that the company collects waste, LG pays US$678. If the company fails to collect waste for a day and is fined US$ 126, its profit is still more than three times the penalty.

Contract Duration

The length of a contract period in SWC is typically related to the life of the underlying technology used in the service provision. In many studies on solid waste services, the normal contract duration is not beyond four years – the viable lifespan of rubbish trucks

(MLGRD1998a; Awortwi 2003, 141; Cointreau-Levine 1994). As a rule of thumb, the shorter the duration of the contract, the stronger the potential for competition in the market, because the contract will be subject to more frequent bidding.

The duration of all the contracts, with the exception of the Litterman, Alphabets and 5 sub-contracts, provide sufficient time for agents to recover investment costs.

Table 5:   **Contract duration and prior notification period for termination**

Name of contract	Contract period (years)	Prior notification period for termination (months)
AMA-Townvil Service Contract	5-7	12
AMA-Sub-contracts with 5 small enterprises	Not specified	Not specified
KMA-Litterman Service Contract	2	6
TMA-Abitod Agreement	3	3
TMA-Keltured Agreement	3	3
TMA-Pitygreen Service Contract	5	Not specified
KMA-Alphabets Agreement	1	Not specified
KMA-Abbens Service Contract	2	3
AMA-Comproj MoU	Not stated	Not stated
AMA-Comproj MoU	Not stated	Not stated

Opportunity for Re-negotiation, Renewal and Termination of Contract

A re-negotiation clause in the Townvil, Litterman and Pitygreen contracts gives the three companies additional assurance that when the financial inducements in their contracts become detrimental to their effective service delivery, they can call for adjustment. The three contracts provide a clear formula to be used in the event of rises in the cost of labour, fuel and lubricant, plant and equipment.

Considering the fact that the prices of these items are unstable, the re-negotiation clause reduces the concern many agents have about investing their money in SWC business. Table 6 shows comparative assessment.

Table 6: **Opportunities for re-negotiation, renewal and termination of contract**

Name of contract	Opportunity for re-negotiation of fees	Renewal of contract period	Condition for termination
AMA-Townvil Contract	Yes	Yes	Yes
AMA- Sub-contracts with 5 small enterprises	Not stated	Not stated	Not stated
KMA-Litterman Service Contract	Yes	Yes	Yes
TMA-Abitod Agreement	Yes	Yes	Yes
TMA-Keltured Agreement	Yes	Yes	Yes
TMA-Pitygreen Service Contract	No	No	Yes
KMA-Alphabets Contract	Unclear	Unclear	Unclear
KMA-Abbens Service Contract	Yes	Yes	Yes
AMA-Comproj MoU	Not stated	Not stated	Not stated

The Pitygreen contract, while providing one of the best financial incentives to the agent, did not have a clause for renewal after the fifth year. This means that regardless of Pitygreen's performance, the contract might not be renewed, implying that while the Townvil and the Litterman are incentivised to invest in and improve their services with the expectation of contract renewal, in the case of Pitygreen ongoing investment and effort, especially in the later stages of the contract, is strongly deterred in business terms. Agreements provide no guarantee of continued business to the small enterprises, nor any opportunity for re-negotiation of contract fee. The inclusion of conditions under which the Townvil, Pitygreen, Litterman, Abitod and Keltured Company contracts were to be terminated, as well as prior notification period, reassures agents that their agreements would not be arbitrarily abrogated. However, the 12-month prior notification clause in the Townvil contract was exceptionally long.

Relationship between Contract Design and Quality of SWC Service Delivery

A comparative analysis of the set of issues that are relevant to any contractual exchange shows that the Pitygreen service contract with TMA was properly written and seems to provide preferential opportunity for the agent. It is followed by the Abitod and Keltured Company (see Table 7).

Table 7: **Assessment of the quality of contract designs in SWC**

Indicators of good contract document	Name of contract			
	Pitygreen	Abitod and Keltured Co.	Abbens	Litterman
Contract Definition (W=3)	27	27	27	24
Contract Process (W=4)	24	8	0	0
Financial Incentives (W=5)	35	45	30	35
Duration, Renewal and Termination (W=2)	16	18	20	20
Monitoring and Sanctions (W=6)	78	60	60	54
Settlement of Disputes (W=1)	6	6	6	6
Total Weighted Score (204)	186	164	143	139
RANK	1st	2nd	3rd	4th

Indicators of good contract document	Name of contract			
	Microcol	Five sub-contracts*	Comproj	Alphabets
Contract Definition (W=3)	27	27	21	15
Contract Process (W=4)	0	0	0	0
Financial Incentives (W=5)	30	27	25	25
Duration, Renewal and Termination (W=2)	0	0	0	4
Monitoring and Sanctions (W=6)	30	36	30	18
Settlement of Disputes (W=1)	6	0	4	0
Total Weighted Score (204)	93	90	80	62
RANK	6th	7th	8th	9th

*Note:

The five sub-contractors had the same contract document

W= Weight of contract clause/variable

Methodology for Assessing Contract Documents

A maximum score of three points was given to indicators that were clearly stated in contract documents. The score allocation reduces to zero for contracts without specific clauses and whose processes seem dubious (not following laid-down rules). Lessons from principal-agent theory suggest that monitoring and sanction are the most important indicators that any agency contract should have. In the analysis of what constitutes a good contract, a higher weight is allotted to monitoring and sanctions. The weight of the indicator is then multiplied by the score.

To compare the effects of contract document on the quality of SWC that agents deliver, a total of 780 households from 43 residential communities in the three cities were asked to assess the quality of SWC services they received from LG agents in their communities. Given that agents are allocated specific communities, households were interviewed in their houses using a report card method. The respondents (majority of whom were women) could identify particular agents that collected their waste, based on either where they dumped their waste or by their collection vehicles. They were asked to score specific quality of services using an ordinary scale of 1– 4. A score of 1 indicates poor; 2 fair, 3 good, and 4 very good. Aggregation of the scores provides a clue to the differences in quality of services delivery by agents. The results of the quality assessment survey are shown in Table 8. Note: one of the weaknesses of the report card method is that it does not take into consideration differences in expectations of community members.

Table 8: **Assessment of the quality of SWC by users of contracted agents**

Agent	No. of households interviewed	Quality of Service delivery				Average Score (%)	Rank
		Frequency (%)	Reliability (%)	Prompt Response (%)	Cleanliness (%)		
Hensworth Sub-contracting	23	61	61	84	61	67	1st
KBC Sub-contracting	48	63	66	64	61	64	2nd
Townvil	160	58	62	58	53	58	3rd
Keltured	20	67	62	58	42	57	4th
Comproj	30	53	49	71	47	55	5th
Alphabets-Ksi	45	56	55	65	41	54	6th
Microcol	45	57	42	54	48	50	7th
Abitod	20	63	48	45	30	47	8th
Tee Waste	15	40	45	57	38	45	9th
Litterman	137	45	45	53	31	44	10th
Alcapune Sub-contracting	15	38	48	45	37	42	11th
Freedom Waste Sub-contracting	18	43	50	38	34	41	12th
Abbens sub-contracting	59	28	29	43	30	33	13th
Pitygreen	100	31	30	42	26	32	14th
TMA in-house delivery	45	25	26	41	25	29	15th

Note: Report Card Score: Poor=1; Fair=2; Good=3; Very Good=4

The number of households interviewed corresponds to the size and population of the community that the agent serves.

A cursory comparison shows that properly written contracts did not provide the best-quality services. Statistically, the correlation between contract design and quality of service delivery is weak (see rank correlation in Table 9). Not only is the correlation weak, but also it does not confirm the assertion that a properly written contract document (with all the important terms) is positively related with high-quality outputs. Indeed, with Pearson's r of 0.410,[1] the analysis shows a negative correlation between contract and service quality. For instance, the Pitygreen contract in Tema that provided the best financial incentives to the private agent delivered the nearly-worst SWC service; next to the LG own 'in-house' delivery.

Table 9: **Correlation between quality of contract and quality of service delivery**

		Total score of contract document	Score of quality of service delivery by agents
Total score of contract document	Pearson correlation	1.000	-.410
	Sig. (2-tailed)	–	.146
	N	14	14
Score of quality of service delivery by agents	Pearson correlation	-.410	1.000
	Sig. (2-tailed)	.146	–
	N	14	14

In fact, the relationship between contract design and performance is not well understood and has attracted little research. Domberger and Hensher constructed a simple model relating contractual performance (contract compliance, users' perception of delivery quality and composite performance index) to four variables (bid selection, contract type, monitoring and enforcement). The results show that contracts awarded to the lowest bidder did not have a significant influence on any of the performance indicators. However, when contractors were screened prior to tendering, the recorded performance rating was between 1 and 2 points higher on average than when they were not. Similarly, when reputation was applied as the dominant selection criterion, performance was up between 1 and 1.5 points. They concluded that contractor selection and contract enforcement mechanisms appeared to be the significant factors that influence contractual performance. Relying on positive incentives and negotiation rather than financial penalties also appears to be an effective way of raising contractual performance. The monitoring variable turned out to be an insignificant influence on performance, which was contrary to *priorimonopsony* expectations. They explained that 'this is not entirely surprising when the lack of precision in the measurement of monitoring activities is taken into account' (Domberger and Hensher 1993,447). In the Ghanaian study, none of the six indicators of a good contract document had any positive correlation with the quality of service delivery as assessed by users instead of LG. The reasons for the negative relationship seem to be many: contract management problems; collusion, conflict of interest and corruption; and LG inability to restructure and manage a monopsony (single-buyer) market.

Contract Management Problems

The act of writing a good contract document is different from the act of managing it. The writing was given a model; management details were left to chances. LG contracts, once signed by public administrators, had been neglected.

In Accra and Kumasi, LGs monitoring of private agents was so poorly managed that private contractors assumed the role of the LG in some instances, undermining the principal-agent relationship. Although many of the contracts make agents liable to pay fines if they default, all failed to create any incentives for the staff of LGs to properly follow up complaints by residents. Logistics to facilitate monitoring were poor in all LGs. Considering that many LG waste management employees were poorly remunerated, vigilance was unlikely. The inability of LGs to regularly pay the agents undermined their ability to enforce sanctions or terminate contracts when agents breached terms of the agreements. In fact, the survey found no record in any of the LGs to indicate that a contractor had ever been sanctioned.

LG managers had little latitude. If unhappy, they could not terminate the contract because many of their agents had connections with people in higher authority in CG. Funds used to pay private agents came from CG grants, so LGs as principals in SWC had little leverage in using the threat of non-payment to persuade agents to deliver (or, conversely, to ensure regular payments). Furthermore, LGs could not impose sanctions unless they had the capacity to take the service over – in Accra and Kumasi, the LGs did not reserve any contingency capacity. In all the three cities, there were many providers that LGs could solicit delivery from, but they preferred to negotiate with existing providers for continuous delivery. LG managers argued that trust and reciprocity were at the centre of their contract management with private agents.

Conflict of Interest, Collusion and Corruption

The "properly written" contracts were tainted with collusion and corruption. For instance, the Townvil service contract was intended to be confidential, but when it leaked out to the public, serious questions on conflict-of-interest were raised. The chief executive of the LG in Accra (AMA) was a member of the board of directors of the Townvil when the contract was awarded. Other members of the board of the company were known members or sympathisers of the ruling political party.. without any experience or expertise in waste management. Townvil became an untouchable private agent to Accra LG in a supposedly principal-agent relationship.

Several episodes of conflict of interest and corruption were told during the field survey. LGs and agents evidently disregarded most of the clauses in the contracts because both felt unaccountable to anyone. The outcome seems to be consistent with a World Bank report which suggests that 'contractual provision of services is most likely to succeed when the contract increases transparency and accountability' (World Bank 1994,60). It was no wonder that four months after a change of government, the Townvil contract was terminated and a fraud investigation was launched into the involvement of many of the directors, including a former president (Crusading Guide 2002). Yet when the new government took over, it mandated all LGs in the major cities to sign a monopolised contract with another big private company called Zoomlion. The cost of the company's waste collection is paid at source through CG deductions of LG grants.

LG Inability to Restructure the Monopsonic Market of SWC

The market for SWC in Ghana can be described as monopsonic - where the LG is the sole buyer facing a few suppliers. While this can compromise open-market competition, a monopsony market does empower the buyer to stimulate competition through the use of competitive bidding and short-term contract durations, with renewal of contract depending on previous performance. Domberger et al.(1986,83) conclude that where tendering has been introduced, it has resulted in significant improvement in the efficiency with which refuse services are provided. Their finding is consistent with the growing body of literature that points to the importance of competition in inducing agents to act efficiently. However, the findings of this study show that LGs did not use this mechanism. Only one out of the eleven commercial contracts was competitively bid. In addition, many of the agents were given absolute monopoly - not because there were no other competitive agents, but because of rent-seeking behaviour by CG politicians. Furthermore, instead of the two-to-four year duration normally required for out-sourcing agreements, Townvil and Pitygreen contracts were signed for five years. This immediately shut out competition for an inordinate period and, once awarded, contracts were routinely renewed. When contracting out merely replaces a government monopoly with a private one, efficiency gains are limited. The poor quality of SWC by Pitygreen, Litterman and the Townvil confirms the widespread assertion that, in the absence of competition, providers become sluggish.

Legally Binding Agents' Contracts versus Collaborative Stewardship Arrangements

Although the correlation analysis showed a negative relationship between a good contract document and quality of service delivery, it did not suggest that agents without written contracts did better. The worst agent happened to be the LG 'in-house' delivery in Tema, which operated without any contract. What the results did suggest is that in certain specific circumstances, negotiation, mutual planning, goal alignment, and flexibility in contractual relationship is good for service delivery. The agency model which operates in the form of command-and-control regulation, accords limited moral responsibility to the agent. In contrast, negotiated stewardship agreements can commit agents morally because of their active participation in the target-setting and design of the scheme (Hansen *et al.* 2002). In Accra and Kumasi, the LGs "collaborated" with CBOs to collect solid waste in low-income areas. The CBOs wanted to do a good job for its own sake – all they sought from LGs was permission to do it, and a mandate to police against indiscriminate waste disposal. They used low-cost technology that was affordable to the households in their area. The negative side for CBO operations in cities was lack of resource support from LG managers and politicians. As a result, by 2008 Comproj and Microcol had collapsed.

Cost Savings to LG from Contracting out SWC Service to Private Agents

The literature shows that, in the presence of competition, out-sourcing should result in cost savings (Averch 1990; Ferris 1986). The studies of Savas (1977, 1981); Eggers and O'Leary (1995) and Savas (2000) report cost-saving efficiencies. McDavid (1985) found public collection was 50.9 per cent more expensive than private collection in a sample of 205 Canadian cities. Savas's report, based on a variety of studies from different nations, shows that "savings average about 25 per cent for the same level and quality of services, after taking into account the cost of administering and monitoring the contract' (2000, 147). Hodge's (2000, 128–29, 155) meta-analysis of contracting studies yields similar estimates of 8 to 14 per cent cost savings through out-sourcing. However, other researches by Praeger (1994); and Sclar (2000) find cost overruns, corruption, and erosion of citizen voice. Ghana's experience conforms to that pattern. Analysis shows that LGs in Ghana are now paying more for SWC than before. For instance, at the time of signing the Townvil service contract, the AMA was paying its local agents US$7.55 per tonne. Since the Townvil contract was signed, the AMA has been paying US$22.17- (about three times higher) per tonne.

Furthermore, one of the most cited pieces of evidence that contracting out SWC reduces costs is the study by Domberger *et al.* (1986). They found costs dropped circa 22 per cent through competitively bid out-sourcing. Even authorities who chose the existing 'in-house' operator among all the bidders secured a cost-saving of 17 per cent. They concluded that competitive tendering was the key. Szymanski and Wilkins' (1993) findings are broadly in line, with a saving of 20 per cent reported. Chaundy and Uttley (1993) concluded that compulsory competitive tendering (CCT) in refuse collection services leads to nominal gross cost-savings of 22 per cent. After deducting tendering costs, net saving amounts to 18.4 per cent (1993:38).

These findings do not hold for Ghana. The Pitygreen contract, which was awarded after competitive bidding, set charges between three and five times higher than contracts which were not competitively bid. A plausible explanation for over-charging the LG in Tema was that the Pitygreen contract was financed extensively by the World Bank, and among the five bidders Pitygreen's overwhelmingly superior capacity made bidding ineffective. Where TMA used its own money, SWC was out-sourced to Ebenk Company at less than half the price: US$ 10.13 per tonne.

Conclusion and Theoretical Reflections

In many cities in Africa, SWC is increasingly being out-sourced to private agents. The evidence from Ghana may be useful to many African countries who are assessing their own systems or who are about to start the process. While poor contracts may increase the chance of failure, good contracts do not guarantee success. For many of the so-called Africa analysts and believers in neo-patrimonial literature, the outcome of Ghana's study will not be surprising; a great many of the failures in public services and reforms are attributable to patron-client relationships that pervade African public management. They argue that politicians use public services to buy votes rather than earn them.

While this may be true in many instances (including examples in Ghana) it is too simplistic. Kettl found similar outcomes in the USA – ineptitude, poor planning and inadequate auditing on the one hand, and venality and corruption on the other, cost taxpayers billions of dollars in faulty procurements. He argues that despite the enthusiasm for entrepreneurial government and privatisation, the most egregious tales of waste, fraud and abuse in government programmes have often involved greedy, corrupt and often criminal activity by the government's private partners, exploiting government management that is too weak to detect and correct these problems (Kettl 1993). Schneider (1993) also cites corruption and wastes in contracts in the USA.

In the USA, recent researches have shown that pragmatic LG managers use private agents in a dynamic approach; they contract out and bring unsuccessful contracts back in-house for direct public provision (Warner, Ballard, and Hefetz 2003; Hefetz and Mildred 2004). In Ghana, LGs have to manage out-sourcing very well, and that requires a special set of skills (Moe 1996). LG managers need training not only on designing contracts but also on managing their implementation. Demand for these skills will grow with continued decentralisation and increasing reliance on private agents for government service provision. But training alone will not be enough. There is a need for the CG to cede greater autonomy to LG in awarding contracts, and strengthen institutions that check and punish corrupt practices. In countries where checks and balances are institutionally weak, citizens should be wary of their LGs designing contracts worth millions of taxpayers' money with private agents.

The agency theory assumes that in contractual relationships, only the interests of the principal (no matter how defined) and the agents matter. The direct role of third parties (users or citizens) in the contractual relationship is often neglected. Agency theory also assumes that the principal (LG) has power to control and discipline the agent whenever the principal wishes. The findings show that this master-servant relationship does not always apply and, certainly in African decentralisation, contracting out is bound to face many challenges.

Besides, the agency theory assumes that the interests of the principal are public objectives only, but there is no certainty that this will be so. While it may not be possible to factor variables such as collusion, political connection, principal ineptitude, the role of third parties, and conflict of interest into two-way principal-agent relationship, this very impossibility is itself a crucial factor. It demands reappraisal of presumptions, assumptions, designs and expectations. In contracting out public services, strengthening institutions that regulate principals and agents, including a direct role for third parties (independent regulators or citizens) may help reduce corruption and improve service provision. In recent times, the theories of regulation have not kept up with the complexities of practice. Consequently, controlling opportunistic behaviour, moral hazards and adverse selection on the basis of existing literature on principal-agent relationships has resulted in simultaneous government and market failure. Attributing the failure of out-sourcing in Ghana to factors of neo-patrimonialism ignores similar out-sourcing failures in other parts of the world, even where strong institutions are available. Indeed, the current global financial crisis is partly due to ill-designed and uncontrolled public-private/power-greed practices in the USA and Europe.

There are many reasons why many public sector reform programmes in Africa have not achieved their expected outcomes: technical incapacity of many bureaucrats, inadequate resources, mis-application of the fundamentals that make reforms work, corruption and patronage networks, and so on. Comparison of the results of public sector reforms in sub-Saharan Africa with those in New Zealand, the UK, Australia and the USA clearly shows that competition and regulation, which are the fundamental principles underlying success in cost saving, efficiency gains, quality of service delivery, and so on in public service reforms are universal principles, to which Africa is not an exception (Awortwi 2003). Socio-cultural, political and institutional factors of any country may have some influence on getting some of these fundamentals right, hence reform outcomes may not necessarily go according to plan. But this does not imply that the NPM and other reform approaches that are deduced from market principles are not applicable to Africa, nor that they will automatically lead to failure. This paper has no knowledge of a type of public sector reform that would be suitable only in Africa. However, it confidently asserts that a combination of universal principles such as competition, regulation and motivation — taking into consideration the socio-cultural, political and economic circumstances of the individual country — will be necessary. But, the national peculiarities do not need to be over-stated, nor repeated over and over again but, need to be acknowledged and managed.

Note

1. Pearson's r is a useful descriptor of the degree of linear association between two variables. It ranges from −1 to 1. When it is near zero, there is no correlation, but as it approaches -1 or +1 there is a strong negative or positive relationship between the variables, respectively.

References

Agbemabiawo, L.K. 1996. Socio-economic and institutional dimensions of solid waste management in Tema, Ghana. Master's thesis, Norwegian University of Science and Technology, Trondheim.

AMA/Colan Consult. 1995. Public and private sector management of solid waste in Accra: An evaluation and prospects for sustainable services delivery. Accra: AMA.

Averch, H. A. 1990. *Private markets and public intervention: A primer for policy designers*. Pittsburgh, PA: Univ. of Pittsburgh Press.

Awortwi, N. 2004. Getting the fundamentals wrong: Woes of public-private partnerships in solid waste collection in Ghanaian cities. *Public Administration and Development*, 24:3(213–224).

——.2003. *Getting the fundamentals wrong: Governance of multiple modalities of basic services delivery in three Ghanaian cities*. Maastricht: Shaker Publishing BV.

Batley, R. 1996. Public and private relationships and performance in service provision. *Urban Studies* 33 (4–5): 723–51.

Batley, R. and G. Larbi. 2004. *The changing role of government: The reform of the public services in developing countries*. Basingstoke: Palgrave-Macmillan.

Benneh, E., J. Songsore, J.S. Nabila, A.T. Amuzu, K.A. Tutu, Y. Yangyuoru and G. McGranahan. 1993. *Environmental problems and the urban household in the greater Accra metropolitan area (GAMA)- Ghana*. Stockholm: Stockholm Environment Institute.

Bennett, S. and Mills, A. 1998. Government capacity to contract: health sector experience and lessons. *Public Administration and Development*, 19: 307–326.

Bertelli, A. M. and Smith, C. R. 2009. Relational contracting and network management. *Journal of Public Administration Research and Theory*, 20: 121–140.

Bogart, W. T. 1995. Accountability and nonprofit organizations: An economic perspective. *Nonprofit Management and Leadership*, 6:157–69.

Bratton, M. and van der Walle, N. 1992. Towards governance in Africa: Popular demands and state responses. In G. Hyden and M. Bratton (eds.), *Governance and politics in Africa*, pp.27–55. Boulder, CO and London: Lynne Rienner Publishers.

Brody, E. 1996. Agents without principals: The economic convergence of the nonprofit and for-profit organizational forms. *New York Law School Law Review*, 40:457–536.

Broomberg, J., Masobe, P. and Mills, A. 1997. To purchase or to provide? The relative efficiency of contracting out versus direct public provision of hospital services in South Africa. In Bennett, S., McPake, B. and Mills, A. (eds.), *Private health providers in developing countries: Serving the public interest?* London: Zed Press. pp. 214–236.

Brown, T. L., and M. Potoski. 2003. Contract-management capacity in municipal and county governments. *Public Administration Review*, 63:153–64.

Chabal, P. and J. P. Daloz. 1999. *Africa works: Disorder as political instrument*. 1st ed. Bloomington: James Curry and Indiana University Press.

Chaundy, D. and M. Uttley. 1993. The economics of compulsory competitive tendering: Issues, evidence and the case of municipal refuse collection. *Public Policy and Administration* 8(2):25–41.

Cointreau-Levine, S. 1994. Private sector participation in municipal waste services in developing countries. *Urban Management Programme Discussion Paper* No. 13. Washington D.C: World Bank.

Commons, M., T. G. McGuire, and M. H. Riordan. 1997. Performance contracting for substance abuse treatment. *Health Services Research*, 32 (5): 631–50.

Cooper, P. J. 2003. *Governing by contract: Challenges and opportunities for public managers*. Washington, D.C: C.Q. Press.

Crampes, C. and A. Estache. 1998. Regulatory trade-offs in the design of concession contracts. *Utilities Policy*, 7 (1998): 1–13.

Crook, R and J. Ayee. 2006. Urban service partnerships, 'street-level bureaucrats' and environmental sanitation in Kumasi and Accra, Ghana: Coping with organisational change in the public bureaucracy. *Development Policy Review*, 24 (1): 51–73.

Crusading Guide. 2002. Ghanaian Local Weekly Newspaper, 21–27 February.

Davis, J. H., L. Donaldson, and F. D. Schoorman. 1997. Toward a stewardship theory of management. *Academy of Management Review*, 22: 20–47.

DeHoog, R. H. 1984. *Contracting out for human services: Economic, political, and organizational perspectives*. Albany, NY State Univ: New York Press.

Devas, N., Amis, P., Beall, J., Grant, U., Mitlin, D., Rakodi, C. and Satterthwaite, D. 2001. *Urban governance and poverty: Lessons from a study of ten cities in the South*. Birmingham: The School of Public Policy, University of Birmingham.

Dharwadkar, R., G. George, and P. Brandes. 2000. Privatization in emerging economies: An agency theory perspective. *Academy of Management Review*, 25: 650–69.

Dia, M. 1996. *Africa's management in the 1990s and beyond: Reconciling indigenous and transplanted institutions*. Washington, D.C: World Bank

Dilger, R. J., R. R. Moffett, and L. Struyk. 1997. Privatization of municipal services in America's largest cities. *Public Administration Review*, 57: 21–6.

Domberger, S. and D. Hensher. 1993. On the performance of competitively tendered public sector cleaning contracts. *Public Administration* 71: 441–454.

Domberger, S., S. Meadowcroft and D. Thompson. 1986. Competitive tendering and efficiency: The case of refuse collection. *Fiscal Studies* 7(4): 69–87.

Donahue, J. D. 1989. *The privatization decision: Public ends, private means.* New York: Basic Books.

Donaldson, L. 1990. The ethereal hand: Organizational economics and management theory. *Academy of Management Review*, 15: 369–81.

Eggers, W. and J. O'Leary. 1995. *Revolution at the roots.* New York: The Free Press.

Fernandez, S. 2007. What works best when contracting for services? An analysis of contracting performance at the local level. *Public Administration*, 85:1119–40.

Ferris, J. M. 1986. The decision to contract out: An empirical analysis. *Urban Affairs Quarterly*, 22: 289–311.

Finbar, B. and B. Allen. 2001. Value for money in PPP: Myth and reality. *Administration*, 29(1): 46–58.

Hansen, K., S.J. Katja, A. Larsen. 2002. Recommendations for negotiated agreements. *Government and Policy*, 20: 19–37.

Hefetz, A. and W. Mildred. 2004. Privatization and its reverse: Explaining the dynamics of the government contracting process. *Journal of Public Administration Research and Theory*, 14(2): 171–190.

Hodge, G. A. 2000. *Privatization: An international review of performance.* Boulder, CO: Westview Press.

Hodge, G. A. 1999. Competitive tendering and contracting out. *Public Productivity and Management Review*, 22: 455–69.

Hood, C. 2002. Control, bargains, and cheating: The politics of public-service reform. *Journal of Public Administration Research and Theory*, 12 (3): 309–32.

Kelman, S. J. 2002. Contracting. In *The tools of government: A guide to the new governance'*, Lester M. Salamon (ed.). New York: Oxford Univ. Press.

Kettl, D. F. 1993. *Sharing power: Public governance and private markets.* Washington, D.C: Brookings Institution.

——.1997. The global revolution in public management: Driving themes, missing links. *Journal of Policy Analysis and Management*, 16(3): 446–62.

Kramer, R. M. 1994. Voluntary agencies and the contract culture: Dream or nightmare? *Social Service Review*, 68 (1): 33–60.

Lee, P. M., and H. M. O'Neill. 2003. Ownership structures and R&D investments of U.S. and Japanese firms: Agency and stewardship perspectives. *Academy of Management Journal*, 46:212–25.

McDavid, J.C. 1985. The Canadian experience with privatising residential solid waste collection services. *Public Administration Review* (Sep/Oct).

McPake, B. and Hongoro, C. 1995. Contracting out of clinical services in Zimbabwe. *Social Science and Medicine*, 41(1), 13–24.

Ministry of Local Government and Rural Development (MLGRD). 1998a. *Project-wide capacity-building and training*. Accra: UESP/Carl Bro/PEM Consult/CMS Ltd.

——.1998b. Prequalification document and model contracts: Provision of solid waste management services. Accra: Ministry of Local Government.

——.1999. Environmental sanitation policy. Accra: The Ministry of Local Government and Rural Development.

Moe, R. C. 1996. Managing privatization: A new challenge to public administration. In *Agenda for excellence 2: Administering the state*, B. G. Peters and B. A. Rockman (ed.), 135–48. Chatham, NJ: Chatham House.

——.1987. Exploring the limits of privatization'. *Public Administration Review*, 47: 453–60.

Obirih-Opareh, N. 2002. Solid waste collection in Accra: The impact of decentralization and privatization on the practice and performance of service delivery. PhD dissertation, University of Amsterdam.

Obirih-Opareh, N. and J. Post. 2002. Quality assessment of public and private modes of solid waste collection in Accra, Ghana. *Habitat International*, 26:95–112.

Osborne, D. E., and T. Gaebler. 1992. *Reinventing government: How the entrepreneurial spirit is transforming government*. Reading, MA: Addison-Wesley.

Palmer, N. and Mills, A. 2003. Classical versus relational approaches to understanding controls on a contract with independent GPs in South Africa. *Health Economics*, 12: 1005–20.

Praeger, J. 1994. Contracting out government services: Lessons from the private sector. *Public Administration Review*, 54(2): 176–84.

Romzek, B. S., and J. M. Johnston. 2002. Effective contract implementation and management: A preliminary model. *Journal of Public Administration Research and Theory*, 12: 423–53.

——.2005. State social services contracting: Exploring determinants of effective contract accountability. *Public Administration Review*, 65:436–49.

Saidel, J. R. 1991. Resource interdependence: The relationship between public agencies and nonprofit organizations. *Public Administration Review*, 51 (6): 543–53.

Sappington, D. E. M. 1991. Incentives in principal-agent relationships. *Journal of Economic Perspective*, 5 (2): 45–66.

Savas, E. S. 1987. *Privatization: The key to better government*. Chatham, NJ: Chatham House Publishers, Inc.

——.1977. *The organisation and efficiency of solid waste collection.* Mass.:Lexington Books.

——.2000. *Privatization and public–private partnerships.* Chatham, NJ: Chatham House Publishers, Inc.

Schneider, K. 1992. 'US cites waste in its contracts.' New York: *New York Times*, 2 December 1992.

Sclar, E. D. 2000. *You don't always get what you pay for: The economics of privatization.* Ithaca, NY: Cornell Univ. Press.

——.1981. Intracity competition between public and private service delivery. *Public Administration Review*, 41(1): 46–52.

Smith, S. R., and J. Smyth. 1996. Contracting for services in a decentralized system. *Journal of Public Administration Research and Theory*, 6:277–96.

Smith, S. R., and M. Lipsky. 1993. *Non-profits for hire: The welfare state in the age of contracting.* Cambridge, MA: Harvard Univ. Press.

Szymanski, S. and S. Wilkins. 1993. Cheap rubbish? Competitive tendering and contracting-out in refuse collection –1981–88. *Fiscal Studies*, 14(3): 109–30.

Van Slyke, David M. 2003. The mythology of privatization in contracting for social services. *Public Administration Review*, 63:277–96.

Warner, M. with M. Ballard and A. Hefetz. 2003. Contracting back in — When privatization fails. In *The municipal year book 2003, 30–36.* Washington, D.C.: International City County Management Association.

Waterman, R. W. and K. J. Meier. 1998. Principal-agent models: An expansion? *Journal of Public Administration Research and Theory*, 8:173–202.

World Bank. 1994. *World Development Report 1994: Infrastructure for development.* Oxford and New York: Oxford University Press.

——.2004. *World Development Report 2004: Making services work for poor people.* Oxford and New York: Oxford University Press.

Zanu, S.Y.M. 1999. Implementation of the environmental sanitation policy: A programme of action. In *Selected speeches and papers: Sixth Annual Conference of District Chief Executives* (Sept 5–10, 1999), Ho, Volta Region. Accra: Ministry of Local Government.

Chapter 15

Lessons and Conclusions

Paschal B. Mihyo

The nine countries studied in this book have different histories, geographies and resource endowments, but all share similar objectives of economic, social and political development. All their reform programmes aim at attaining utmost efficiency, accountability and transparency in the delivery of public services; and they all face strikingly similar problems.

The very need for the PSR was accelerated by especially difficult conditions and the challenges of rapid change in the economic, social, political and even physical environments. Prevailing economic crises in the case study countries constrained financial and human resources developments in those countries and limited their capacity to plan properly or ensure strategies to mitigate setbacks. Consequently, they had to rely on development partners for financial and human resources needed to carry out the reforms.

In parallel, reforms had to take place amid climate change, desertification, conflicts and even new diseases. The reforms were also initiated at the time when new developments surfaced in Africa, including globalisation, the world trade system that emerged with the World Trade Organisation, regional integration, which gained higher momentum from the late 1980s, and the increasing importance of public services, all accompanied by a revolution in information technology and a knowledge-driven global economy.

Globalisation and the new world trade system required new skills and more skilled personnel in the public service.

Some of the trade issues were so intertwined that they required networking capabilities across ministries and sectors.

The new diseases, environmental issues and the demand for improved public services required new policy skills, new modes of operation, improved ways and means of conducting government business, and a quantum increase in skilled human power and technology.

Given such difficult conditions, steps taken by African governments to reverse the tide of poor performance in service delivery have been bold, and, not unexpectedly, fraught. The hope of this book is that encouragement can be drawn from successes and lessons can be learned from less effective outcomes. Keynotes emerge for those continuing to implement existing reforms and designing new ones.

Clarity of Concepts

The majority of the reforms aimed to introduce new public management principles and practices. The New Public Management (NPM) concept was taken for granted, rather than being deeply understood, and every change made in management systems was assumed to be part of the NPM. The Business Process Re-engineering (BPR) experiment in Ethiopia, the performance management reforms in higher education in Botswana and performance management in Zimbabwe all plugged into the NPM without full understanding of the major elements and conditions essential for it to become operative.

Similarly, contracting out in Ghana, Tanzania and Zimbabwe were based on assumptions that agency relationships would lead to accountability and that this would automatically lead to efficiency and transparency.

There was insufficient recognition that this "potential" sequence of cause and effect requires the public to exercise power in a principal-agent relationship, to be aware of its rights, to be capable of exercising these rights, to be organised enough to influence decisions in the relationship, and to be capable of imposing sanctions on agents in the event of performance default or abrogation of social contract.

Private Sector Realities

A second lesson is that the private sector is not an immediate paragon of performance virtues. While commercial competition can drive greater efficiency, private sector organisations can also be ill-informed, ill-funded and ill-equipped or downright exploitative. The contracting out efforts of Tanzania in the health systems of Morogoro Hospital and Sokoine University highlight the need for financial capacity, staff capacity (in terms of knowledge and skills) and prior contracting experience. If a public organisation contracts out to private sector suppliers that have financial and capacity constraints, service delivery hurdles get worse, and not better. In Zimbabwe, where services were contracted out to retrenched public sector workers, performance failed; not only because of financial and equipment constraints, but also because they had no experience of being contracted and had no management capacity. And, as a Tanzania case illustrates, if government contracts out services, it must be ready and able to pay fully and promptly; or else corruption sets in, thus amplifying the very problems the reform process is aimed at eradicating.

Institutional Variants

Some institutions are easier to reorganise reforms in than others. Institutions and ministries of finance have embraced reforms more easily and quickly, as seen in Mauritius, Tanzania and Zimbabwe. This may be partly because these institutions are the core ministries that design and supervise reform programmes. On the other hand, universities which are multi-disciplinary in their staff composition and teach about the need for reforms have turned out to be more difficult to change, as has been noted in the cases of the University of Botswana and Makerere University in Uganda. Ironically, the staff in these universities became suspicious of reforms and resisted them in spite of their knowledge that reforms were necessary. Management of these universities — knowing very well that they were managing people who were highly educated and capable of contributing to the planning and implementation of the reform programmes — took a top-down approach as if the staff did not have anything to offer. Many of the chapters in the book show that all organisations are not equally amenable to change and there is a need to consider the context of each organisation while introducing reforms.

Stakeholder Participation

Almost all cases show how important it is to involve stakeholders at all levels and at all stages of the reform process. This means that it is essential not only to plan for change, but also to change the way plans are made by ensuring the participation in the plan formulation of people who are directly affected by the plan and those who implement it (Dodge and Bennett 2011).

In parallel, the front-line implementers must have the authority and autonomy to drive the plan, without excessive state (political) interference or control. South African Telecom was "partially" privatised, with government retaining 39.7 per cent of the shares which it has used to retain a significant role in choosing top management and influencing major decisions. As a result, the institution has remained subject to political interference – a factor that was supposed to be reduced – and its performance has not greatly improved. Reluctance to 'let go' is evident in many of the case study countries. The Ethiopian government considers health as a politically sensitive and important issue, and the chapter on Addis Ababa city health sector governance reforms indicate "government's involvement of public, private and NGO health sectors is somewhat tokenistic – doing something to inform and consult but little to truly transform." In reality, there is no active involvement of citizens, the private sector and NGOs in the planning and budgeting processes of the city's health service delivery. It is important to note that where government has continuing control of services, it will not easily create adequate room for sharing power with important stakeholders unless the citizens and their institutions are strong enough to compel them to do so.

Participation, involvement and engagement of key stakeholders reduces suspicion, galvanises support for reform, infuses new ideas, produces more practical designs and ensures team spirit in implementation. It is clear that top-down approaches were responsible for the failure of many intended reforms, while effective stakeholder involvement and engagement led to some successful implementation. Failure to clearly and adequately communicate the objectives of a reform creates room for multiple interpretations and management by rumours as it is evidenced in the Botswana case study. This exacerbates perception problems and gives detractors opportunity to oppose and misinform.

Importance of Capacity

Organisational capacity in terms of infrastructure, financial resources, equipment, human resources, governance systems, programme development, management and evaluation, information systems, networking and external relations is crucial for sustainable change. In each case study, it is clear that this was a major factor, either as a constraint or as a supportive element in the achievements recorded.

Leadership is Pivotal

Lungu (2005, 84) has noted in his study of public service reforms in Malawi (not included in this book) that, '...Leadership is the engine that drives change'; and according to him, it '...requires a compelling vision that will inspire and mobilise others to achieve their best.' In the case studies, it is clear that where the degree of success was very high, as in Mauritius, it was true that leadership from government provided the necessary space and stewardship (not power and hierarchical control) for that level of success. In other cases, as in Zimbabwe and the fight against corruption in Kenya, it is clear that there was no champion leading the change, and no commitment from empowered authorities to push the reforms forward.

Progressive Progress

For any reform programme to succeed, it has *to gather momentum as it goes*. From the case studies: on universities, as the BPR in Ethiopia, anti-corruption in Kenya and performance management in Zimbabwe, it is clear that the pace of reforms decelerated as implementation progressed and ultimately they were either abandoned, as in Botswana, or lost direction, as in Kenya and Zimbabwe. In the case of Mauritius, it was relentless efforts to keep the reform processes moving forward that enabled substantive success.

The Role of Regulation

Reforming the public sector, in general, and deregulation, in particular, require a *very carefully designed regulatory system*. In Zimbabwe, privatisation was introduced without any governing legislation. This created loopholes that led to the predominance of administrative discretion, selective implementation and personalisation of decisions about what should be privatised, how and at what cost. Contracting out in Tanzania and Ghana was introduced without a clear regulatory framework defining contracting practices, rights and arbitration mechanisms. In all the cases, reforms were not based on a sound framework for power-sharing between governments and markets with room for voice from the public, which is the assumed principal in the emerging structures of market-based governance. The absence of a regulatory framework led to chaotic privatisation, ambiguous objectives of decentralisation and business process re-engineering as well as glaring absence of systems through which governments and markets could be held accountable to the people.

Adaptability

Policies cast in stone cannot respond to frequent and unforeseen changes that will always challenge any reform process. It has been counselled that policy actors should start thinking of policies that 'anticipate and respond to an array of conditions that lie ahead and can navigate towards successful outcomes when surprised by the unforeseen' (Venema and Drexhage 2009, 1). Swanson and Bhadwal (2009, 21–22) have suggested the principles that should be taken into account in the development of flexible policies. These include: "integrated forward-looking analysis; multi-stakeholder deliberations; automatic policy adjustment; enabling self-organisation and social networking; ensuring that policies do not undermine existing social capital; decentralisation of decision-making; promoting variation; formal policy review and continuous learning". It is clear from the case studies that most of these elements were lacking in many of the reform efforts. Very few policies seem to have been based on a careful identification of possible scenarios and possible future surprises.

Lack of multi-stakeholder consultation and prevailing vested-interest interference led to multiple directions of implementation and minimum cooperation from those expected to push reform processes forward. Instead of gaining support incrementally as the reforms progressed, in many cases, existing social capital was lost along the way and reforms either lost momentum or were abandoned.

In short, it is clear from this book that reforms have to be very carefully planned. Policies have to be flexible and adoptive. Stakeholders have to be involved, engaged and continuously informed about the goals, progresses, outcomes and constraints of reforms. To sustainably progress reform, there is a need to build, accumulate and retain capacity in terms of skills, financial resources, materials and equipment; to ensure there are strong leadership and management teams that can provide direction and keep all stakeholders inspired and eager to achieve the desired outcomes. All these elements need to be enshrined in and supported by legislative and regulatory frameworks.

Finally, if future waves of reform benefit from these lessons, there is hope that the public sector in Africa can become more accountable, competitive and comparable with the best in the rest of the world and provide public services that enhance the life and well-being of African societies.

References

Dodge, C.P., and G. Bennett. 2011. The way to change. In *Changing minds: A guide to facilitated participatory planning.* Kampala: Fountain Publishers.

Lungu, P.R. 2005. Public service reforms: The case of Malawi. In K. Kiragu and G. Mutahaba (Eds.), *Public service reform in Eastern and Southern Africa.* Dar es Salaam: Mkuki na Nyota.

Swanson, D. and S. Bhadwal, eds. 2009. *Creating adaptive policies. A guide for policy-making in an uncertain world.* New Delhi: Sage Publications India Pvt Ltd.

Venema, H., and J. Drexhage. 2009. The need for adoptive policies. In *Creating adoptive policies: A guide for policy-making in an uncertain world.* New Delhi: Sage Publications India Pvt Ltd.

Index

Lightning Source UK Ltd.
Milton Keynes UK
UKOW03f0644060617

302788UK00002B/502/P